Bluegills
Biology and Behavior

Bluegills
Biology and Behavior

Stephen Spotte
Mote Marine Laboratory
1600 Ken Thompson Parkway
Sarasota, Florida 34236

American Fisheries Society
Bethesda, Maryland
2007

Suggested citation format is

Spotte, S. 2007. Bluegills: biology and behavior. American Fisheries Society, Bethesda, Maryland.

Printed in the United States of America on acid-free paper.

Library of Congress Control Number 2007925726
ISBN 978-1-888569-93-3

American Fisheries Society Web site address: *www.fisheries.org*

American Fisheries Society
5410 Grosvenor Lane, Suite 100
Bethesda, Maryland 20814
USA

For Keith Reynolds

Fishing is pals

Contents

Introduction

I was fishing one summer day at Lake Istokpoga in central Florida with the marine artist Keith L. Reynolds, whose pen and ink drawing graces the dedication page. In Keith's perceptual world of light and shadow a fly rod becomes an extended brush, a metaphorical tool for painting distant patches of water using a small hairy creature of his own creation. At that moment my own world seemed pale and dull in comparison, a sweaty arena limited to distilling nature's complexities. Art seemed far more exciting than science.

Keith wandered off and I was alone, although not for long. The air was hot and sticky. Frogs croaked dully from the tepid water while gnats gyrated above it, driven insane by the heat. An alligator popped up near my feet wearing a scarf of duckweed. Ever so lightly an insect touched the surface and was quickly eaten by a bluegill. I cast a small grasshopper pattern to that spot and watched it float, then gave it an almost imperceptible twitch. The bluegill was small, but it fought with fierce determination, and when I lifted it out it gazed at me calmly. I returned the look, admiring its finny shape and glistening colors before tossing it back, one of thousands living in the weedy depths. I wondered vaguely what they were doing down there and how they went about doing it, and so the idea for this book was born, a sort of blank canvas to be painted later with words.

The text you are about to read is unconventional in both organization and content. My intended audience is not specifically freshwater ecologists, fishery managers, ichthyologists, experimental biologists, or other specialists but rather biologists of diverse backgrounds. Readers must be willing to undertake an intellectual challenge, that of examining the bluegill by first understanding *how* it lives in its world as a prelude to assessing *what* it does there. My premise is that a book on the biology and behavior of bluegills would be sadly incomplete if, say, only ecological aspects were included. Trophic relationships, reproductive potential, habitat use, and so forth help explain *what* bluegills do, but such information is useful only descriptively. Answering *how* requires knowledge of deeper processes like hydrodynamics, anatomy, physiology, and sensory biology. I believe that an image of the essential bluegill can emerge only by weaving what we understand into a crude narrative in which mechanism is subsumed in event. For example, reporting that bluegills sometimes remain motionless in the presence of a predator is tautologous, the *what* having been included in the observation. We need to know *how* this behavior enhances survival and not simply measure what we see, or think we see. Having watched bluegills navigate nimbly through stands of aquatic weeds might be worth mentioning, but only once. To possess scientific value, subsequent observations must describe the anatomical features and fin movements of *how* this is accomplished.

What you are about to read is not a monograph but an overview of the biology and behavior of *living* bluegills. I make no claim of completeness. With a few exceptions I declined to cite the gray literature and narrowed refereed reports to those that extend a holistic understanding of the different subjects. This meant excluding most of fishery management, induced hybridization, and all of aquaculture and toxicity testing. Parasitism[1] and chronology of the bluegill's nomenclature[2] are documented elsewhere. Information on evolution and distribution—subjects that deal respectively with history and geography—has also been excluded.

Taxonomic keys to the sunfishes (family Centrarchidae) can be found in several publications,[3] and I could think of no reason to reproduce one of them. Lacking expertise in fish taxonomy, I have assumed that bluegills everywhere belong to the species *Lepomis macrochirus* without further subdivision. This is apparently a matter of choice. Some ichthyologists recognize the subspecies *Lepomis m. macrochirus*, *Lepomis m. purpurescens*, and *Lepomis m. speciosus*;[4] others are more conservative, listing only *L. macrochirus*.[5] Authors who refer to two or more individual bluegills in the singular evidently see them as commodities. Carlton Ogburn Jr. noticed duck hunters practicing the same tendency: "A hunter would speak not of pintails and teals but of pintail and teal. It is curious that an avicidal intent and the omission of the plural 's' should go together."[6] My use of the plural to denote more than one individual is therefore proper English usage, not an asseveration of subspecies even if they exist.

The lengths of fishes can be expressed as *total length* (TL) from tip of the snout to tip of the caudal fin, *standard length* (SL) from tip of the snout to the posterior end of the hyperurals (the bones at the end of the spine that support the caudal fin), or *fork length* (FL) from tip of the snout to center of the fork of the caudal fin. I report measurements as stated in the original sources. Based on a sample size of 7,300 bluegills, total length measurements convert to standard length by SL = TL/1.278 (bluegills < 12.9 mm), TL/1.261 (bluegills 12.9–20.6 mm) and TL/1.246 (bluegills > 20.6 mm).[7]

Bluegills have long been used in the aquatic sciences as scaly wet laboratory rats. Biologists have studied them in the wild and in containers of all sizes and shapes, sometimes without recognizing the distinction. Oddly, the differences in behavior and resource use between a tiger in the forest and a tiger in a cage, while obvious to everyone, somehow disappear when applied to fishes. In my reading I came across many statements in which results obtained from captive bluegills were applied uncritically to wild ones. In the text I have been careful to report whether someone's experiment was performed in a lake, enclosure in a lake, aquarium, or "mesocosm" (i.e., a pool).

Overall, the bluegill literature offers much to admire. Hundreds of dedicated scientists, technicians, and students have waded into lakes and ponds with nets or ventured out in boats, day and night, to study bluegills. Some have devised clever experiments to illuminate some aspect of bluegill biology or behavior. Impatient readers might wonder why certain experiments have been described here when a simple overview would seem sufficient. But simple overviews, by definition, omit both important details and the critical evaluation required by scholarship. One of my duties has been to evaluate the relevant literature, not merely collect and summarize it, and sometimes this required synopses of specific experiments.

Having now placed the book's contents in perspective, my hope is that you, its readers, come away with renewed appreciation for the extraordinary qualities of an ordinary little fish.

Stephen Spotte
Longboat Key, Florida
November 2006

Movement

1

Fishes move about by bending their bodies and using their fins. Depending on the situation the fins can act as thrusters, steering devices, or brakes. To a casual observer a swimming fish appears to leave no trace of its movements, but in fact it disrupts the section of water through which it swims, temporarily altering its shape and leaving behind a wake, or area of turbulence.

Some standard features of hydrodynamics require explanation before being applicable to living bluegills. The starting vortex, or detached eddy, has a counter clockwise rotation (+K). The bound vortex, or bound circulation, which has a clockwise (-K) rotation, remains attached until the starting vortex has been shed. Kelvin's theorem requires that the total vorticity, or circulation, must have a neutral charge balance over time. Thus any variation in the bound vorticity necessitates a vortex having the opposite sign being released into the wake. If the bound vorticity varies with time, $\Gamma(t)$, then in the brief interval δt the total vorticity released into the wake will be $(\partial\Gamma/\partial t)\delta t$, and once separated from the fish it assumes the form of a continuous vortex sheet.[8] Because relevant motions made by a fish are periodic, the resultant variations in vorticity are periodic too.

Vortex sheets are dynamic, containing places of positive, negative, and coalesced vortices. A von Kármán vortex street describes two infinitely long rows of vortices with alternating signs (Figure 1). In the figure, flow is left to right. The wake indicates a momentum deficit compared to the incoming flow, and the subsequent wake creates drag on the organism producing it.

Figure 2 shows a reverse von Kármán vortex street resulting in a wake, or jet, having an excess of momentum and generating thrust instead of drag. Drag and thrust increase in direct proportion to the vertical distance between rows, and either is eliminated if this distance is reduced to zero. The fins of swimming bluegills produce wakes of reverse von Kármán vortex streets.

A swimming fish exerts some control over incoming vortices, whether self-generated or extraneous in origin, by altering their locations and strength. Three situations are possible.[9] All can result in either drag or thrust that is always maximized. In vortex annihilation a vortex generated by a fin or body interacts destructively with an incoming vortex, weakening the downstream vortex street. Constructive interference is a situation in which the generated and incoming vortices produce an additive effect, strengthening the vortex street downstream. During vortex pairing the vortex that is generated interacts with another of opposite sign and results in pairs, or four per cycle.

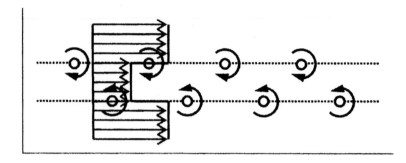

Figure 1. Von Kármán vortex street. Upper vortices rotate clockwise (-K), lower vortices counter clockwise (+K). Source: Young (2005).

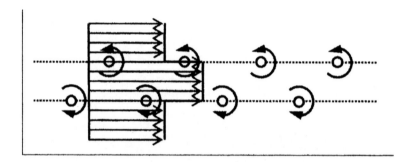

Figure 2. Reverse von Kármán vortex street. Upper vortices rotate counter clockwise (+K), lower vortices clockwise (-K). Source: Young (2005).

Pectoral Fin Kinematics and Wake Dynamics

Many teleosts rely extensively on their pectoral fins for maneuvering, but the bluegill also uses them when swimming in labriform (wrasselike) fashion. Labriform swimming by the bluegill involves a cycle of fin movements in which the pectorals are in several sequential positions with respect to the body's axes.[10] These are lateral (abduction–adduction), longitudinal (protraction–retraction), and vertical (levation–depression). Abduction is movement toward the body; adduction is movement away from it. The other movements: forward (protraction), backward (retraction), up (levation), down (depression). The cycling, or oscillation, of the fins through these positions is (1) anteroventral (downstroke), (2) rotation at the end of the downstroke and stroke reversal ("fin flip"), (3) posterodorsal (upstroke), and (4) a pause at the end of the cycle when the fins are held tightly against the body.[11]

Swimming speed affects wake morphology. At a slow speed (0.5 L/s, or total body lengths per second) the downstroke and stroke reversal segments generate most of the wake vorticity.[12] Partway through the downstroke a single vortex is produced posterior to the pectoral fin and another upon stroke reversal (Figure 3). At 1.0 L/s, the maximum sustainable speed by a bluegill for purely labriform swimming, the wake is composed of a vortex pair plus another pair generated on the upstroke after the fin reverses and begins to adduct (Figure 4). The vortex rings, are toroidal (doughnut-shaped). They rotate in opposite directions, intertwine like the links of a chain, and between each pair is a jet flow of strong momentum oriented posteroventrally and laterally.

Wake dynamics based on patterns of pectoral fin movement and observed fluid flows (de-

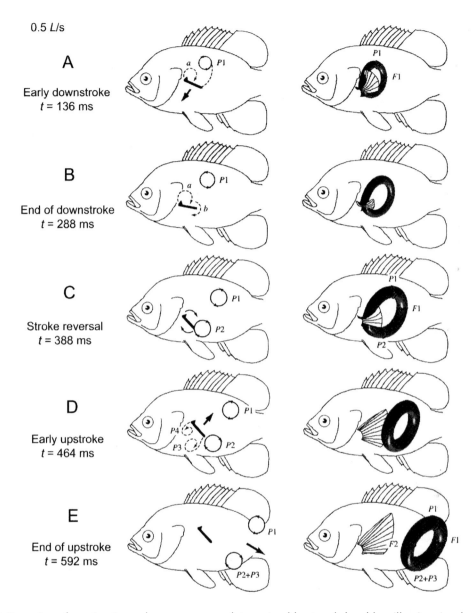

0.5 L/s

A
Early downstroke
t = 136 ms

B
End of downstroke
t = 288 ms

C
Stroke reversal
t = 388 ms

D
Early upstroke
t = 464 ms

E
End of upstroke
t = 592 ms

Figure 3. Formation of a vortex ring wake over one complete pectoral-beat cycle by a bluegill swimming slowly (0.5 L/s, or total body lengths per second). *Left column*: sequential time elapsed at each stage in the cycle. *Center column*: proposed mechanism for development of wake circulation in the parasagittal plane. Fin movement is indicated by straight-line arrows (curved arrows in C), rotational flow by solid-line circular arrows. Broken lines indicate predicted flows. *Right column*: hypothetical three-dimensional reconstructions of fluid flow predicated on flow patterns observed in perpendicular planar sections of the wake. Each fin-beat cycle results in a single discrete vortex ring with a central fluid jet. Time was measured from start of the pectoral fin downstroke ($t = 0$ ms). a = attached leading-edge vortex, b =clockwise flow around fin induced by the acceleration reaction. $F1$, $P1$, $T1$ = starting vortices on downstroke; $F2$, $P2$, $T2$ = downstroke stopping vortices. Letters represent the different planes from which hydrodynamic factors were measured: F (frontal), P (parasagittal), T (transverse, not shown). Source: Drucker and Lauder (1999).

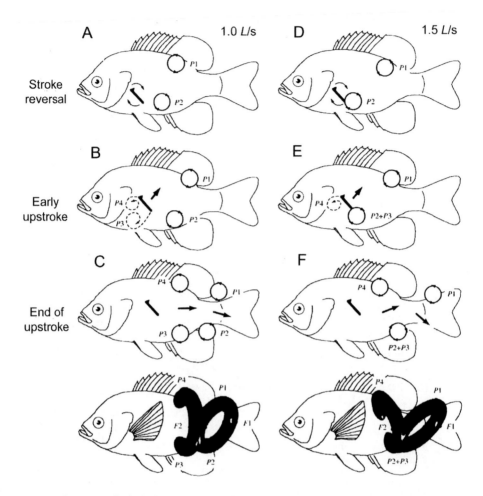

FIGURE 4. Development of a linked-pair vortex wake during the second half of a pectoral fin stroke at high swimming speeds (1.0 and 1.5 L/s) by the bluegill. Columns show mechanisms by which circulation is generated within the parasagittal plane from stroke reversal through end of the upstroke (vortex dynamics during the downstroke are similar to those illustrated in Figures 3A-B). Schemes representing three-dimensional wake structure, inferred from flow patterns observed in orthogonal planar sections of the wake, are depicted in the two bottom images. The appearance of three or four vortices in the parasagittal plane but just two in the frontal plane (see original report) suggests the production of linked pairs of vortex rings by each fin during a stroke cycle. As swimming speed increases the ring linkage shifts from mainly lateral (1.0 L/s) to ventrolateral (1.5 L/s), which alters the orientation of the fluid jets and the wake forces generated. Abbreviations and symbols as in Figure 3. Source: Drucker and Lauder (1999).

picted schematically in Figures 3 and 4) work as follows, starting at the slow swimming speed with the pectorals fully adducted and flat against the body (Figure 3A).[13] At the onset of abduction (the downstroke) a space forms in the crevice between fin and body, which water quickly fills. Upon further abduction a vortex forms and begins to spin counter clockwise (Figure 3A, *P1*). This is partly a result of the acceleration reaction (see below), which acts against deceleration of the fin at the end of the downstroke and alters fluid flow to the opposite (ventrolateral) side of the fin (Figure 3B). Commensurate with vortex formation is initiation of a clockwise rotation (Figure 3B, *b*). The downstroke then ends and a vortex ring shoots downstream. During stroke reversal accumulated vorticity (Figure 3B, $a + b$) is squeezed to the ventrolateral side of the fin and into the wake, and a second vortex appears (Figure 3C, $P2$). The hydrodynamics of the upstroke mirror those of the downstroke: adduction produces a clockwise ring released from the back edge of the fin (Figure 3D, $P3$) and another moving counter clockwise from the fin's leading edge (Figure 3D, $P4$). The details vary with swimming speed. In one configuration the rings fuse (Figure 3E, $P2 + P3$).

Vortex formation at even higher swimming speeds (≥ 1.0 L/s) is partly a result of stronger, quicker fin beats. The downstroke is also shorter, and a vortex that spins clockwise during stroke reversal is swept away more rapidly (Figure 4A, $P2$). Its quick departure allows another clockwise vortex to form on the upstroke (Figure 4B, $P3$). The shorter, more powerful upstroke at 1.0 L/s creates a well defined ring (Figure 4B, $P4$) that despite being close to $P3$ is nonetheless released into the wake (Figure 4C). At 1.5 L/s the vortices $P2$ and $P3$ should release separately, but the shortened period of the upstroke causes them to fuse instead (Figure 4E). Other factors (see the original report) allow $P4$ to survive despite the orientation of its spin (Figure 4F).

Propulsion

Bluegills propel themselves, in part, using a combination of drag and lift: the force applied to the pectoral fin is the vector sum of these factors directed forward.[14] In drag propulsion the fins rotate from the vertical until their broadest surfaces are perpendicular to the body's midline and then pull posteriorly like oars. In lift propulsion the fins move up and down like a bird's wings instead of rotating. The fact that depression and protraction of the pectorals of bluegills cause no obvious deceleration of the fish indicates that lift force is perhaps adequate to induce a forward-directed vector.[15]

Still a third mechanism—acceleration reaction—is force produced by resistance of the water in response to changes in the velocity of the fins.[16] The bluegill pectoral fin contributes to thrust and lift. The lift is positive on the downstroke, negative on the upstroke.[17] A bluegill swimming at high speed releases vortex rings during each half-stroke up and down. The second ring, aimed posteroventrally, also increases the force needed for propulsion. In addition, circulation is enhanced at completion of the downstroke when the fin decelerates and the entrained water "rolls up" (Figure 3B, flow b).

The acceleration reaction probably contributes to thrust as the pectorals cycle through brief periods of acceleration (adduction) and deceleration (retraction).[18] At the termination of abduction the force of acceleration is a vector directed toward the fish's anterior end. The force of water (its added mass) surrounding the fin resists deceleration, moving the fish forward. Conversely, when adduction stops the added mass of water shoves the pectoral fin toward the fish's posterior end, which also results in forward propulsion.

Direct supporting evidence of an acceleration reaction can be seen in how a bluegill swims, which is smooth and straight and devoid of the lift-based bouncing motion of many wrasses and parrotfishes. Such vertical undulation is reminiscent of penguins as they "fly" through the water and of the jerky aerial flight of many small songbirds (e.g., nuthatches). Also missing from the bluegill's swimming pattern is a visible propulsive-recovery (stroke and glide) motion characteristic of fishes that might rely more on drag-based propulsion.

Changes in fluid momentum create force, which is characterized by the release of vorticity and signals a shift of momentum into the wake.[19] The dynamic morphology of the wake illuminates the connection between swimming speed and force.[20] For example, upstroke formation of a posterior-facing second vortex ring (Figure 4, bottom right) accounts for the increase (by 5×) in forward thrust as swimming speed increases from 0.5 to 1.0 L/s. Thrust evens out at the highest speeds, coinciding with intervention by the caudal fin.[21] This is the gait transition speed, an odd

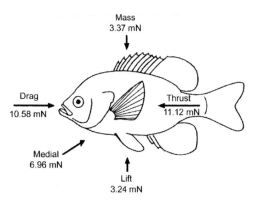

Figure 5. Synopsis of the hydrodynamic balance of forces determined empirically for bluegills swimming at 0.5 L/s. Thrust and lift values are mean reaction forces of both pectoral fins averaged over the cycle. Propulsive forces calculated from the wake velocity do not differ significantly from measured resistive forces of total body drag and mass (see Table 2, original report). The large reaction force directed medially might aid in stability during swimming. Source: Drucker and Lauder (1999).

term considering that bluegills have no legs. It defines the point at which labriform propulsion is augmented by thrust from the soft dorsal and tail fins (see below).

Similar vortices formed on the downstroke between 0.5 and 1.0 L/s serve as counterbalances, smoothing out net lift.[22] When a bluegill is swimming slowly each half-stroke of a pectoral fin (abduction and adduction) aids in producing a single vortex ring. Lift doubles between 1.0 and 1.5 L/s, attributable to the greater tilt of the vortex ring generated on the downstroke, and by its downward force (Figure 4, bottom images). Added upward force produced by the pectorals might be needed to balance the increasingly negative lift caused by the bluegill's frontal profile; alternatively, positive lift could be produced posteriorly by oscillating sweeps of the tail.[23]

Force might be affected by the bluegill's deep compressiform shape, which effectively separates one side from the other. According to this hypothesis the sides act as walls, becoming hydrodynamic barriers that lessen their mutual involvement in the wake.[24] Separate wakes might help in stabilization during swimming and turning.[25] This possibility is based on empirical findings showing that the force directed medially by the pectorals, and which makes no contribution to lift or thrust, is large for the bluegill (Figure 5). In this sense the pectorals could function as "thrusters," preventing the body from rolling in turbulence produced extraneously or by its own wake. Additional thrust might be provided when the pectorals adduct against the body at termination of the upstroke, transferring vorticity quickly into the wake.

A kinematic investigation of how the pectoral fins generate propulsion based on movements during the fin cycle was made using three-dimensional imaging.[26] For a slowly swimming bluegill the cycle proceeds uninterrupted (Figure 6). Transitions at the highest swimming speed (longitudinal and lateral) were more erratic and sometimes followed brief pauses. This is evident at 0.4–0.6 s (Figure 6B). The figures show that at both swimming speeds the highest values of abduction at the fin tip mirror those of maximum depression. Furthermore, during abduction the fin tip is often depressed and protracted simultaneously. In like manner the tendency during adduction was simultaneous retraction and levation. The steepest slopes of the curves show that adduction and retraction occur fastest in the halfway periods between adduction and abduction.

Pectoral fin beats of a bluegill swimming at 0.5 L/s average 0.83 s.[27] However, the pattern of pectoral fin movements changes with swimming speed. Most noticeable is the frequency of fin beats (Figure 7), which nearly doubles (1.2–2.1 Hz) as swimming speed increases from 0.3 to 1.0 L/s.[28] At 1.0–1.1 L/s a swimming bluegill begins augmenting pectoral fin locomotion by using its median and tail fins.

Median Fins

The homocercal tail of a steadily swimming bluegill produces lift.[29] It works as follows.[30] Lateral movement is ~50% greater in the dorsal lobe, meaning that instead of acting as a vertical

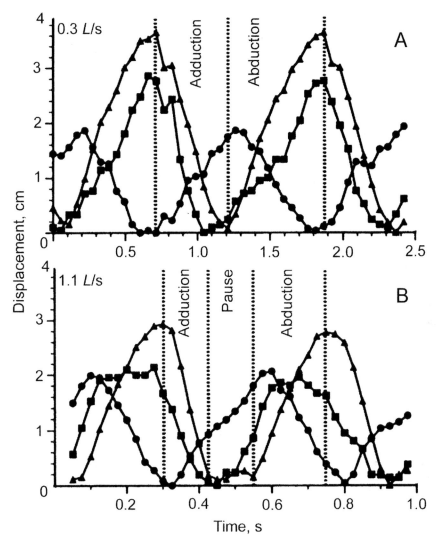

Figure 6. Orthogonal displacement of the tip of the pectoral fin relative to the body of a bluegill through one cycle at two swimming speeds. A: The slowest (0.3 *L/s*). B: The fastest (1.1 *L/s*). Negative slopes of the curves for *x* (■), *y* (●), and *z* (▲) represent fin retraction, adduction, and depression. See original report for details. Source: Gibb et al. (1994).

paddle with thrust distributed evenly along its posterior edges, the actual movement is asymmetric. During steady swimming the ventral lobe of the tail fin expands in the first third of the oscillation; the dorsal lobe expands in the last third.[31] These observations are reinforced by analysis of the musculature.[32] Each half-stroke produces a vortex ring, and each full stroke generates two counter rotating vortices.[33] The vortex wake probably spins off as a chain of linked toroidal rings tilted ventrally and accompanied by a jet inclined both behind and below the moving fish (Figure 8). The resulting torque is offset by lift produced from the fish's head or perhaps its pectoral fins.

Relative to thrust, lateral forces of the major median fins (caudal and dorsal) are high in many teleosts.[34] In the bluegill such forces produced by the caudal fin are almost twice the thrust force, which is not atypical. No teleost fin, including the pectoral, is an efficient propulsion device. Propulsion efficiency (represented by η) can be measured in terms of mechanical performance, in

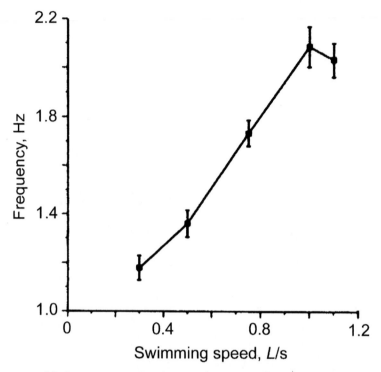

Figure 7. Frequency of fin beats versus swimming speed. Data points are $\bar{x} \pm SE$. Source: Gibb et al. (1994).

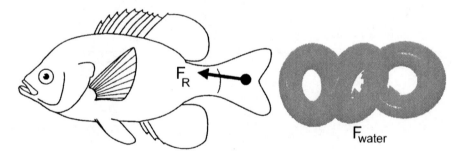

Figure 8. Schematic illustration of the vortex wake behind a bluegill swimming steadily. The oscillatory motion of the tail is thought to produce a chain of linked vortex rings (here shown for simplicity as circular and enlarged relative to tail height). The rings are tilted, and their outside diameter closely matches the height of the expanded tail. The fish's reactive force (F_R) is oriented anterodorsally. According to this hypothesis the homocercal tail generates lift forces and torques that must be balanced by anterior forces generated during orientation or movement of the body and by the pectoral or pelvic fins. Source: Lauder (2000).

this discussion the fraction of the total force generated by a fin that represents thrust. Computationally, η is the ratio of mean thrust multiplied by speed and the mean power output. For the bluegill caudal and pectoral fins $\eta = 0.38$ and 0.39.[35] The caudal's low value derives from large lateral forces, that of the pectorals from both lift and lateral forces. Large lateral forces are thought to assist stability and maneuverability, allowing a fish to continuously correct its position about its center of mass (CM).[36]

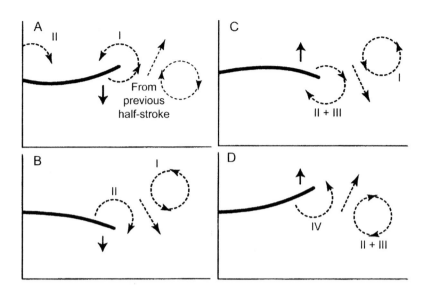

Figure 9. Schematic representations (dorsal view) of flow fields in the wake of the oscillating soft dorsal fin of a bluegill swimming steadily at 1.1 L/s. Frontal plane view intersecting the fin in the middle. See text for explanations. Source: Drucker and Lauder (2001).

The caudal fin manipulates vortices received from the anterior end of the fish, including those generated along the body, shed from other moving fins, or from any projecting spines or edges of stationary fins. Whether they all affect propulsion is unknown. The ability of the tail to reposition them suggests an additive thrust effect, although the reposition maneuver produces drag.[37] The bluegill caudal fin is known to intercept the wake shed by the soft dorsal and manipulate it to advantage.[38] This action potentially increases thrust, evidently by constructive interference.[39]

The other major median fin of the bluegill is the dorsal, divided into a spiny anterior portion and a soft-rayed posterior section. The spiny part of the fin has limited lateral movement and remains depressed while the fish is swimming,[40] but the soft-rayed portion of the dorsal has musculature that extends considerably more control over its conformation.[41] Until recently the soft dorsal of the bluegill was not thought to generate thrust independently, but it actually sheds a reverse von Kármán vortex street from its trailing edge, accounting for 12% of the total thrust in excess of drag.[42]

During steady swimming above the speed at which the caudal fin is recruited (> 1.0 L/s), the soft dorsal undulates continuously, and its wake, a reverse von Kármán vortex street, generates thrust.[43] The resemblance of the wake pattern and oscillatory motion to the caudal's implies a similar function. Abduction of the soft dorsal is driven by dorsal inclinator muscles originating in the fascia and attached at the lateral base of each fin ray.[44] Their proposed function is to provide stiffness and uniformity to the fin, enabling it to better resist the force of the water.[45] The observation that the soft dorsal undulates only when the body undulates, and that its oscillatory period coincides with the caudal's (see below), reinforce this hypothesis.[46]

Each full stroke of the soft dorsal (Figure 9) generates a pair of counter-rotating free vortices (I, II + III) between which flows a central jet. The pattern is a typical reverse von Kármán vortex street generating thrust. As the fin sweeps medially (Figure 9A, beginning of a half-stroke) a counter clockwise starting vortex forms at its trailing edge while a clockwise bound vorticity develops upstream, and the two roll onto the concave side of the fin. Vortex II now slides poste-

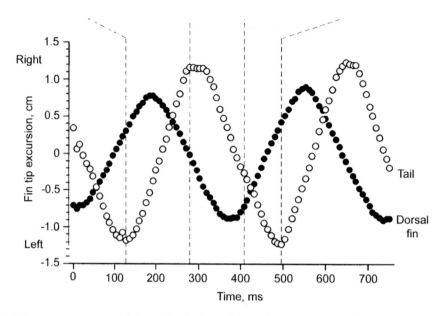

Figure 10. Lateral movements of the trailing edges of the soft dorsal and caudal fins versus time over two consecutive stroke cycles. The tail's abducted amplitude on each half-stroke exceeded that of the soft dorsal, averaging 5.1 mm, or 19% of the tail's total sweep amplitude. Fish used in the experiments measured 210 ±12 mm TL ($\bar{x}$±SEM). Source: Drucker and Lauder (2001)

riorly forming a "stopping" vortex at termination of the half-stroke (Figure 9B, vortex II). At the end of the half-stroke vortex I, rotating counter clockwise, is shed into the wake. Initiation of the return stroke produces a new starting vortex (vortex III, analogous to vortex I in Figure 9A), which merges with vortex II (the "stopping" vortex from the earlier half-stroke) to form II + III (Figure 9C). At completion of the full stroke this combined vorticity (II + III), now rotating clockwise, is shed into the wake while a bound vortex of opposite sign forms at the fin's trailing edge (Figure 9D).

As mentioned, axial undulation of the soft dorsal and caudal fins commences above gait transition speed. The two curves then become sinusoidal and similar (Figure 10), having beat frequencies of ~2.5 Hz at 1.1 L/s.[47] Oscillation of their trailing edges has a mean lag phase of 121.4 ms with the soft dorsal preceding the tail by ~30% of the stroke cycle. The amplitude of its lateral sweep (1.66 cm) is significantly less than the tail's (2.69 cm).

The bluegill propels itself forward using the pectoral fins, caudal fin, and soft dorsal fin acting in synchrony (Figure 11). The vortex sheet released into the wake by an upstream fin is imbued with momentum and energy.[48] A fin positioned downstream can potentially intercept a passing vortex sheet, assimilate its vorticity, and subsequently lower the loss of wake energy. If the fins oscillate out of phase the upstream fin perhaps enhances total thrust and propulsive effectiveness. Alternatively, each fin might release vortices that coalesce with those of another fin nearby, producing additive thrust.

A soft dorsal fin sweeping laterally (Figure 12A, 12B) spins off a vortex (Figure 12B, vortex *a*) consisting of part of its reverse von Kármán vortex street as in Figure 9A, 9B, vortex I. This vortex is intercepted by the tail's dorsal lobe, the excursion of which exceeds that of the soft dorsal. Vortex *a* then slides across the dorsal lobe of the tail, where bound vorticity is presently being formed, and shed as vortex *b* (Figure 12C). Vortices *a* and *b* merge to become *c* (Figure 12D). However, vortex *c*, having developed in the tail's wake, doubtfully contributes to thrust. More likely the rotation and increased velocity of vortices *a* and *b* perform this function as they pass across the surface of the tail.

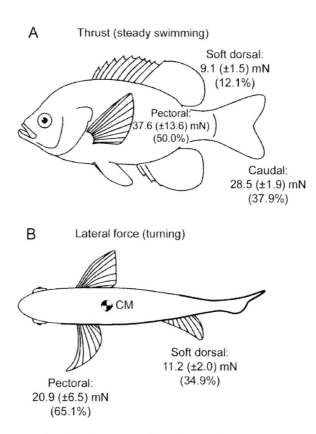

A Thrust (steady swimming)

Soft dorsal:
9.1 (±1.5) mN
(12.1%)

Pectoral:
37.6 (±13.6) mN
(50.0%)

Caudal:
28.5 (±1.9) mN
(37.9%)

B Lateral force (turning)

CM

Soft dorsal:
11.2 (±2.0) mN
(34.9%)

Pectoral:
20.9 (±6.5) mN
(65.1%)

Figure 11. Summary of forces produced by the system of three fins used in locomotion by the bluegill. A: Thrust produced while swimming steadily at 1.1 *L*/s. B: Lateral force produced while turning after steady swimming at 0.5 *L*/s. See original report for details. CM = center of mass, which in the adult bluegill is considered to be 0.36 *L* posterior to the end of the snout (Webb and Weihs 1994). Source: Drucker and Lauder (2001).

The explanation so far stops short of addressing how a fish overcomes its inherent instability. The bluegill's center of buoyancy is below its center of mass, causing a tendency to roll. The oscillations of the soft dorsal fin, which acting alone could tip over a swimming bluegill, are countered by synchronous movements of the soft posterior portion of the anal fin.[49] At swimming speeds equalling or exceeding 1.5 *L*/s both the body and median fins start to oscillate, attaining maximum excursion as steady swimming commences. At this time anal fin, body, and dorsal fin demonstrate significantly different phase lags. During maneuvers both fins expand and shift to the same side, excursion of the soft dorsal intensifying. Their fins act in ways similar to the flexible stays in a sail, providing stability and controlling the fin's curvature. Maximum curvature is similar in the two fins during steady swimming, although even adjacent rays bend differently depending on momentary stresses. Control over fin shape by the fin rays is therefore complex, dynamic, and subtle.

Turning

Turning is a controlled dynamic maneuver, momentarily disrupting the steady-state locomotion of swimming straight ahead. As labriform swimmers bluegills rely heavily on their

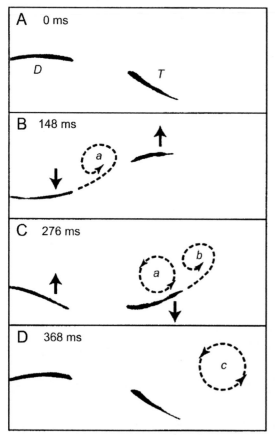

Figure 12. Proposed mechanism (dorsal view) of wake interaction between the soft dorsal fin (*D*) and tail (*T*) of a bluegill swimming steadily at 1.1 *L*/s. Fin silhouettes in plan view are depicted as they move through one stroke cycle. Solid arrows indicate the direction of fin movement. This sequence, repeated on alternate sides of the fins, induces a reverse von Kármán vortex street wake. See text for explanations. Source: Drucker and Lauder (2001).

pectoral fins when maneuvering. Simplified biomechanics of the forces involve elements of the equation

$$\overline{F} = M / \tau$$

in which $\overline{F}$ = total average force produced by fin strokes; M = fluid momentum distributed into the wake through a complete fin stroke, representing the product of water density, mean vortex flow, and the area occupied by the vortex rings; and τ = the time during which the body rotates and then translates as a result of pectoral fin movements.[50]

As described previously, wakes generated by the pectorals take the shape of toroidal vortex rings. The strong-side pectoral fin is on the side of the body facing the stimulus. The weak-side fin is on the opposite side. Both fins are used when turning. However, unlike in swimming their movements are asymmetrical. Presentation of a stimulus results in instantaneous abduction (downstroke) of the strong-side fin. Abduction by the weak-side fin is delayed and its movements offset, not reaching maximum position until the strong-side fin commences adduction. Concurrent with these events the body rotates in the direction of the weak side, but with very little translation.

As rotation proceeds, the weak-side fin stays in the fully abducted position, then is rapidly adducted in synchrony with the strong side. With the weak-side adduction the axis of the body rotates ~26°, and the fish translates away from the stimulus. "During the turning response... early abduction of the strong-side fin is associated with body rotation, and late adduction of the weak-side fin is correlated with body translation."[51] When turning, the force developed laterally by the strong-side fin is 4× the mean values seen during steady swimming; the posterior forces generated by the weak-side fin exceeds that of steady swimming by 9×. Their relative magnitudes should not surprise anyone familiar with maneuvering a boat equipped with twin propellers. During turns the fluid forces exerted laterally exceed those of slowly cruising straight ahead, an observation apparent from the surface disturbance.

The wake patterns generated while swimming are changed upon turning. Compared to vortices produced during forward motion, those resulting from a complete downstroke–upstroke cycle by the strong-side pectoral are paired and also much larger. The central jet of the wake is now aimed laterally, and its speed is twice that produced during steady swimming. During adduction the weak-side fin releases a desultory wake consisting of paired vortices.

As shown here (Figure 13), the base of the bluegill's pectoral fin is inclined toward the vertical (mean θ = 74°) and demonstrates anteroposterior motions within a horizontal plane. The pectoral fin base of a rainbow trout *Oncorhynchus mykiss*, being oriented more toward the horizontal (mean θ = 10°), moves dorsoventrally within a vertical plane. These differences in range of motion, tested during turning maneuvers involving the pectoral fins, show that the bluegill's laterally directed forces are substantially greater than the trout's. The wake, directed perpendicular to the body's axis, is also substantial during swimming at both low and high speeds. Consequently, force of the lateral wake is heightened during turns when the momentum of lateral fluid flows impinges on the turning moment around the body's CM. This is made possible by the vertical orientation of the pectorals, which sweep back and forth perpendicular with the horizontal plane, subsequently generating greater turning force than fins oriented horizontally and beating dorsoventrally. The laterally force generated by a bluegill making a turn is ~8× that of a rainbow trout. Pectoral fins like the trout's that beat up and down are more destabilizing during turns, causing the body to roll. The bluegill pectoral, with its wide range of motion, has largely overcome this problem by generating greater laterally directed forces.

Turning maneuvers are initiated by the strong-side pectoral fin, but with subsequent recruitment of the soft dorsal. The soft dorsal's participation provides 35% of the total lateral force, and its moment about the fish's CM is large.[52] Immediately following rotation and the start of adduction of the pectoral fin (beginning of the translational phase), abduction is apparent along the trailing edge of the soft dorsal (Figure 14). Once set in motion abduction is commensurate with a free vortex shed from the trailing edge (Figure 14A) while vorticity of opposite sign (clockwise) forms in its place. As the soft dorsal's distal edge returns to the midline and straightens, bound vorticity is shed into the wake as a second free vortex (Figure 14B). Turning is an unbalanced maneuver, and the reaction force impinging on the soft dorsal at a location posterior to the CM slows the rotation induced earlier by the pectorals. In addition, the fish is pushed forward and away from the stimulus.

Braking

The bluegill is a master of maneuverability. Its short compressiform shape, large and vertically oriented pectoral fins capable of a wide range of motions, and location of the pectorals near the CM provide excellent stability for rapid turning, braking, and maneuvering in tight places. Turns can be accomplished on a short axis with minimal bending of the trunk. Bending of the body, which accompanies pectoral fin movements during turning in trout and many sagittiform fishes, influences forward propulsion and braking. Braking in combination with suction feeding (Chapter 3) is important to bluegills during foraging.[53]

Location of the pectoral fins impinges on braking ability (Figure 15). To decelerate, a swimming bluegill must produce force directed in front, and it does this by protracting the pectoral fins and exposing their entire surfaces perpendicular to the incident flow. According to hypothesis 1 (Figure 15A), when the fins are located ventrally the wake momentum is predicted to be horizontal, and the line of braking force occurs below the body's CM. A later model, hypothesis 2 (Figure 15B), predicts that in species with pectorals positioned higher on the body, braking force is directed so that the reaction force intersects the CM. Recent experiments tested both hypotheses. A braking force reaction oriented arbitrarily depicts two angles in parasagittal view (Figure 15C): angle α between the longitudinal axis of the fish and the line of action of the braking force acting on the fin (reaction force angle), and angle β between the longitudinal axis of the fish and the line connecting CM with the centroid of the pectoral as completely extended while braking (angle of inclination). Hypothesis 1 is supported if α is significantly less than β, hypothesis 2 if the difference is not significant.

Significance was not detected in tests using bluegills, indicating that pectoral fins located higher on the body can direct braking reactions through the CM. As confirmation, bluegills

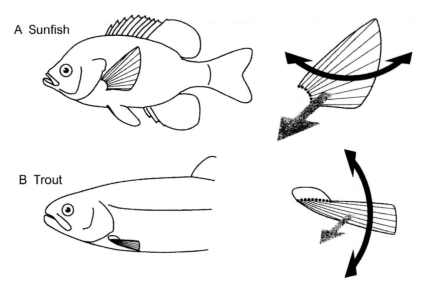

Figure 13. Comparative orientation of base of the pectoral fin in the bluegill and rainbow trout. Points of insertion are indicated by rows of dots. Double-headed arrows represent a fin's stroke plane, shaded arrows the relative magnitudes of predicted force vectors oriented laterally. Angles of inclination of fin bases were measured relative to the longitudinal body axis. Source: Drucker and Lauder (2002).

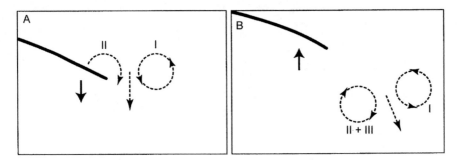

Figure 14. Wake produced by the soft dorsal fin (dorsal view) of a bluegill making a slow turn in response to a stimulus applied to its left side. Solid-line arrows show direction of fin motion. See text for explanations. Source: Drucker and Lauder (2001).

experience minimal forward pitch, or somersaulting, when braking. In rainbow trout the vector of the reaction force is positioned at an angle (angle α) underneath angle β, or below the CM. A trout brakes by bending its pectoral fins so that the trailing edge is protracted but also raised, much like ailerons. Both fishes release a braking wake comprising paired counter rotating vortices, both of which are well developed in the bluegill but uneven in the trout. The bluegill's wake momentum is directed downward and forward, courtesy of its vertically oriented pectorals, that of the trout is angled upward and forward.

When a trout abducts its pectoral fins to brake it has a tendency to pitch. This directed moment is countered by abducting the dorsal fin to one side. In addition, the trailing edges of the pelvic fins are protracted and raised, mimicking motions of the pectorals. Nonetheless, pitch is obvious upon abrupt deceleration. In contrast, the pectoral fins of bluegills direct braking forces closer to the CM.

The additional surface area of the bluegill's large pectoral fins was thought to enhance

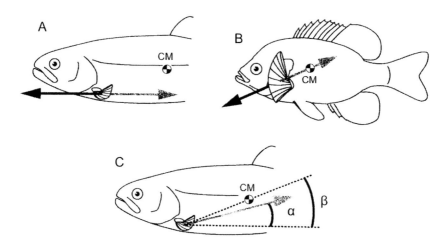

Figure 15. Location of the pectoral fin and implications for braking force. Fins are depicted at maximum extension. Black vectors represent braking forces exerted by the pectoral fin; shaded vectors represent reaction forces impinging on the fin. A: Previously untested model of pectoral fin braking (hypothesis 1) proposed by Breder (1926). B: Braking model (hypothesis 2) of Harris (1938). C: Experimental measurements used to evaluate these hypotheses. CM = center of mass. Source: Drucker and Lauder (2002).

braking. However, captive specimens with the distal 65% of the pectorals ablated are able to brake as efficiently as before, falsifying this hypothesis.[54] Bluegills with ablated fins quickly learn to incorporate more displacement and faster protraction of the pectorals into their braking movements, using a combination of glide, propulsion, and maximum protraction to sustain both speed and control when approaching prey, much like maintaining forward speed when docking a boat while simultaneously applying reverse thrust.

Braking in the bluegill also involves the medial fins. As the fish decelerates the dorsal inclinators cause abduction of both the soft dorsal and caudal fins, but in opposite directions.[55] This configuration, implemented to induce drag, has been likened to a sea anchor.[56]

Sensory Perception

2

Hydrodynamic and Acoustic Detection

Underwater, sound reception and hydrodynamic forces are not only difficult to distinguish, but their functions vary with level of organization. At the level of the receptor, hair cells of the lateral line and inner ear, or labyrinth, act as displacement detectors.[57] At the organ level the simple lateral line neuromasts detect velocity,[58] the movements of their cupulae being stimulated by drag forces proportional to the velocity of the water flowing past.[59] At the system level, arrays of neuromasts are detectors intermediate between velocity and acceleration, neuromasts of the lateral line canal ordinarily operating to detect acceleration.[60] The superficial neuromasts are sensitive only in still waters,[61] such as those inhabited by bluegills; in running waters these organs are stimulated at all times, making them useful mainly for rheotaxis[62] but not for detecting hydrodynamic movements.[63] Over short distances—that is, close to moving prey or predators—the vectors of acceleration vary in strength and direction and readily stimulate the lateral line.[64]

The otoliths of the inner ear (utriculus, sacculus, and lagena) are linear acceleration detectors, their displacements occurring during displacement of the fish; the three semicircular canals and their components work as angular acceleration detectors.[65] The hydrodynamic field moves toward uniformity with distance from the source, and the absence of local disturbances leaves cupulae of the lateral line unstimulated.[66] In this situation the denser otoliths are more adapted to detect displacements of neutrally buoyant fishes.[67] Therefore, both the lateral line canals and their constituents, along with the otolith organs, have evolved to detect acceleration, the first associated with acceleration of water relative to the fish, the second with acceleration of the fish itself.[68] In addition, the lateral line senses spatial differences along its arrays; the otoliths monitor acceleration of the water as an average over the volume occupied by the fish as it swims.[69]

Although the lateral line acts operationally as a hydrodynamic receiver, it also detects low-frequency sounds originating from nearby objects in motion.[70] Together, hydrodynamic reception and low-frequency detection aid in schooling, avoiding obstacles, capturing prey, and escaping predators.[71] The lateral line's detection limit is thought to extend into the water no farther than a few body lengths of the receiver, with about one body length or less being the most effective distance.[72] If a prominent hypothesis depicting the lateral line as a particle acceleration

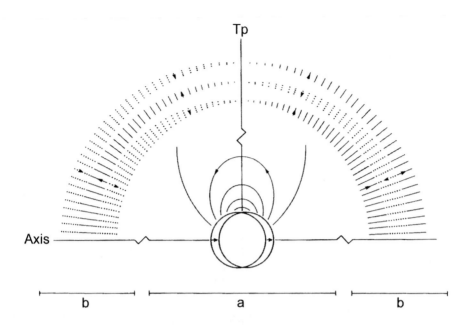

Figure 16. Dipole field of a vibrating sphere. a = dipolar local flow, b = radial propagating sound wave. Arrows = particle velocities, solid lines = compression, broken lines = rarefaction. Dipolar and radial regions are separated by a broad and complex transition zone (not shown). Axis = axis of vibration, Tp = transverse plane. Not to scale. Source: Kalmijn (1989).

detector responding to low frequencies is correct,[73] this organ's restricted range of effectiveness results not from predatory fishes detecting acceleration specifically, but from their sensing of spatial differences in the acceleration of particles radiating outward from swimming prey—that is, to spatial differences in the hydrodynamic fields surrounding a prey organism as it moves.[74] Moreover, differences in acceleration along the lateral line arrays fall away steeply (approximately the fourth power of distance from the source).[75] Lateral line organs extend nearly the length of a fish, enabling it to more easily detect differences in acceleration and accurately pinpoint the location of targets.

The hydrodynamic vortices around a swimming fish (Chapter 1) resemble the dipole field of a submerged vibrating sphere in which pressure gradients cause fluid particles to fall off and accelerate away from the sides, disengaging with the cube of the distance and proportional to the volume of the moving object (Figure 16). As the model sphere moves forward it pushes water ahead. The water directly in front banks up, displaced by the slight compression, before spilling away. Once in motion it floods vacant spaces that arise continuously along trailing edges in rarefactive patterns, streaming to the sides, pushing laterally into broad arcs, and finally emerging behind as a turbulent wake. This pattern remains as a sphere (or swimming fish) moves ahead, but the fluid particles change. The formation and dissolution of these configurations are dynamic and instantaneous, although nonetheless detectable by predators able to discern from their prey's movements whether it is accelerating or moving steadily. Within striking range these hydrodynamic models dissolve in a swirling pool of vortices and turbulence, and how the lateral line operates at this point is unknown. We can say only that its stimulation and the fish's subsequent response might be undemanding, the disruption of any recognizable flow fields irrelevant.

The wake left by a swimming fish or other aquatic animal slowly attenuates, but not without

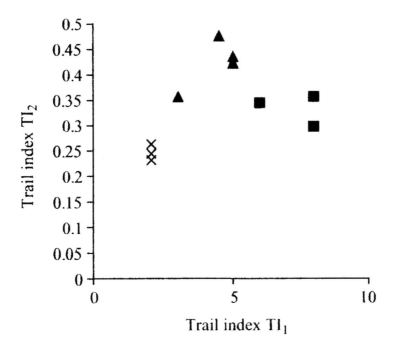

Figure 17. Trails measured in one aquarium plotted by trail indices (see original report). **x** = banded puffer, ■ = five-spot African cichlid, ▲ = pumpkinseed. Source: Hanke and Bleckmann (2004).

alerting intercepting predators or prey of its owner's location and distance. These hydrodynamic "trails" have been playfully called "fish footprints."[76] The size of a wake depends on the size of the fish, but its morphology varies by species.[77] If "fish footprints" are indeed unique to species, and if they can be recognized and used to advantage by conspecifics or predators, they might better be named "fish fingerprints."

Vortex sheets released into the wake (Chapter 1) decay quickly but remain distinguishable from the background noise for several minutes.[78] Captive wels (also known as European catfish) *Silurus glanis* held in complete darkness can track a guppy *Poecilia reticulata* by its wake even when the vortices are 10 s old and the guppy 55 body lengths away.[79] The wakes of a pumpkinseed *Lepomis gibbosus* in still water remained detectable after 5 min, and the vortices themselves lasted more than 60 s.[80] During trials in which the extended trails of pumpkinseeds were tested, maximum values of both vorticity and velocity decayed within the first 10 s, although remnants persisted.[81]

Such wakes remain distinctive even while disintegrating. Pumpkinseed wakes are measurably different from those made by the banded puffer *Colomesus psittacus* and five-spot African cichlid *Thysochromis ansorgii*, which are distinguishable from each other. Hydrodynamic trails of the pumpkinseed and cichlid have greater lateral spread than the trail of the banded puffer, a tetraodontiform swimmer that relies on its dorsal and anal fins for propulsion. There are other identifiable differences, like maximum width and the distribution of velocity. The pumpkinseed's trail has sharp contours; that of the cichlid is diffuse. The extent of the separation is apparent in Figure 17.

The shed vorticity is associated with velocity gradients, which cupulae in the lateral lines of fishes have evolved to detect; neuromasts of the lateral line detect acceleration of the water relative to the fish.[82] The mechanisms by which fishes might use vortices to advantage are just now being discovered. One other use has been found: machine-generated vortex rings introduced into channels downstream of pump intakes have successfully repelled fishes.[83]

Fishes have provided considerable behavioral evidence for the hydrodynamic detection of prey.[84] Captive fishes continue to feed on live prey in the absence of visual cues, although feeding ceases upon inactivation of the lateral line sensors. An unmanipulated captive muskellunge *Esox masquinongy* feeds in two phases: it skulks stealthily toward its prey using the pectoral and caudal fins, then strikes quickly.[85] The process involves vision for initial target detection, but the lateral line assumes dominance during the strike. Vision might even be the less important sensory function throughout the attack sequence: growth of the closely related northern pike *Esox lucius* correlates negatively with water clarity.[86] When feeding on fathead minnows *Pimephales promelas*, muskies with their lateral lines blocked reversibly by cobalt approached minnows significantly closer before striking, compared with control muskies with intact vision and unblocked lateral lines. Controls approached from a larger angle, probably to expose a greater number of the linear lateral line receptors to the target in anticipation of striking. Blinded muskies with their lateral lines intact were still successful predators but unable to initiate the stalking phase of the repertoire, remaining motionless until a minnow came within close range. Muskies that were both blinded and lateral line-suppressed ignored minnows even when close.

Dark-adapted captive bluegills of 120–150 mm moved toward small goldfish *Carassius auratus*, but did not attack until closing the distance to 2 cm or less. However, bluegills detected goldfish and subsequently approached them from 10 cm away, evidently in response to hydrodynamic vortex fields generated by their movements and mediated by the inner ear.[87] As mentioned, the inner ear otoliths, like the lateral line neuromasts, are acceleration detectors, although of a different sort.[88] Vibrating spheres and wires were also attacked at distances of 2 cm or less, but only if their frequencies were below 10 Hz. Those vibrating at higher frequencies (10–100 Hz) were ignored. This is consistent with the acceleration spectrum of a slowly moving goldfish, which shows a maximum amplitude of 10 Hz,[89] and with slowly moving fishes generally, which produce frequencies predominantly less than 20 Hz.[90]

Bluegills with their lateral lines blocked reversibly by cobalt could not detect either goldfish or vibrating spheres at close range, but still approached goldfish from 10 cm away, indicating no disruption of hearing. In the dark, blocked bluegills did not attack goldfish unless touched. In the light, both blocked and unblocked bluegills approached low-frequency sources from 10 cm away, but did not attack. Both also located goldfish visually from distances greater than 10 cm and rushed forward to attack them. This was in marked contrast to their behavior at night, which was to glide slowly in midwater using their tail fins sparingly, behavior consistent with enhancing the lateral line's effectiveness by minimizing local water movement, and like that of adult bluegills observed at night in Lake Cazenovia, New York.[91] Similar stroke and glide behavior has been reported in captive juvenile alewives *Alosa pseudoharengus*, a species that like the bluegill feeds mainly in daylight but at night can detect other organisms (zooplankters) using its lateral line.[92] Evidence that the lateral line can override vision has also been found in the green sunfish *Lepomis cyanellus* and largemouth bass *Micropterus salmoides*.[93] The inner ear's eminently useful but inexact directional hearing might guide night-feeding fishes to the vicinity of their prey before being superseded by the lateral line.[94]

The wake of a swimming insect larva telegraphs its presence and ought to be detectable by the lateral line of a drifting bluegill even in complete darkness. Damselfly larvae *Enallagma cyathigerum* are active swimmers, and their maneuvers are typical of other aquatic insect larvae.[95] A swimming damselfly releases alternating vortex rings with every half-stroke of its tail (Figure 18). The vortex arises much as it does in caudal-swimming fishes, forming anteriorly before sliding down the body and being shed into the wake. However, unlike vortices originat-

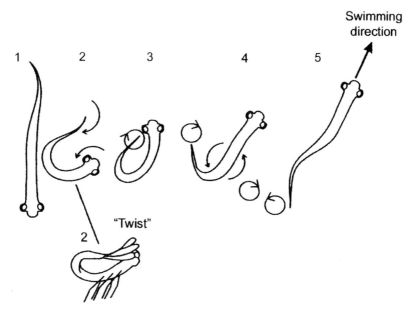

Figure 18. Schematic representation of how a thrust vortex is generated by a larval damselfly during a simple flex maneuver. Source: Brackenbury (2003).

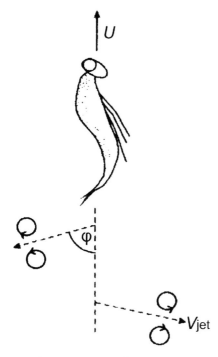

Figure 19. Schematic pattern of ring vortices shed into the wake of a swimming mayfly larva. U = forward velocity, ϕ = momentum axis of the ring vortex in the medial plane of the body, V_{jet} = velocity of jet relative to the surrounding water measured at the plane of the vortex ring. Source: Brackenbury (2004).

ing from the tail sweeps of fishes, insect vortex rings are not von Kármán street, which are released as a pair on each side of the body with alternate half-strokes and come together in the wake like links of a chain.

A swimming mayfly larva *Chloeon dipterum* exhibits a similar pattern. Vortex rings are shed separately from the dorsal and ventral surfaces with alternate half-strokes and propagated at 90° to the direction of forward thrust (Figure 19).

The labyrinth has two sensory functions: vestibular for posture and balance and auditory for hearing.[96] Fishes vary in hearing ability, the differences falling partly along phylogenetic lines. However, as exemplified by the squirrelfishes, large disparities sometimes occur within a single taxonomic group.[97] Fishes are thought of as hearing specialists or hearing generalists.[98] Hearing specialists are sensitive to sound over extended frequencies, having low auditory thresholds and greater susceptibility to hearing damage when exposed to sounds of high intensity. This group includes the otophysans (cypriniforms, characiforms, siluriforms, and gymnotiforms). Many percids and other hearing generalists detect sounds over a narrower frequency range at higher auditory thresholds and appear to be harmed less by sustained exposure to high-intensity sounds.

A fish's sensitivity to sound depends to some extent on possession of a swim bladder, although other gas-retaining structures have been identified. Some species have evolved bony connections that provide a bridge to the inner ear, thus serving as hearing aids. Among these ancillary accoutrements are otophysic extensions that push the swim bladder anteriorly and therefore closer to the inner ear (e.g., mormyrids), extensions of bone from the pelvic girdle or skull to the swim bladder (e.g., squirrelfishes, triggerfishes), and suprabranchial chambers and bullae where air is retained (e.g., gouramis).[99] The Weberian ossicles of otophysans bestow superior hearing. These consist of a series of small bones (modified vertebrae) linking the anterior end of the swim bladder directly with the inner ear. In many other hearing generalists, such as the percids, the swim bladder is isolated, and in these its role in audition is doubtful.[100] One such species is the bluegill.

Fishes no doubt hear what they need to hear. If some appear auditorily challenged, it seems not to have affected their survival and evolution. Biologists have questioned why certain fishes even have hearing, especially those unable to communicate with conspecifics using sound.[101] One such species is the goldfish, which is mute but certainly not deaf: it hears tones from 50 to 3,000 Hz.[102] Sensitivity to sound pressure and the capability to hear over a wide bandwidth have no demonstrated relationship for detecting signals from conspecifics. In fact, "The correlation between communication sound production and auditory sensitivity is poor or nonexistent."[103]

Some fishes exposed to high-intensity sounds show auditory threshold effects; that is, audiograms made after exposure reveal a shift upward from baseline levels, indicating hearing damage. Species with enhanced hearing sensitivity (hearing specialists) are affected more severely than hearing generalists. When bluegills and fathead minnows were exposed to high-intensity white noise for 2, 4, 8, or 24 h, auditory thresholds for bluegills before and after exposure were statistically indistinguishable (Figure 20, data for 24 h). Note from the curves that the bluegill, a hearing generalist, has a higher baseline auditory threshold than the fathead minnow, a hearing specialist. The minnows sustained measurable hearing loss following exposure, as seen by the higher and statistically significant upward shift in its auditory threshold.

Vision

With exception of the optimal foraging model (Chapter 3), which stipulates no particular sensory mode for acquiring energy from the habitat, the implication is that bluegills forage using only vision. As described in the above section, this seems unlikely. More accurately, bluegills can be said to rely heavily—but not exclusively—on vision to locate food, but also to recognize conspecifics and detect predators. A bluegill's visual acuity, or its capacity to see shapes and details, is limited by—and defined as—the angle subtended by the target object at detection and by the minimum separable angle between cones in the retina.[104] Because focal length increases with lens diameter, visual acuity improves as the fish grows.[105] However, cone numbers decrease slightly with age, which tends to lessen visual acuity.[106]

Visual acuity increases in curvilinear fashion with body length.[107] Its development, synonymous in pragmatic terms with a decreasing visual angle,[108] depends on the diameter of the lens and on cone numbers.[109] The measured angle is 2.7 min of arc for bluegills of 120 mm SL.[110] Prey organisms of larger bluegills subtend smaller angles, which are associated with smaller measured distances between cones.[111] Therefore, bigger bluegills ought to have better visual acuity than smaller conspecifics, and the visual angle should diminish with growth (Figure 21). Reduced visual angles allow a fish to see prey from farther away, thus enlarging its foraging space.[112]

Intercone distance varies little with changes in body length, although this observation can be misleading. With growth, a bluegill's retina grows too, but it also recedes from the center of the

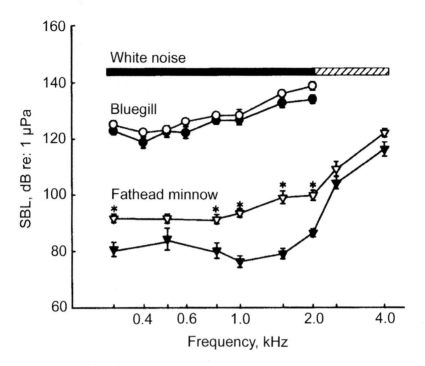

Figure 20. Audiograms of bluegills and fathead minnows depicting baseline and threshold shifts caused by exposure to white noise for 24 hours. Closed symbols = controls (baseline data for fish not exposed to noise), open symbols = test fish exposed to white noise (0.3-2.0 kHz, 142 dB, re: µPa). Asterisks indicate significance at $p < 0.01$. Horizontal bar represents white noise SPL received by both species, with solid section representing bandwith of exposure for bluegills, hatched section the extended bandwith for fathead minnows. SPL = sound pressure level; frequency range is $\log_{10}$. Source: Scholik and Yan (2002).

lens.[113] As a consequence, the retina's magnification factor (distance on the retinal surface per degree of visual angle) increases. The result is that the viewed object projects a larger image, although in a larger eye. The unchanging numbers of micrometers separating cones correlates with the diminishing number of minutes of visual angle (Figure 22). Comparing the slopes of the two regression lines in the Figure shows that the visual angle decreases by ~50% as a bluegill grows from 35 to 60 mm SL. That larger fish used in this experiment attacked smaller prey was attributed to improved visual acuity.

As a fish grows, so does its lens. Lens diameter in bluegills is allometric with body length.[114] Visual acuity is thought to increase too because, as mentioned previously, focal length increases with lens diameter.[115] This allows larger bluegills to detect prey at a greater distance. For bluegills of 22.9–126.5 mm SL the association of lens diameter versus body length (log-transformed data) is shown by the linear regression equation

$$\ln(y) = -2.745 + 0.901 \ln(x)$$

where y = diameter of the lens (mm) and x = SL (mm): $R^2 = 0.96$, $n = 64$. Lens diameter is nearly proportional to standard length (SL).

From aquarium experiments reaction distance (RD), or the distance at which a prey organism can be detected, increases with size of the prey and increasing length of the predatory fish, but attenuates in bigger fish.[116] Simple optics define the visual angle, α, as extending in straight

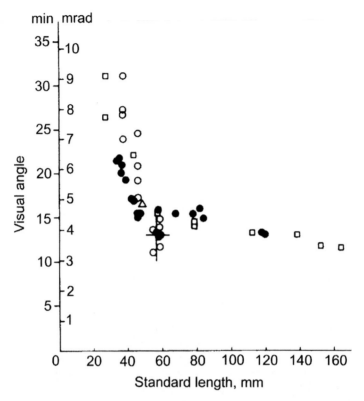

Figure 21. Visual acuity versus body length in the bluegill. Symbols are from different sources (see Li et al. 1985 for references). Source: Li et al. (1985).

lines from the prey's outer periphery to the center of the fish's eye. Thus, $\alpha = 2$ arctan $(0.5\,h/RD)$, where h = height of the prey and RD represents one reaction distance. Reaction distance in these experiments was based on behavior of pumpkinseeds.[117] Upon sighting prey a sunfish (1) stops, (2) erects its dorsal fin slightly, (3) swims directly to the object, and (4) sucks it in. One unit of reaction distance (1 RD) was therefore defined as the distance (cm) between the occurrence of behaviors 2 and 4. The median visual angle decreased with increasing size of the fish, indicating improvement in visual acuity with length. These findings assume cone number to be relatively constant.

A measure of visual acuity versus length in bluegills has been described by a quadratic regression using the natural logarithm of visual acuity regressed against the natural logarithm of standard length in the form

$$\ln(a) = a + b(\ln L) + c(\ln L)^2$$

in which α = visual angle (minutes of arc), L = SL (mm), and a, b, and c are coeffients ($a = 9.14$, $b = -2.40$, and $c = 0.229$); $R^2 = 0.42$, $n = 342$, $p < 0.0001$.[118] From this equation visual volume could be calculated for zooplankton of six sizes based on length of the fish (Figure 23). Visual volume in this case is the hemispheric space with a radius defined by the reaction distance between the eye and the object;[119] in other words, the volume of water within which prey organisms of a particular size can be detected. The curves show that a bluegill of 40 mm SL has a visual volume ~3.5× smaller than one twice that length. An increase should raise the encounter rate, leading to improved foraging efficiency.

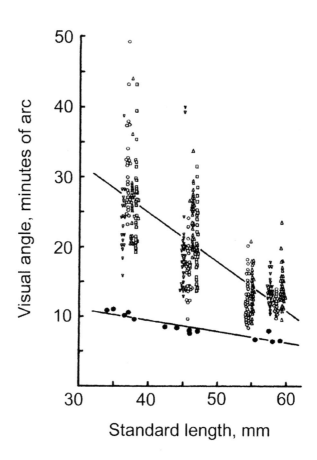

Figure 22. Two independent measures of vision in the bluegill based on length. Open symbols are reaction angles measured on bluegills of 37, 46, 55, and 58 mm SL feeding on water fleas of different sizes (∇ = 1.1, O =1.6 mm, Δ = 2.0 mm, $\square$= 2.4 mm). Data are spread for clarity. The reaction angle declined from $\bar{x}$ = 27.8 minutes of arc in small fish to $\bar{x}$= 14.2 in bigger ones (n = 12). The reaction angle represents the angular distance of a bluegill's head just before attacking a water flea of known diameter and the moment when its jaws snapped, as determined from x, y coordinates taken from an overhead video. Filled circles depict intercone spacing (6.3 ±0.5 µm, $\bar{x}$ ±SD) measured from histological sections. Source: Hairston et al. (1982).

Assuming light and turbidity are not limiting, the capacity of a fish to detect a prey organism is dependent on its distance and the angle at which it appears. The number of cones (6,000–7,000/ mm²) and their distribution in the bluegill retina is greatest dorsotemporally and ventronasally, but generally uniform, and cone counts do not predict better vision in any particular axis.[120] Behavioral investigations indicate that a bluegill's vision is best in both the vertical and horizontal planes from 0 to 45° (Figures 24 and 25) with maximum resolution closer to 45°.[121] Prey items at 90° or positioned behind the fish at 135° are ignored in favor of those in front, unless their apparent size is much greater. These observations are consistent with the extensive accommodative range of the bluegill lens in the pupillary plane, which is mainly along the rostral-caudal axis instead of the lateral axis, as it is in the goldfish.[122] Accommodation in this plane accompanies stretching of the lens toward the rostrum, which would be necessary for good vision not only nearby but directly in front.

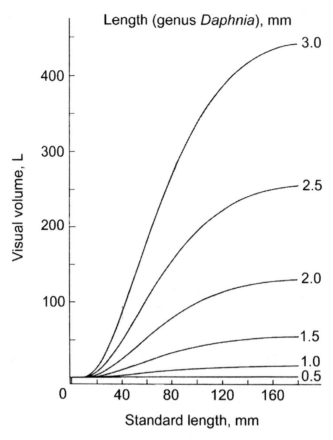

Figure 23. Predicted visual volume versus length (mm SL) in bluegills. Visual volume is assumed to be hemispheric with a radius equal to the reaction distance. Source: Breck and Gitter (1983).

Bluegills are mainly diurnal.[123] The combination of superior contrast detection, even dispersal of cones throughout the retina,[124] low ratios of bipolar cells to ganglion cells,[125] dynamic lens accommodation in the rostral-caudal plane,[126] and excellent acuity in the forward hemisphere[127] are adaptations for detecting small mobile prey in bright environments. However, vision is doubtfully useful in dim light or turbid water where the lateral line and inner ear are likely to be important. A bluegill's reaction time diminishes as a negative power function of turbidity from less than 2 m in clear water to 9 cm at 50 NTUs (nephelometric turbidity units).[128] Enclosure experiments using larval bluegills of 12.5 mm TL revealed that capture rate declined with increasing turbidity (11–64 NTUs) at low levels of illumination (< 100–300 lx), rising as turbidity and light intensity increased (> 460 lx).[129] Larval bluegills chose small zooplankters at high levels of illumination and increasing turbidity, but large ones during conditions of low light and high turbidity. Other experiments showed that for prey of given size the reaction distance of bluegills decreases at light intensities less than 10 lx and low turbidity (1 JTU, Jackson turbidity unit).[130] Above 10 lx reaction distance increases with increasing prey size. However, at 0.70 lx the reaction distance for 2-mm prey was ~6.5× less than at 10.8 lx. At low illumination and high turbidity the value falls substantially from ~21 cm at 6.25 JTUs to ~4.5 cm at 30 JTUs. How closely these results extrapolate to nature is unknown (e.g., the growth of larval bluegills in 21 Illinois reservoirs was unaffected by water transparency).[131]

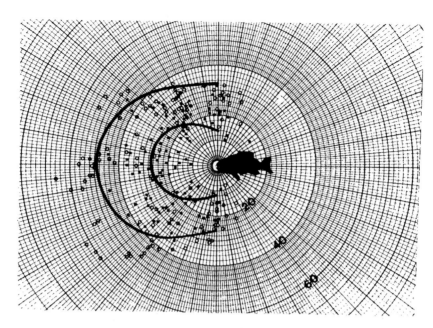

Figure 24. Location of 2-mm specimens of water fleas (*Daphnia magna*) in the forward-directed vertical plane surrounding a bluegill at light intensities of ~5,900 lx. ■ = where water fleas were located, ○ = where they were not located. Line closest to the fish encompasses the region where finding prey is 95% certain; outer line marks the region beyond which prey organisms are located < 5% of the time. Within the intervening space the chance of location increases gradually toward the inner line. Numbers are distance from the fish (cm). Source: Luecke and O'Brien (1981).

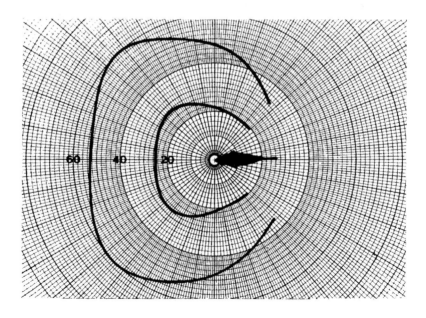

Figure 25. Location of 2-mm specimens of water fleas (*Daphnia magna*) in the horizontal plane surrounding a bluegill at light intensities of ~5,900 lx. Numbers are distance from the fish (cm). Source: Luecke and O'Brien (1981).

Light intensity ameliorates turbidity, but this is of little consequence at night. As discussed elsewhere, bluegills sometimes feed in darkness. When foraging in water of low illumination and high turbidity, or in darkness, visual detection of prey is likely overridden by the lateral line and inner ear. Even at 35 lx, a typical level of illumination in lakes at midday, a bluegill's ability to locate prey is reduced ~25%.[132] At 0.91 lx, or the equivalent of lake water at twilight, the loss can reach ~66%. This suggests that RD measurements underestimate how well bluegills find prey, representing the greatest distance at which food is identifiable but not the distance at which the object is first seen.[133]

An object is invisible and without any contrast if the light it reflects matches the color and intensity of light in the background. This background spacelight, or veiling radiance, comprises the coloration seen underwater. It arises when light is scattered in all directions by water molecules and suspended particulate matter. Scattering causes photons to be everywhere, coloring the water in all directions. Waters vary in their spectral quality of light and in the light transmitted through them. Wavelengths that excite a fish's visual pigments are often different from those illuminating the ambient environment. Such mismatched, or offset, visual pigments provide advantages to diurnal fishes inhabiting shallow waters, enabling them to filter out the background spacelight and see targets with greater contrast. They work as follows.[134]

Water selectively absorbs light, lessening its intensity by subtracting wavelengths, and, with depth, turning it increasingly monochromatic. In combination, absorption and scattering attenuate the light needed to form retinal images, lessening a target's distinction with the background spacelight. A pigment matching the dominant wavelength of the background is not always optimal for detecting contrast. A bluegill swimming in shallow water and looking horizontally can distinguish objects only if they are contrasted against the background spacelight either by being darker or brighter. (Brightness, or luminance, is the perceptual quality of light intensity.[135]) The reflected light from a bright object, having traveled only a short vertical distance from the surface, is less monochromatic than light in the horizontal plane and therefore contains more bandwidths than the background spacelight. This is because, in the horizontal, the intervening water contributes a spacelight of its own.[136] As horizontal distance increases, the radiance from the target eventually merges with the background spacelight until it disappears. The light radiated from the object is least for the dominant wavelength behind it.

With depth, the spectral distribution of the downwelling light eventually merges with that of the background spacelight until the light reflected from the target and that of the background have identical values of luminance, or perceived brightness, at all wavelengths.[137] Photoreceptors having a spectral sensitivity that matches the background luminance most closely will have the best target detection. Therefore, photoreceptors possessing sensitivity matched to the spectrum of the background spacelight are most effective for detecting distant targets and targets that are darker when projected against the background. However, bright objects in shallower water require receptors with sensitivity focused at wavelengths that are offset from the maximum light transmission.

A fish's visual pigments are adapted to provide the best contrast of objects against the background,[138] and bluegills perform this function remarkably well: both the minimum time span of a perceived target and the contrast threshold are 1/55 that of humans[139] and remain superior even at low temperature (15°C). The ratio of light absorbed by the bluegill's visual pigments (the light reflected from the object) and the background spacelight (the contrast) is less for a matched pigment than one that is offset. This is because its maximum wavelength is mismatched with the maximum wavelength transmitted through the water. The waters of North American lakes and ponds tend to be green, ordinarily with a yellow component. Yellow pigments, largely refractory remnants of decomposing plants and bacteria (e.g., tannins, lignins, fulvic and humic acids), absorb all wavelengths of incoming light, but especially ultraviolet, violet, and blue, acting collectively as a "minus-blue" filter and shifting the underwater spectrum toward 600 nm.[140] Typically, such waters are dominated by wavelengths of 540–560 nm.[141]

Having more than one color receptor allows a fish to discriminate different wavelengths matched for brightness,[142] enhancing contrast perception. Bluegills have two types of cones containing predominately green- and red-sensitive pigments. These are single green-sensitive cones with a mean λ_{max} of 536 nm and double red-sensitive cones having a mean λ_{max} of 620 nm.[143] The green-red combination seems tailored to the bluegill's diurnal activities, enhancing contrast during feeding at dawn and dusk near the surface and in deeper water at midday.[144] Red-sensitive cells enhance contrast in the yellow-pigmented waters typical of most lakes and ponds, but also allows bluegills to see into the near-infrared background spacelight of darkly pigmented, or "black," waters that characterize some lowland rivers and sluggish streams of the southeastern United States. Bluegills apparently lack cones that are sensitive to the short wavelengths, and this improves sensitivity by lowering the effects of scatter and chromatic aberration, both of which are intensified at the short end of the spectrum.[145] In addition, the ocular media of a bluegill's eyes filter potentially harmful ultraviolet radiation.[146]

Contrast sensitivity in bluegills varies with intensity of the background spacelight. Below a certain threshold the target contrast falls exponentially with further diminution of the background spacelight.[147] Nonetheless, bluegills can detect prey organisms that are < 1% brighter than the background and continue to do so over a range of background intensities. This remarkable capacity is evidence of Weber's Law in which the detection threshold of radiance remains constant over the range of background values. Within this context, contrast sensitivity is the smallest difference in radiance between R_o (an object) and R_b (the background spacelight) detectable as a result of the background space light, or $(R_o-R_b)/R_b$.

Bluegills probably do see best in bright habitats. Prey detection and therefore reaction distance declines as the light level falls.[148] This seems straightforward. However, when light levels exceed 1 mW/cm², green- and red-sensitive reception follows Weber's law.[149] Below this level the brightness of the target must be greater than the predicted contrast sensitivity before becoming detectable. At 0.01 mW/cm² its brightness must exceed that of the background spacelight by 50–70%. At values below 1 mW/cm² a bluegill's capacity to detect contrast falls off rapidly, causing a simultaneous decrease in reaction distance.

Spatial summation is the visual capacity to sum the photons of light received, and the stimulated region of the eye over which this occurs is the critical diameter. The area of a target and the contrast necessary to detect it are explained by Ricco's law, which states that targets are equally detectable if the product of their luminance and area is constant. Increasing the luminance until the target is barely detectable is the detection (contrast) threshold. Increasing the area of the target results in more photons summed, thus lowering the amount of light required to maintain the detection threshold. This relationship stays proportional (and the product a constant) until area expands beyond the middle of the receptive field. Because foveal fields are small, spatial summation might occur within a minute or two of arc. The bluegill's cones obey Ricco's law, sensitive to critical diameters of 5.6° (green) and 5.5° (red).[150] Below these values the decline in sensitivity is linear and rapid. In practical terms the target contrast of a tiny object at fixed distances must be ~10× that of a target equal in size to the critical diameter.

The contrast of objects against the background spacelight is crucial to bluegills, especially when they feed on nearly transparent zooplankton in open water. Sensitivity declines when targets are less than the critical diameter, and with spatial summation occurring in a progressively smaller region of the retina more photons are needed to activate a threshold detection response. The reaction distance of adult bluegills feeding on water fleas of 1 mm is greater than 16 cm[151] at a subtended visual angle of 0.36°.[152] To provide sufficient contrast a 1–mm water flea would require illumination of, at minimum, 1 log unit greater than the threshold for the critical diameter.[153]

The visual acuity of juvenile bluegills (32 mm SL or longer) is not independent of prey size as

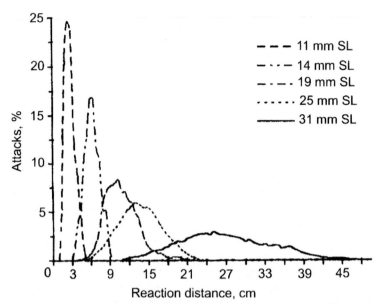

Figure 26. Distribution of reaction distances among juvenile bluegills of different size-categories. Distributions are moving averages of three fish (≤ 20 mm SL) or 10 points (fish ≥ 20 mm SL) for equivalent numbers of attacks on three prey size-categories of water fleas: small (~0.8 mm), medium (~1.1 mm), and large (~2.3 mm). Reaction distances for fish 18–20 mm SL are summed and plotted as 19 mm SL, those for fish 30-32 mm as 31 mm SL. Source: Walton et al. (1997).

it is in larger fish.[154] Because visual angles increase size of the prey, an age-0 bluegill needs to project retinal images more than twice the mean space between cones to see a 2-mm water flea. Such images are probably blurred in a developing fish, worsened by poor lens accommodation (the capacity to move the lens for focusing images on the retina) and a shortage of neuronal connections. Behavioral experiments showed the greatest incidence of detection to be for the smallest water fleas tested (~0.8 mm). Reaction distance increased with fish length (Figure 26), the range for 11-mm bluegills being restricted to 5 cm or less but expanding from 11 to 46 cm in bluegills of 30–32 mm SL.

Foraging

3

The information in this chapter and the next two unavoidably intermingle, and the titles of all three are simply arbitrary divisions lacking clean edges. Foraging can be impossible to separate from competition and predation, predation is sometimes competitive, competition typically drives foraging, fishes often forage where the likelihood of predation is less, and so forth. Some things are more certain: organisms happen to be in water because they live there, fall from the sky, or topple in from the land, and a bluegill thinks of them all as food. While mulling over what bluegills eat it occurred to me that a list of what they reject might be shorter. For obvious reasons this species has been described as insectivorous, planktivorous, omnivorous, and piscivorous.[155] Bluegills fit all these classifications. Different age-classes eat the same things, variation being in the proportions.[156] The diet ranges from detritus to other fishes[157] to the larvae and eggs of amphibians.[158] Little else is passed up, even bryozoans.[159] Ostracods occur commonly in bluegill stomachs, but whether they offer any food value is uncertain. Their shells are sometimes unopened, in which case they pass intact into the intestine.[160]

Bluegills also eat plants. Stomachs of specimens caught in Illinois had 24% plant material by volume,[161] Wisconsin fish (mostly adults) held 20%,[162] a sample from Minnesota yielded 16%,[163] and some bluegills from Ontario contained 26%.[164] Algae constituted 50% of the stomach contents of 42 Mississippi bluegills,[165] but whether algae alone can meet metabolic requirements is questionable.[166] Of 81 specimens averaging 128 mm FL (94–175 mm FL) caught by angling in Wyland Lake, Indiana, 29 had consumed algae or dead aquatic macrophytes.[167] At some locations plant seeds are a substantial part of the diet,[168] especially for larger bluegills. Bluegills introduced into Lake Biwa, Japan, in 1963, have evolved into at least three trophic morphs, one specialized for feeding on aquatic vegetation.[169]

Aquatic insect larvae are staples, but adult insects qualify too, if only serendipitously. Flies, grasshoppers, ants, spiders, terrestrial mites—any small creature that wriggles or twitches—is at least examined for its gustatory possibilities. Floating woodchips are nibbled speculatively, but so are toes dangled from a canoe[170] and the fingers and toes of bathers.[171] Cannibalism? Of course. Even the eggs and young of its principal antagonist, the largemouth bass, are attacked indiscriminately,[172] perhaps assuaging future regret at being treated in kind.

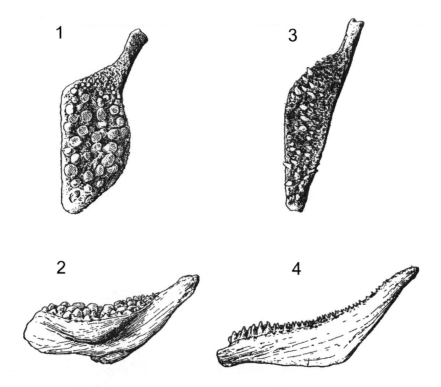

Figure 27. 1: Lower left pharyngeal pad of the pumpkinseed, top view. 2: Side view. 3: Lower left pharyngeal pad of the bluegill, top view. 4: Side view. Source: Richardson (1910).

Bluegills living in coastal rivers and bayous along the southeastern Atlantic and Gulf coasts demonstrate no aversion to brackish water.[173] During aquarium experiments extending over 2 months, juveniles behaved normally when kept in diluted artificial seawater of 10 ppt and fed a casein-based diet containing up to 4% table salt by mass.[174] Bluegills in saline environments routinely forage on sponges *Ephydatia fluviatilis*, barnacle *Balanus subalbidus* cirri, mud crabs *Rhithropanopeus harrisii*, and blue crabs *Callinectes sapidus*,[175] all isosmotic with the surrounding water. Not excluded from the diet are brackish-water plants (trachaeophytes, genera *Ceratophyllum* and *Vallisneria*).[176] Unlike most freshwater fishes, the gill tissues of bluegills apparently do not take up chloride from the environment.[177] Bluegills entering Chesapeake Bay are tolerant of salinities to at least 18.[178] Those in tidal waters of the Escambia River, Florida, can exist where the benthic salinity is 11.8;[179] others from the Ochlockonee River, Florida and Georgia, have been caught in water of 4.7.[180] Specimens described as "subadults" were captured in a stretch of the Aransas River, Texas, at 17.4,[181] or half the salinity value of seawater.

Feeding Adaptations

The bluegill's mouth opening is narrow, 8.0 mm (6% of a fish of 125–150 mm SL), or about one-third that of a largemouth bass the same size.[182] The pharyngeal pads of pumpkinseeds are covered with molarform teeth, enabling them to crush and grind the hard parts of mollusks and isopods (Figure 27). With exceptions,[183] mollusks ordinarily are unimportant dietary items for bluegills,[184] and, as shown in Figure 27, the bluegill's pads are covered with fine needlelike teeth adapted for feeding on small soft prey.[185]

The bluegill is a more efficient facultative planktivore than the pumpkinseed, in part be-

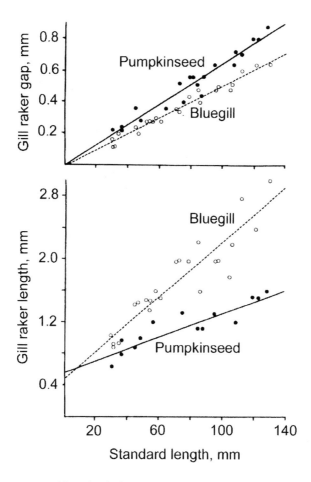

Figure 28. Mean spacing and length of gill rakers on the first gill arch. Linear regressions for gill-raker gap: bluegills, $y = 0.009 + 0.005x$ ($R^2 = 0.96$, $n = 23$ fish); pumpkinseeds, $y = -0.003 + 0.007x$ ($R^2 = 0.94$). Linear regressions for gill raker length: bluegills, $y = 0.493 + 0.017x$ ($R^2 = 0.82$); pumpkinseeds, $y = 0.551 + 0.008x$ ($R^2 = 0.86$). Regression slopes for bluegills and pumpkinseeds are significantly different (ANCOVA, $p < 0.01$). Source: Mittelbach (1984).

cause its longer and more closely spaced gill rakers permit entrapment of finer particles (Figure 28). Further evidence is seen by the shorter handling time when capturing tiny organisms like water fleas (Figure 29). Handling time is the interval between capturing an item of prey and swallowing it, although some definitions include stalking, striking, manipulating, and swallowing the prey.[186] Except for the smallest specimens of the genus *Physa*, a group of aquatic snails, pumpkinseeds longer than 75 mm SL were significantly faster than bluegills of equal size at handling gastropods. Pumpkinseeds needed more time when feeding on gastropods with stronger shells (genera *Gyraulus*, *Helisoma*).[187] These were often refused by captive bluegills, which mouthed them briefly before spitting them out.

The terminal mouth of a bluegill is said to be protrusible as a tube, and prey organisms are then sucked in by expansion of the pharynx.[188] This is a true but simplified description. Inertial suction—rapidly expanding the oral cavity to induce an abrupt surge of water into the mouth—is the common means of predation in most teleost fishes.[189] Variations depend on the relative body masses of predator and prey, the speed at which the process occurs, and the absolute

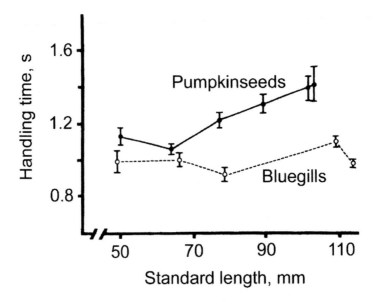

Figure 29. Mean handling times (±SE) for bluegills and pumpkinseeds feeding on the water flea *Daphnia pulex* (2.0 ±0.03 mm body length). Mean handling times for all bluegills and pumpkinseeds > 75 mm SL differed significantly (independent *t*-test, $p < 0.01$). Source: Mittelbach (1984).

change in volume inside the mouth.[190] All contributing factors, which evolved as means of overcoming water's density, are now entirely dependent on it.

Inertial suction is driven by alternating pressures of different origin, each displaying several waveforms. The process begins with buccal pressure, which decreases abruptly as the mouth opens and subsequently attains a peak negative pressure within 10–60 ms (Figure 30, BU: A, B, D).[191] The pressure then becomes briefly positive before declining. In the bluegill the rapid drop in pressure probably initiates forces of acceleration substantial enough to dislodge aquatic insects attached to stems and leaves.[192] Opercular pressure jumps quickly to positive at the point at which pressure in the buccal cavity begins to fall (Figure 30, OP: A, B). The subsequent phase is negative, bottoming out at 10–25 ms after peaking of the negative buccal pressure. The pressure then returns to baseline levels, in the end demonstrating a final positive phase (Figure 30 A, D).

Waveforms vary, sometimes indicating just the negative phase, in which case buccal pressure falls rapidly back to ambient (Figure 30, BU: G, I). Other patterns are negative-positive (Figure 30, BU: I, J) or multiple spikes of negative pressure (Figure 30, BU: B, F). Opercular pressures are less variable. During lazy strikes at stationary prey items there might not be a positive phase. However, positive pressure is always involved when the prey is moving and strikes are rapid. Maximum negative pressure in the gill cavity follows, or is simultaneous with, the peak in negative buccal pressure. Note the occasional preparative phase just before water in the buccal cavity is compressed (Figure 30, H, J). Positive buccal pressures sometimes occur in series after a prey organism has been captured (Figure 30, F), attributable to chewing movements. These pulses range from 100 to 400 ms and +20 to +250 cm H_2O. The opercular cavity, meanwhile, remains at equilibrium (Figure 30, F). The patterns are similar in form and duration for the bluegill, redbreast sunfish *L. auritus*, and pumpkinseed. Suction feeding from beginning to end lasts 20–100 ms and involves a single pulse of water.[193] The magnitude of the buccal pressure determines feeding performance.[194]

The bluegill is a high-performance suction feeder, balancing the hydrodynamics of water

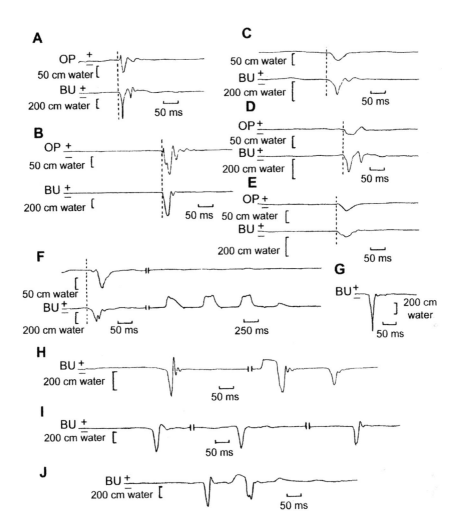

Figure 30. Buccal and opercular cavity pressures recorded in synchrony from sunfishes (including bluegills) during feeding. BU = buccal cavity pressures; OP = opercular cavity pressures. A, B = pressure waveforms during feeding on goldfish. C, D, E = different pressure waveforms during feeding on earthworms. F = buccal and opercular cavity pressures while making a strike (left) and chewing (right) after prey capture. Note that time scales are different. G = very rapid buccal pressure reduction during capture of a prey organism. H, I, J = variability in buccal pressure waveform in each of three recording sessions. Note occurrence of a preparatory phase in two feeding attempts and variability in waveform after initial pressure reduction. Source: Lauder (1980).

intake against the potentially negative fluid movements generated as it swims.[195] The bow wave accompanying a swimming fish ought to interfere substantially with suction feeding, but the bluegill circumvents this by combining suction with ram feeding. Upon detecting prey at the reaction distance a bluegill swims toward it, decelerating to ~30% of approach speed at the instant before capture and then slowing to a momentary stop after peak gape. Time to peak gape in captive specimens averages 32.0 ms, and average ram speed at the instant of peak gape is 8.4 cm/s. When a feeding bluegill is stationary it sucks in water from all directions. However, with increasing ram speed the volume taken in becomes concentrated in front of the mouth, and as ram speed increases still more the shape of the fluid intake narrows and lengthens, becoming more focused. The high-performance aspect is this: a bluegill swimming toward its prey experiences no decrement in the rate at which water is sucked in despite bow wave and other hydrodynamic interferences. Closing speed is instead made more effective by the additive processes of suction and ram, the whole sequence orchestrated by the bluegill's exquisite control over braking (Chapter 1).

Foraging Models

Bluegills perform poorly during academic exercises like moving toward a light to avoid an electric shock,[196] but excel in such practical matters as eating. Captive bluegills learn to accept previously unknown foods more quickly than pumpkinseeds,[197] and unlike pumpkinseeds and rock bass *Ambloplites rupestris* they can distinguish between familiar and unfamiliar conspecifics.[198] Bluegills spend more time with conspecifics they recognize[199] and forage with them more often.[200] Foraging bluegills can astutely track and sample changing resources for at least 40 min.[201] Their time at a given location depends on how rapidly food items are encountered. Once assessed, this information is used to devise a foraging pattern for exploiting the available resources predicated on their availability.

Related nuances attempting to explain the ways in which bluegills obtain food have been the subjects of foraging models. These can be placed in two groups, those emphasizing *why* fishes select certain foods and others attempting to discern *how* the selection works. Although each model is supported by separate theoretical pillars, testing any of them requires a toolkit containing a few standard items. A traditional way of considering habitat–diet relationships is to assess the foods eaten and then determine whether the diet is wide (lots of different items) or narrow (just a few). Diet width is then compared against measures of relative habitat complexity. The literature contains evidence for both wide[202] and narrow diets[203] as habitats become increasingly intricate. According to one version of the wide diet hypothesis a bluegill foraging in a structured habitat becomes less selective than a fish in open water because no species of prey is more available than the others, especially as summer advances; that is, the availability of all prey organisms has diminished uniformly. Consequently, they are scarce, encountered less frequently, or more difficult to capture. A fish in this situation forages opportunistically with little selectivity, and its diet widens. Although the availability of food ordinarily is associated negatively with diet width, a greater variety of items is consumed as the habitat becomes increasingly complex.[204]

The narrow diet hypothesis again starts with a foraging fish in a habitat of structural complexity. This time some items of prey are more available than others by being differentially abundant, encountered more often, or less difficult to capture. A fish forages selectively in this situation, and its diet narrows. Although the availability of food correlates positively with diet width, a lesser variety of items is consumed.

Changes in diet width can also be apparent in fishes foraging in open water. The prediction is the same: foraging fishes narrow their diets as prey becomes more abundant.[205] Bluegills select larger organisms as the total number of zooplankters increases.[206] When the standing crop is low they become less selective, ingesting prey of several sizes, and their diet widens.

Handling time has important implications in calculating foraging efficiency. For example, bluegills manipulated small zooplankters in less than 1 s,[207] but when feeding on midge larvae (genus *Chironomus*) buried in sediment the feeding rate rose to 10 s/larva.[208] Early instar chironomids can be either planktonic or benthic,[209] but a bluegill extracting one from a soft bottom pays the price of a mouthful of sediment. Larger larvae burrow deeper,[210] and their handling time is even longer. Before a midge larva can be swallowed the sediment must first be separated and expelled through the gills, which increases handling time.[211] For each type of prey the handling time stays more or less constant below a critical prey-length/fish-length ratio, but increases exponentially above it,[212] shown by

$$H = 0.639e^{9.966l/L}$$

in which H = handling time, l = length of prey, and L = length of the bluegill (mm SL).[213] In other experiments handling times for small bluegills were about twice those predicted by the optimal foraging model (see below), but the exponential equation

$$H = 0.566e^{21.83l/L}$$

underestimated the time necessary to handle prey smaller than 0.13 mm.[214] For small bluegills a logarithmic equation fit better.

$$\ln H = 0.264 \times 10^{7.0151(l)}$$

(This equation is an odd mix of natural and base-10 logarithms, but I was unable to write it in a form that made better sense.) An optimal handling time doubtfully exists, and actual time is the only measurement possible. Animals are under physical constraints that lengthen the time necessary to handle prey despite the prospect of higher rewards.[215]

Prey items are captured at a rate dependent partly on their concentration and length, and on the size of the predator. Prey encounter rate is sometimes defined as the mean number of prey items captured over a period of time minus handling time.[216] Other authors treat encounter rate and feeding rate (prey capture per unit of time) as separate acts,[217] which has considerably more utility, or leave the relationship ambiguous.

As discussed in Chapter 2, a predator reacts upon detecting prey, and its distance away at this moment is the reaction distance (RD). Another definition specifies RD as the greatest distance that an object of prey can be recognized by a predator.[218] Most tests of prey encounter rates have used zooplankters in open water of good clarity and assumed that RD is proportional (or nearly so) to the size of the object.[219] This relationship is not always valid.[220] For example, phantom midges (genus *Chaoborus*) are nearly transparent except for a few darkly pigmented areas—notably the eyes, hydrostatic organs, and gut—and a predator probably focuses on these and not total length.[221] Even so, a reduced area of target contrast must be many times more visible than a target equal to the critical diameter before a bluegill can see it. The measurement of RD in one dimension ignores the fact that fishes search in three dimensions, meaning that tiny changes in prey size greatly alter the likelihood of the prey being detected.[222] An example emphasizes this point: if the visual field is described as a sphere of radius equal to RD, a water flea of 2 mm is 27× more likely to be seen than one measuring 1 mm.[223]

Transparency is strongly advantageous to zooplankters in avoiding predation by fishes.[224] Motion increases a transparent organism's visibility independent of total length. A moving phantom midge increases the RD up to 2.7× in the white crappie *Pomoxis annularis*, a planktivorous centrarchid.[225] Phantom midges are ambush predators. They hang motionless before moving with a darting motion to capture a prey organism. As mentioned, specimens containing ingested prey are themselves more susceptible to predation.[226]

Water fleas (e.g., *Daphnia magna*) have dark pigmentation, and the gut, which typically is filled with algae, also stands out. Any pigmentation on a transparent animal raises the likelihood of target detection by improving contrast against the background spacelight. Contrast is further resolved if the target's coloration stands in contrast with that of the background spacelight.[227] Populations of one species of water flea *(D. dentifera)* in northern lakes become seasonally and synchronously infected by the bacterium *Spirobacillus cienkowskii* as water temperatures start to drop in autumn.[228] Infected specimens turn red, and bluegills feed on them preferentially. Summer epidemics are repressed by the high mortality of infected water fleas but flourish in autumn as bluegills slow their foraging.

Optimal Foraging Model (OFM)—The OFM has come under criticism,[229] but remains the gold standard of the *why* genre. However, it ignores the important matter of *how* predators make their pertinent selections.[230] Some attempts to falsify the OFM have been unsuccessful[231] and others have yielded mixed results.[232] The model's basic premise states that animals select foods offering a net gain in energy above the costs of foraging for them, and that sustaining this positive balance necessitates periodic switching to more energetically profitable habitats. Foods available to bluegills occur cyclically through the growing season and are usually exploited according to age-class. The OFM incorporates such factors as prey encounter rates, prey handling times, relative sizes of prey and predator, and estimated return in energy. The objective is to predict shifts in foraging emphasis as the abundance of prey organisms sequentially rises and falls. Two elements of the toolkit are specific to the OFM, so I have included them here.

Optimal foraging rate is the activity producing the maximum net energy gained per unit time, E_n/t. Zooplankters are small, making their handling times short and their E_n/t low.[233] However, a zooplankter's energy content is also small. Based on equal mass the energy content of zooplankters and aquatic insects is similar. The water flea *Daphnia pulex* and larvae of the damselfly (genus *Enallagma*) both yield ~21 J/mg dry mass,[234] but the damselfly is 3–5× longer. Zooplankters (0.2–1.2 mm) are considered to contain 2,300 J/g wet mass, insect larvae in the sediments (3–20 mm) a comparable 2,510 J/g wet mass.[235]

The OFM's key element is behavioral: prey are actively selected, not merely consumed as encountered.[236] When E_n/t is plotted against prey length (larger prey contain more energy per unit mass), the optimal diet is the sum of all sizes of prey equal to or exceeding the prey size at which E_n/t is maximized.[237] This varies with size of the fish (Figure 31). The sloping shoulders and eventual flattening of the curves in the figure are evidence that an optimal diet (more easily defined in the largest bluegills) includes a range of prey sizes of less than optimal energy content, but which nonetheless has little effect on the net gain of energy. This has been reinforced by experiments showing that younger age-classes of bluegills consume prey below the predicted size.[238]

In the context here, I define profitable habitats as those containing the food resources necessary to temporarily sustain optimal foraging rates. The qualifier temporary is important: all other mitigating factors being constant, a habitat's profitability is seasonal. As mentioned, lacustrine environments are dynamic, gaining and losing energy resources from spring through autumn. Open waters of northern lakes contain little life in spring, but by late June the profitability of their zooplankton populations exceeds that of the sediments and stands of macrophytes, and this superiority continues through August. Consequently, larger bluegills use vegetated habitats exclusively until moving into the limnos to forage. Smaller fish under threat of predation remain in the vegetation (Chapter 4), considered to be a less profitable habitat as summer progresses and its once substantial populations of insect larvae metamorphose and depart.

The OFM is an interesting and well conceived approach to testing questions about energy partitioning, but doubts have shadowed its steps, notably when the fishes tested preferentially selected smaller prey than considered optimal.[239] Nor have certain indirect measurements proved reliable. Mean masses of food in bluegill stomachs have correlated both positively[240] and negatively[241] with the predicted rate of energy return, probably because age is a continuum, and bluegills (and fishes generally) require less food in proportion to body mass as they age.[242]

Other nuances of growth and morphology are potentially confounding. As pumpkinseeds

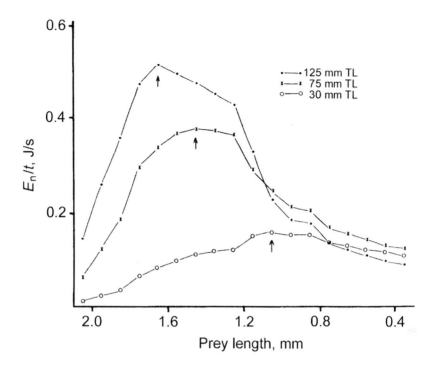

Figure 31. Mean optimal foraging rates (E_n/t) for bluegills of three size-classes (30, 75, and 125 mm SL) plotted against length of zooplankters from Lawrence Lake, Michigan, 19 July 1979. Optimal diets are indicated by arrows. Source: Mittelbach (1981b).

grow the average size of prey items they depend on does not keep pace, increasing only slightly.[243] However, the number of items and their total mass increase progressively with growth, even though some that might differ in energy content are substituted along the way. Examples are mollusks and ephemeropteran (mayfly) nymphs for chironomid larvae and isopods.[244] Finally, mouth width is similar in pumpkinseeds and bluegills, but prey size is not. The pumpkinseed consumes prey larger than 50% of mouth width; most of a bluegill's prey items are smaller than 25% of mouth width.[245]

The average work performed by a bluegill swimming slowly at $0.5 L/s$ over a mean stride length of 0.082 m is 0.91 mJ.[246] It has yet to be demonstrated that such minimal energy lost intermittently during foraging and handling of prey exerts any measurable effect on growth and nutritional status. Bluegills rarely fill their stomachs completely despite foraging for extended periods.[247] Also, diel sampling has shown that the range over which bluegill stomachs are full far exceeds the population mean; that is, the mean is considerably below the value of an individual fish with the fullest stomach. This is illustrated in Figures 35 and 36. As the range bars show, the upper limits of fish with the fullest stomachs are 0.045 g/g of body mass for pumpkinseeds and a little less for bluegills, although the respective mean fractions exceed 40% lower (0.026 and 0.025).

The OFM might have gained theoretical space had it first set minimal thresholds against which the silhouette of optimal could later be illuminated. Bluegills regularly eat less than the optimal amount, evidently without jeopardizing fitness. The competitive relegation of juvenile bluegills to thick vegetation (Chapter 4) is thought to compromise fitness by denying them access to more profitable foraging in open water.[248] However, juveniles regularly select prey organisms smaller than predicted for optimal energy gain.[249] Nonetheless, enough survive to reach maturity, reproduce, and often dominate the fish fauna in terms of their numbers. In Three Lakes III, Michigan, where water fleas were rare, the diet of bluegills longer than 75 mm SL consisted of 24% zooplankton and 67% organisms inhabiting vegetation.[250] In two Minnesota lakes the respective diets were 19% crustaceans (mostly planktonic) and 78% organisms associated with vegetation.

Survival of larvae and juveniles appears unrelated to the zooplankton concentration,[251] and the OFM might not apply to early age-0 bluegills during the first phase of rapid growth (Chapter 7), a period when suboptimal food intake is evidently adequate.[252] Over the first 120 d, which encompasses both phases of early growth (fast and slow), the concentration of age-0 fish competing for food, not the foraging mode, determines growth and survival. Diminishing concentrations of prey stretch diet width during the slow growth phase. At Lake Opinicon, Ontario, for example, zooplankton concentrations greater than 600/L in May will have declined to 60–100/L by late summer.[253] Suboptimal foraging is still sufficient. Thus, "At sufficiently low prey density, consumption of all encountered prey *is* the optimal behavior."[254]

Behavioral Thermoregulation Model (BTM)—In devising and testing foraging hypotheses a habitat is a heterogeneous environment where an organism forages, and a patch is a homogeneous part of the habitat.[255] The length of time a bluegill spends foraging at one patch before moving to another depends on how often it encounters an item of prey. This quitting, or giving-up, time is the duration spent at a patch without finding something to eat before leaving.[256] Bluegills, like many animals, have shorter quitting times (i.e., they stay longer) where food is abundant. In addition, food abundance and the time spent at a patch is linear (i.e., the proportion of time spent foraging matches the proportion of food available),[257] except that that memory makes the initial quitting time at a specific site less predictable.[258] One reason for this could be experience (learning), which increases foraging efficiency up to 4× in just 6–8 foraging bouts.[259] Selection of the day's first foraging site is based on memory from the previous day.[260] Quitting times are updated continuously as foraging progresses, depending on present success and knowledge or perception of the general surrounding quality.[261]

Bluegills are obviously familiar with where they forage. Home range is variable, evidently influenced by body size and physical constraints of the habitat. At Talisheek Creek, Louisiana, bluegills (size unstated) marked by fin clipping had maximum home ranges of 38 m.[262] At Cedar Lake, Illinois, bluegills of 160–190 mm TL monitored by radio telemetry ranged over 0.15–0.75 ha.[263] No seasonal effect was evident. Adult bluegills (211–271 mm TL) were followed at Pelican Lake, Nebraska, by radio telemetry from April–September 2000.[264] Movement peaked in mid-summer, and the pattern was similar throughout the diel cycle. Pelican Lake is 332 ha, and home ranges were as large as 172 ha; only 8.5% were less than 1 ha.

Bluegills use sun-compass orientation for homing[265] and navigation.[266] Juveniles (15–31 mm SL) moved in predictable patterns during experiments in outdoor pools. For example, specimens captured at locations in the pond from which offshore vegetation was absent moved toward the fake shore. Those from areas where the offshore vegetation was thin demonstrated bimodal movement, some moving toward the shore, others offshore. Movements became random on overcast days.

Other models assume that foraging fishes are constrained spatially by the distributions of predators or food but otherwise free to make decisions. The behavioral energetics model attempted to integrate the interactions of food and temperature in habitat choice, but it proved equivocal.[267] The BTM demonstrated that temperature sometimes overrides both food (the OFM) and predators in determining where a fish chooses to forage.[268] Aquarium experiments provided bluegills of 60–70 mm TL with a choice of two spaces connected by a short tunnel. The spaces could be controlled for food availability and temperature. For bluegills the optimal temperature for growth is 25°C, and highest food conversion efficiency occurs at ~31°C, which also represents the preferred, or eccritic, temperature (Chapter 7). One section of the aquariums was set at 25°C, the other at 30°C. Whether feeding or not, the fish spent more time in the warmer sections. In one experiment bluegills were fed equally on both sides, in another the food was made more plentiful on the cooler side. The fish spent more time in the cooler section when feeding, but then returned to the warm section. They stayed in the warm part when the food was divided equally. Overall, the BTM was a better short-term predictor (minutes to weeks) of the behavior observed than the OFM.

Assuming these results are valid, movement into habitats by bluegills is driven by a preference for temperature over food, not energetics and temperature[269] or an innate knowledge of which choice is the most energetically favorable. They seek habitats where body temperature can be sustained near 31°C and move away only when the influence of food is immediate and direct.[270] For a decline of 2°C the drop in proportional use of a location was 13%.[271] Thus a decline of ~1°C from the eccritic temperature initiates a 5% decline in foraging time spent in the cooler patch, so long as the warmer section is not more than 31°C. The driving force, it seems, is selecting a location based not on its energetic potential but on its temperature. Having fed, bluegills then seek places where the temperature is near the preferred value, despite the higher energy conversion (and subsequent reduction in growth).

Apparent Size Model (ASM)—The ASM is a prevalent hypothesis of the *how* genre, but it takes more risks by also proposing mechanisms addressing *why* planktivorous predators make certain selections. The ASM predicts that a fish's diet reflects the probability of encountering prey organisms of different sizes and concentrations inside the field of vision.[272] A predator's diet should shift to increasingly larger prey items, based on their apparent sizes, with increasing total concentrations of prey.[273] Conflicting work has falsified this distinction, finding no concentration-dependent selection based on apparent size.[274] Furthermore, apparent size choices might be irrelevant in waters of high turbidity or low illumination where only one or a few prey organisms are visible simultaneously.[275]

Apparent size is defined as the arc tangent of the quotient obtained from dividing the length of the prey by the fish's reaction distance.[276] Optically, it represents the greatest distance from which an object can be detected by the subtended angle it makes with the fish's eye.[277] A nearby object, which might be small, appears larger than one farther away because it subtends a larger visual angle between itself and the eye of the predator.[278] Prey length in this case actually brackets the edges of the object. Because objects that appear large often are, the ASM directs a predator toward prey that might be the most profitable.[279]

An early version of the OFM involving bluegills tried to reconcile the apparent size selection of zooplankters with their concentrations.[280] The result was optimal prey choice, and it presumed to define the boundaries of optimal diet width when prey organisms of various sizes were available at different concentrations. The OFM predicts that bluegills become increasingly prey-selective as they grow, eventually choosing large zooplankters over small ones commensurate with a decline in prey concentration.[281] Prey selectivity indeed increases with increased visual acuity, consistent with provisions of the ASM.[282] Size preferences for planktonic prey undergo a noticeable shift in captive bluegills between 10 and 29 mm SL (Figure 32).[283] Fish from 29 to 38 mm SL could capture water fleas of three size-classes at concentrations of 9–20/L; those exceeding 38 mm SL preferred the larger water fleas.

However, the ASM requires a fish to forage on prey items that at the instant of selection represent the largest visual angles. This stipulation seems based on the presumed inability of planktivorous fishes to distinguish objects at their actual sizes. Although no direct contradictory evidence has come forth,[284] captive bluegills longer than 60 mm SL choose more large water fleas than the ASM predicts, and this could doubtfully happen unless they were assessing their

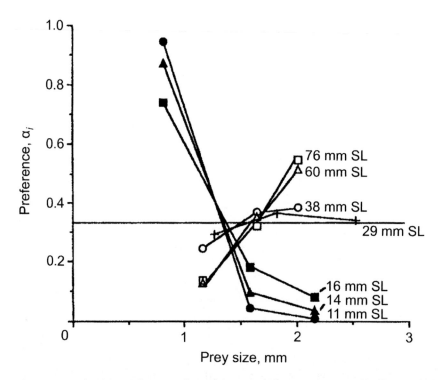

Figure 32. Change in preference (α_i) for water fleas of three size-classes, i, by bluegills of six size-classes during growth (mm SL). Approximate prey sizes were 0.8, 1.1, and 2.3 mm. Preference values were calculated from data in Li et al. (1983) and Walton et al. (1992). $\alpha_i = 0.33$ represents no selectivity. Above this value the prey are attacked in greater proportion than encountered, below it in lesser proportion. Source: Walton et al. (1997).

true sizes.[285] Other species have demonstrated this capability. Goldfish display size constancy, a measure of perception that like visual acuity is obtained from determining the distance to a target and its angular subtense. Goldfish trained to distinguish white disks differing only in diameter and presented at 20 cm could still tell the disks apart after they had been moved until both subtended the same visual angle.[286]

Implementation of the ASM is active; that is, the fish actively selects (or pursues) whichever prey item appears to be largest.[287] Selection at high concentrations would be limited to prey items nearby.[288] According to the ASM, small bluegills, because their visual resolution is poor, tend to choose prey organisms based on their apparent size instead of their actual size, although evidence that adults choose differently has not been given.[289] Whether or not juveniles do this, the ASM has so far proved incapable of predicting changes in foraging selectivity with differences in visual resolution.[290] Nonetheless, this model appeals because it conforms with some of what we know about the bluegill's visual system. To forage effectively in the limnos bluegills need levels of illumination well above the contrast threshold (Chapter 2).[291] At or below this level a fish has no choice except to close the reaction distance, which enlarges the apparent size of the target, bringing it closer to the critical diameter. A shorter RD also increases contrast sensitivity, enlarges the area of spatial summation, and reduces the number of photons required to activate a threshold detection response.

If a fish's visual field is filled with images of zooplankters, some larger than others, their proportions both seen and encountered depend on reaction distance.[292] The fish will see relatively more large zooplankters provided the concentrations of all sizes are the same. The rate of encounter depends mainly on the prey organisms (their sizes and concentrations) and on the

Table 1. Reaction distance (RD) and size-related probability (S_t) of successful prey capture by bluegills of four mean size-classes. Prey items were water fleas *Daphnia pulex* sieved to three lengths ($\bar{x}\pm$SD): small (0.73 ±0.04 mm), medium (1.86 ±0.10 mm), and large (2.12 ±0.07 mm), and presented at concentrations of 110-225/L. Source: Walton et al. (1992).

Mean fish size (mm SL)	Small RD (cm)	S_t	Medium RD (cm)	S_t	Large RD (cm)	S_t
11.2	2.9	0.60	5.6	0.10	7.7	0
14.1	3.7	0.72	7.1	0.32	9.7	0.13
16.6	4.3	0.79	8.4	0.65	11.4	0.28
29.3	13.6	1.00	19.5	1.00	27.1	1.00

size of the fish.[293] Smaller bluegills have shorter RDs, and their probability of successful captures diminishes as prey organisms become larger (Table 1). In fact, a larval bluegill of 11 mm can doubtfully focus on an item of prey more than 2 mm long[294] and has almost no chance of capturing it.[295] Larger fish extend the probability of encounters over longer RDs, presumably because their eyesight is better, and a bluegill of 29 mm SL catches even the largest water flea every time (values of S_t, bottom row). Nonetheless, the probability of a prey item actually being consumed is the sum of probabilities of every step in the predation sequence (location, identification, pursuit or stalk, and capture).[296]

The ASM predicts that bluegills of all size-classes should prefer large water fleas. This has proved generally true for fish of 38 mm SL in wading pools.[297] However, larger ones (60 and 76 mm SL) diverged substantially from the expected results. Fish less than 12 mm SL in aquarium experiments chose small prey even when bigger ones were more visible.[298] In keeping with the OFM this preference weakened with increasing size of the fish and their improving visual resolution. Ultimately, the ASM matched exactly in bluegills averaging 29.3 mm SL. Those of all size-classes preferred smaller prey than predicted. The OFM correctly demonstrated a shift to increasingly larger prey with growth, although diet widths were never as narrow as predicted.

Choice experiments to test the ASM gave these results.[299] Two water fleas of different sizes (range 0.7–2.5 mm) were placed in an aquarium less than 10 cm from a bluegill of 60–70 mm TL. Apparent size was controlled by varying the horizontal distance. Test fish chose two water fleas of similar apparent size about equally. The apparently larger water flea was chosen preferentially as the ratio of apparent size increased, a trend that continued until, at a size ratio of ~1.35, the apparently larger specimen was selected more than 90% of the time (Figure 33). When two water fleas, one actually smaller but apparently larger, the other the reverse, were placed less than 10 cm from a bluegill neither was selected preferentially. Choice at greater distances (20–35 cm) was based mainly on apparent size when the actual size ratio was less than 1.6, but this was reversed at actual size ratios greater than 1.6. Bluegills generally chose the prey item that was actually larger when both were nearby, and especially when the alternative was considerably smaller.

According to the ASM a bluegill's pattern of feeding and size of the prey it selects should remain constant for fish of given length,[300] but this is not necessarily true. Small fish, which have poorer vision, are not just more selective than predicted, they also prefer smaller prey than expected. Bluegills feeding where prey organisms are concentrated choose larger individuals preferentially, skewing the expected range of sizes. This behavior agrees with the OFM in which larger organisms offer greater energy return, but applies only to larger fish.[301] Across all size-classes bluegills tend to select prey in rough agreement with the OFM, although fish of all sizes also forage routinely on suboptimal prey.[302] The same is true of common carp *Cyprinus carpio*[303]

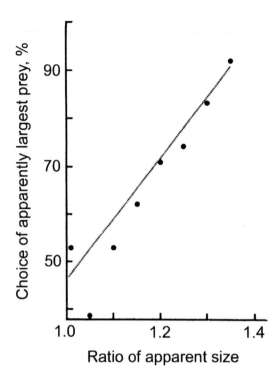

Figure 33. Choice between two live water fleas *Daphnia pulex* of different actual and varying apparent sizes placed at different distances (1-35 cm) from a bluegill. Source: O'Brien et al. (1985).

and no doubt other species. In addition, the choice of prey depends on proximity, location in the horizontal and vertical fields,[304] and other factors to be mentioned shortly.

Experience partly determines the size of prey selected.[305] Bluegills of 54 mm SL were divided into two groups, those experienced at capturing water fleas and those that were not, and tested in a wading pool with water fleas of two size-classes. The preference for large water fleas was strong even though small ones were twice as common. Experienced and inexperienced fish both matched the ASM at low concentrations of prey. Fish in both groups foraging at high concentrations consumed more water fleas than predicted by the ASM, and this was especially true of the experienced group.

Reaction Field Volume Model (RFVM)—The RFVM is similar to the ASM,[306] but its implementation is passive instead of active. For prey objects that differ in size, the distance of detection is roughly proportional to the object's length.[307] Based on this assumption the predation rate should be proportional to the volume immediately around the fish within which prey organisms are close enough to be visible.[308] This reaction volume is roughly proportional to length of the prey cubed.[309] Accordingly, a bluegill consumes prey organisms as it encounters them in direct proportion to the number entering its visual field.[310] Prey selection in the RFVM stays constant and independent of the total or relative concentration of prey.[311] In principle, the prediction that a fish should select numbers of prey proportional to their concentrations times the cube of their lengths renders the RFVM indistinguishable from the ASM.[312] In practice, differences depend on prey concentrations, numbers, and types of prey.[313] When just a few types are available, as reproduced during laboratory experiments, the models diverge, but they converge at prey concentrations starting at ~100 organisms/L.

Informed Decision Model (IDM)—Still not fully answered is whether size selection is deliberate or random. In some simulations the ASM is difficult to distinguish from randomness[314] or from the RFVM. The ingestion of larger prey could still be passive, in which case apparent size selection is simply an artifact of differential encounter rates. A foraging bias is then introduced by the interacting consequences of RD and the relative proportions of zooplankton size-classes, causing encounter rates to increase with prey size. The result would be a tendency to favor large zooplankters, requiring no decision by the fish.[315] The IDM is an attempt to address this problem.

A fish foraging in dim light or turbid water is presumably disadvantaged because its rate of encounter with prey—and therefore its feeding rate—is reduced. The attenuation of light in water affects both the encounter rate and size frequency of suspended objects.[316] Light attenuates exponentially with distance, and objects in the distant visual field are affected most strongly. Larger prey that might be visible in clear water disappears from view during high turbidity with the result that encounter rates of small prey are affected comparatively less. Reaction distance, having become nearly independent of prey size, should eliminate perceptual bias and instead give a closer measure of the true size distributions of zooplankters.[317] In such situations a predator could be expected to select the nearest object in its visual field. However, bluegills in turbid water apparently still choose large water fleas in preference to small ones, which suggests some level of active decision making.[318]

A fish in turbid water is unlikely to encounter two objects of prey simultaneously.[319] Bluegills averaging 75.3 mm TL in plastic pools having turbidity levels of 1 nephelometric turbidity unit (NTU) captured 41 water fleas in 3 min, but only 22 when the turbidity was 190 NTUs.[320] The number captured was proportional to the number encountered, invoking the conclusion that size selection was independent of prey concentration. However, the actual number of organisms consumed declined with increasing turbidity.[321] Consequently, the stable proportions of total prey eaten suggest the opposite: a decrement in the selection of large organisms with increasing turbidity.[322] Neither the encounter rate nor the rate at which water fleas were eaten could be proportional to the visual volume, which was much reduced and lacking any visual field filled with prey. Instead, these were proportional to the volume of water through which the fish swam. In the case of bluegills, which appear to stop swimming when searching for prey,[323] the notion of a moving visual volume might not be appropriate.

I named this hypothesis the Informed Decision Model because the choices made by a bluegill in turbid water are presumably based on previous rates of encounter. For a fish to implement the required behaviors reliably it must have a notion of interrupted time and the capacity to recall the comparative sizes of prey likely to be met. It then has to assemble the information instantaneously into a format appropriate for rapid decisions. An alternative sensory mechanism to vision under these conditions might be more plausible (Chapter 2).

Greatest Stimulus Model (GSM)—The GSM presumes that a foraging fish will pursue whichever item of prey offers the greatest visual stimulus.[324] As an alternative to size the stimulus can be movement,[325] speed,[326] contrast,[327] degree of opaqueness,[328] degree of pigmentation,[329] and perhaps even texture.[330] These last two factors probably stimulate by affecting visual contrast. A moving image offers more information than a static one.[331] Bluegills prefer moving prey and apparently learn to recognize specific organisms by their movements.[332] In aquarium experiments bluegills presented with dead specimens of *Daphnia pulex*, either motionless or moving, chose the moving specimen unless the other was considerably larger.[333]

Some zooplankters are able to evade predators by darting quickly out of their visual field.[334] Others use different evasive techniques: phantom midge larvae (genus *Chaoborus*) and many copepods swim in bursts but spend most of their time not moving at all. Copepods of the genus *Diaptomus* move only 3.2% of the time.[335] By staying stationary they increased the reaction distance of white crappies 3×. Pumpkinseeds in aquarium experiments were nearly 100% successful at capturing water fleas (genus *Daphnia*),[336] which move almost continuously.[337] However, capture success was only 39% for copepods *Diaptomus ashlandi*. Copepods sometimes experience minimal mortality from bluegills because they are more evasive[338] or simply less preferred. However, in an experiment set up in 500-L tanks and lasting 28 d bluegills had a significant impact not just on the cladocerans (genera *Daphnia*, *Ceriodaphnia*), but also on the calanoid and cyclopoid copepodids and copepod nauplii.[339] Small bluegills are generally less effective at capturing mobile prey.[340] For example, the rapid upward spirals of water fleas in the presence of predators[341] might give them an advantage against small sunfishes.

Negative stimuli also influence foraging. Small bluegills learn from experience not to take certain prey. The exotic cladoceran *D. lumholtzi* has a sharp head spine and a long spiny tail; an indigenous species *D. magna* lacks the head spine, or helmet, and has a shorter tail (Figure 34). Both were tested in aquarium experiments using bluegills of 20–25, 26–30, and 31–35 mm (TL?).[342] Fish of the smallest size-class rejected specimens of *D. lumholtzi* significantly more often. They also consumed 90.2% of the indigenous water fleas compared with only 40.8% of the helmeted species. Some even stopped attacking the exotic form. Captures of this species by all size-classes were made with the head spine oriented toward the mouth. Sometimes the spine lodged in the roof of a fish's mouth, causing instant expulsion. On one occasion these unpleasant events induced bluegills of the smallest size-class to stop feeding completely. Small bluegills (< 50 mm TL) in another study selected specimens of *D. pulex* over those of *D. lumholtzi*, but larger conspecifics actually preferred the last-mentioned, tentative evidence that foraging constraints weigh more heavily against small fish.[343]

Most models attempting to reconcile foraging behavior with energy gain and expenditure are predicated on the premise that, given choices, animals act in ways that maximize benefits while minimizing costs.[344] The models just described are no different, having assumed decision making to be coupled tightly and preferentially with energy maximization, and, by extension, to the enhancement of fitness. The presumption is that bluegills correlate size of the food item with energy content and make selections accordingly. Although compelling, other tests offering the possibility of alternative explanations, or even refutation, can be devised. For example, preferences derived from learning can affect later food choice more than timing of the choice itself. State-dependent valuation, or valuation based on current nutritional status, and value assignment in decision making, have been identified in mammals, birds, and insects.[345] Past investment in a choice, even if inferior, can override expected returns.[346] Factors other than energy rewards are clearly in play, and sometimes the outcome is in conflict with prevalent hypotheses.

For example, European starlings *Sturnus vulgaris* selected the option requiring more work (and presumably greater energy expenditure) for the same reward.[347] Desert locusts *Schistocera gregaria* were conditioned to a stimulus associated with starvation and another with being well fed. Previous selections took precedence over later ones despite present nutritional state, and grasshoppers of one group later favored the starvation-associated stimulus significantly more often regardless of their body condition.[348] Selecting and then failing to capture an item of prey also affects the encounter rate,[349] a possibility usually ignored. A large zooplankter attacked by a small fish can escape more easily than a small zooplankter. The escaped organism, having been nearby when attacked, stood a high probability of being encountered. Therefore, reduced capture efficiency can increase the encounter rate.

How does a bluegill decide when to quit a patch and move to another? A strategy of some kind directs decisions based on available information and distribution of the prey.[350] The capture rate of prey naturally declines with time, and quitting time is thought to involve a choice of

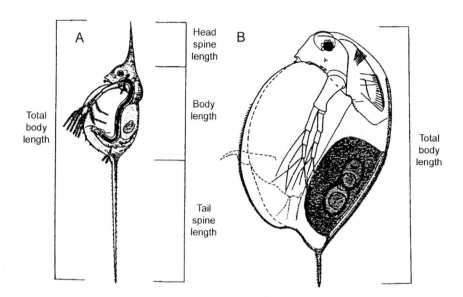

Figure 34. Comparative external morphologies of two cladocerans. *Left: Daphnia lumholtzi. Right: D. magna.* Source: Swaffar and O'Brien (1996).

decision rules: (1) time (the forager leaves after having spent a given amount of time), (2) number (the forager stays until it captures *n* items of prey), or (3) rate (the forager stays until the capture rate declines to a threshold level). Bluegills (45–80 mm TL) foraged in a pool among fake vegetation having stem concentrations of 1000/m². Specimens of frozen and freshly thawed midge larvae *Chironomus riparius* had been attached to the stems. The pool was divided into four habitats. Quality (total concentration of prey) differed across them but patch quality (number of organisms in all patches within given habitats) was the same. Results showed bluegills to use rate of capture to decide when to quit a patch and move to another. In a parallel experiment the design variables were reversed: habitat was held constant, and patch quality was varied.[351] The bluegills were of similar size (50–65 mm TL). Although a few of the other design features were different, the time decision rule fit best, and the fish stopped foraging after a certain amount of time.

Combined, these results indicate that bluegills search haphazardly within patches and that a certain flexibility might allow them to modify decisions concerning exploitation of a habitat. Foraging is stochastic, the models used to describe it mechanistic with little room allowed for dynamic behaviors. The limnos constitutes a foraging habitat in which the distribution of zooplankters is clumped, or patchy, rather than random or uniform. Experienced bluegills ($\bar{x}$ = 49 mm TL) can distinguish differences among zooplankters and make foraging decisions accordingly.[352] They select water fleas of the genus *Daphnia* even when the apparent size of individuals of another genus (*Diaptomus*) is larger and the probability of detection is the same when both are encountered simultaneously. During aquarium experiments the capture success was 100% for the first (genus *Daphnia*) but only 49.9% for specimens of the more evasive *Diaptomus*. Bluegills selected the evasive organism as its size increased relative to the other despite a capture rate only half as successful.

The OFM and ASM are the most widely tested foraging models in which bluegills have been the experimental animals. The OFM would have a fish focus on the nonevasive prey until the size of the evasive one became twice as large, presumably the point at which the energy return would be greater despite the increased effort. The ASM would merely restrict selection to the prey item that looked the biggest. Bluegills, in assessing the relative rate of return, appear to violate both models.

Diel Foraging

Lake Opinicon in southern Ontario is 890 ha and has a maximum depth of 11 m.[353] Two spikes in feeding activity were apparent by foraging bluegills of ages 2–3, the larger occurring at 1500 hours after which stomachs emptied progressively until 2030 hours when foraging resumed (Figure 35).[354] Bluegills foraged intermittently at night, and a second spike occurred shortly after 0100 hours, although 20% of the fish collected by 0730 had empty stomachs. Bluegills browse more or less continuously, the evidence being that fewer than 20% had empty stomachs at any hour, and by the fact that stomach contents per gram of fish were never less than 0.4%.

Pumpkinseeds revealed three spikes in the amount of food in the stomachs, one at 1800, another at 0800, and a third (lower than the others) at 0300 (Figure 36).[355] The pumpkinseeds' foraging patterns were more strictly diurnal than those of bluegills. Foraging commenced ~0500 and continued until 0730, after which the stomachs emptied until 0930 when sustained feeding began once again. Foraging then increased rapidly between 1500 and 1730. The stomachs then emptied decrementally until midnight, at which time foraging resumed briefly followed by prolonged emptying until daylight. The range in degree of stomach fullness was more pronounced than in bluegills. Stomachs emptied at night, and some stomachs were empty at all sampling periods.

A similar study of bluegills (25–134 mm SL) in two heated Texas reservoirs showed minimal feeding to occur at 0200–0800.[356] As in Lake Opinicon, feeding increased after sunrise. Also in rough conformity with Lake Opinicon there were two major peaks, one in the morning at 0900–1000 and a larger one in the afternoon at 1800–1900, after which stomach fullness declined until 2200 hours and then began a sharp downward trend an hour later. In both Ontario (Table 2) and Texas planktivorous activity ceased at night. Note that cladocerans were prominent dietary items during early morning and late afternoon, times when a bluegill's visual pigments are apparently sensitive to contrast in open water. At night the important food organisms were aquatic insect larvae. Most of the summer diet in the Texas reservoirs consisted of aquatic insects and arachnids consumed between 0700 and 2200.[357] In winter, entomostracans (cladocerans, copepods, ostracods) contributed significantly. Plants were seldom eaten at one location (Lake Nasworthy) but were second in importance in nearby Lake Bastrop. Plant material consumed included the cattail (genus *Typha*), pondweed (genus *Potamogeton*), waterweed (genus *Elodea*), and a green filamentous alga (genus *Spirogyra*).

In contrast with these investigations both age-0 and adult bluegills in Lake Onalaska, Wisconsin, a northern Mississippi River backwater lake, are reported to feed actively at all hours, mostly in the vegetation.[358] Stomach contents of adult bluegills (78–198 mm TL) were dominated (60% by mass) by chydorids (branchiopods), chironomids, and gastropods, although by count chydorids, cladocerans, and amphipods were most numerous. Mean total biomass of the stomach contents did not differ either by month or time of day. Individual prey items varied seasonally according to their abundance. Mean volumes of stomach contents of age-0 bluegills (19–65 mm TL) were chydorids (12%), chironomids (35%), cladocerans excluding water fleas (e.g., genera *Simocephalus, Ceriodaphnia, Sida*, 12%), water fleas (genus *Daphnia*, 6%), amphipods (5%), and other taxa (20%). The most numerous prey organisms were copepods, specimens of the genus *Bosmina*, and chydorids. Mean total biomass was greatest in August; total biomass did not vary throughout the diel period. The diversity of prey was invariant between adult and age-0

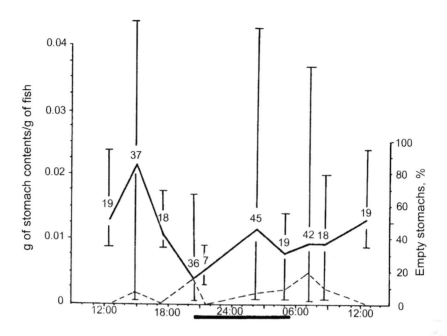

Figure 35. Daily feeding by bluegills in Lake Opinicon, Ontario. Solid curve represents mean mass (g) of stomach contents per gram of fish, broken line the percentage of empty stomachs. Vertical lines above means are ranges, numbers on curves are sample sizes (total n = 271 fish of ages 2–3, 90-140 mm TL, 11.1-58.0 g). Solid bar depicts hours of darkness. Data were obtained over two 48-h periods, 1–2 June and 15–16 July 1966. Source: Keast and Welsh (1968).

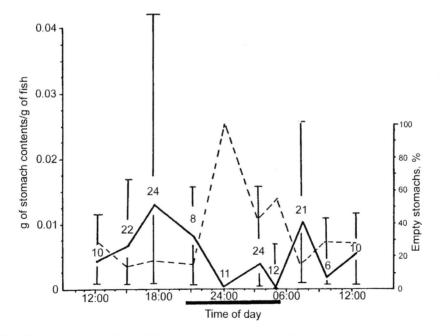

Figure 36. Daily feeding by pumpkinseeds in Lake Opinicon, Ontario. Solid curve represents mean mass (g) of stomach contents per gram of fish, broken line the percentage of empty stomachs. Vertical lines above means are ranges, numbers on curves are sample sizes (total n = 148 fish of ages 2–3, 100–140 mm TL, 18.0–62.0 g). Solid bar depicts hours of darkness. Data were obtained over two 48-h periods, 1–2 June and 15–16 July 1966. Source: Keast and Welsh (1968).

Table 2. Numbers of food organisms taken from bluegills caught at two depth ranges in Lake Opinicon, Ontario (mean values for 10 fish taken in two 48-h periods, 1-2 and 15-16 June 1966). Volume percent encompasses the entire sample. Sample sizes (numbers of fish) are in parentheses. L = larvae, P = pupae, A = adults. Source: Keast and Welsh (1968).

Food organisms	0.6-1.5 m						1.8-4.6 m					
	15:00-17:30 (34)		0200-0300 (23)		0500-0900 (38)		1500-1730 (21)		0200-0300 (22)		0500-0900 (41)	
	No.	Vol %	No.	Vol %	No.	Vol %	No.	Vol %	No.	Vol %	No.	Vol %
Cladocerans	518	12	10		507	30	28	5	2		57	
Copepods	3				3	2					1	
Ostracods			1		1		13	2			8	10
Amphipods	4		5	3	2	2	2				3	7
Isopods					1		35	10	1		2	4
Ephemeropterans (N)					14	25	2	2			12	15
Zygopterans (N)	8	35	1	2	3	5	1	5			5	15
Anisopterans (N)	18	3	1	2	1				2	15	1	2
Trichopterans (L)	13		4	3	7	4	19	10	36	55	8	20
Chironomids (L)	29	5	3	2	11	2	17	2	2		1	
Chironomids (P)			5	5	13	12	74	55	72	20	7	10
Chaoborus (L)					1						1	
Chaoborus (P)					1						2	
Ceratopogonids (L)	125	25	215	70	15	12	7	4	7	3	1	
Ceratopogonids (P)			12	3	1						10	6
Simulium (L)			1	2								
Dipterans (A)			1	2								
Hymenopterans (A)	3	3	1				2				1	
Hemipterans			1									
Coleopterans	3	5			1						1	
Gastropods					2	2			1	2	1	
Pelecypods									3	5		
Hydracarinians	4		1		7		4	2			2	
Araneidans					1							
Fish eggs	187	10										

bluegills, and niche overlap[359] was high (general overlap index = 0.98).

In Maple and Grove lakes, Minnesota, adult bluegills (152–203 mm) foraged throughout the diel period with mean volumes of stomach contents ranging over values that were high at noon (54%), low at 1500 (24%), and intermediate at 0300 (39%).[360] The lakes are shallow with large limnetic areas thick with macrophytes; as in Lake Onalaska, most foraging took place in vegetation. Consumption by adult bluegills ($\bar{x}$ = 157 mm): juvenile fishes (6%), insects (4%), crustaceans (19%), snails (6%), plant material (16%), and miscellaneous (13%).

At Lake Cazenovia, foraging aggregations of small bluegills (mostly < 130 mm TL) break up at twilight, and the fish assume nighttime coloration, which includes darkened median and pelvic fins.[361] They move into shallower water (1.6–2.5 m) where many remain just above the bottom. Larger bluegills (generally >170 mm TL) typically seen in daylight above and along the margins of weed beds continued to feed well after dark. Similar nocturnal behavior has been reported in southern Michigan lakes.[362]

Influence of Structural Complexity

Structural complexity affects foraging efficiency. How fishes perform in structured habitats with their interrupted lines of sight is complicated. In general, large fishes in all habitats perform more efficiently than small ones. The reason is attributed to their superior visual acuity. For example, captive bluegills of 110 mm SL caught significantly more prey (coenagrionid naiads on vegetation, midge larvae in sediment, water fleas in open water) than fish of 65 mm SL.[363] When the sizes of prey organisms and their concentrations were held constant, encounter rates were substantially greater in open water than in vegetation and sediments. Prey organisms in these and similar habitats are larger and more profitable, but have lower encounter rates and more extended handling times.

Macroinvertebrates increase in number with increasing complexity of the habitat, but foraging efficiency declines (Chapter 4). Foraging is easier at low structural complexity, although food is scarcer. The most efficient foraging is thought to occur at intermediate structural complexities,[364] but whether growth is improved is doubtful (Chapter 8).

Macrophytes provide substrata for epiphytic invertebrates,[365] which are important foods of many juvenile and adult bluegills, especially when zooplankters are scarce. Plant architecture, or growth form, also influences foraging efficacy, as shown by aquarium and pond experiments. Pumpkinseeds averaging 89 mm SL were allowed to forage for cladocerans *Sida crystallina* and larval damselflies (coenagrionids) among live specimens of soft-stem bulrush *Scirpus validus* with its leafless cylindrical stems and big-leaf pondweed *Potamogeton amplifolius* with its leafy stems.[366] Capture rates were significantly greater among bulrushes.

Surface area appears to be an important factor affecting invertebrate numbers. Finely divided leaves have more surfaces for attachment than simple ones, and pondweeds like the stonewort *Chara delicatula* tend to support more epiphytic invertebrates than grass-leaved pondweed *Potamogeton gramineus* and water smartweed *Polygonum amphibium* (= *P. natans*).[367] Invertebrate abundance on long-leaf pondweed *Potamogeton nodosus* in Eau Galle Lake, Wisconsin, correlates positively with surface area of the plant.[368] By August the amount of leaf damage affects invertebrate abundance. One plant collected in June had 555 invertebrates, including 177 larval chironomids and 143 naidid worms. A stand of long-leaf pondweed measuring 20 × 20 m was estimated to contain ~33 million invertebrates in June and 30 million in August.

Individual sizes, population structures, abundance, biomass, and habitat preferences of prey organisms in lacustrine environments vary widely. An assessment made in July and August 1984 of 10 lakes within 150 km of Montréal, Québec, showed the invertebrates on macrophytes to correlate best with individual species of plants, although total plant biomass sometimes gave equivalent results.[369] Gastropods, water mites (hydracarinians), ostracods, and tri-chopteran (caddisfly) larvae correlated most closely with certain plants. The cladoceran *Sida crystallina* and some branchiopods (genus *Diaphanosoma*) for example, were found most often on broad-leaved pondweed *Potamogeton amplifolius*. However, the abundance of most cladocerans and chironomids related just as well to total plant biomass and to the biomass of individual plant species. Cladocerans were most numerous where the areal cover of macrophytes was extensive, as were chironomids and trichopterans. Most invertebrate taxa increased as summer progressed, but gastropods decreased significantly. The abundance of invertebrate taxa corre-lated positively with total phosphorus, probably because vegetative growth depends directly on sufficient concentrations of phosphate. Most invertebrates declined in abundance with depth, but gastropods increased. In this investigation the numbers of chironomids, cladocerans, cyclopoid copepods, and trichopterans became more numerous between 1 July and 26 August.

The range of prey size in temperate lakes is typically greatest in vegetation and least in open water, with the sediments intermediate.[370] Prey organisms on vegetation tend to decrease in size from spring through summer, at least in some northern lakes.[371] In Lawrence Lake, Michigan, the biomass also declines as summer progresses, exclusive of gastropods, which increase.[372] The concentrations of organisms larger than 3.0 mm in the vegetation (number/m³) show a steady and significant decline: 6,540 (May), 2,965 (June), 3,938 (July), and 1,408 (August), mostly attrib-uted to increasing scarcity of larger instars of ephemeropterans, trichopterans, odonatans (dam-selflies), and amphipods (genus *Hyalella*). Bluegills that obtained more than 80% of their prey from the vegetation had a three-fold decline in stomach contents over the summer; simulta-neously, the biomass of organisms available in the vegetation diminished by 2.5×. The sedi-ments of Lawrence Lake showed a similar trend.[373] Concentrations of prey larger than 3 mm fell significantly from 32,358/m³ in May to 11,287/m³ in August, although the biomass stayed constant.

Larger bluegills were selective when foraging in the limnetic zone of Lawrence Lake. Those exceeding 100 mm SL fed almost entirely on large water fleas, ignoring smaller zooplankters like copepods, certain cladocerans (genera *Ceriodaphnia* and *Bosmina*), and water fleas at the low end of the size range (Table 3).[374] An abundance of prey narrowed their diet. In Lawrence Lake and nearby Three Lakes II and Three Lakes III, bluegills and pumpkinseeds less than 75 mm SL ate 76–91% prey dwelling in the vegetation, and pumpkinseeds averaged 16–22% snails. The per-centage of snails in the diet increased sharply at 45 mm SL and steadily thereafter.[375] When small pumpkinseeds did eat snails they focused on tiny specimens of *Physa* available only in July and August. Pumpkinseeds of 53–77 mm TL in Lake Opinicon also fed on small gastropods.[376] Snails composed 63–73% of the diet of pumpkinseeds greater than 75 mm SL in the three Michigan lakes,[377] a trend also reported from two lakes in Minnesota.[378] The smaller size-class of Michigan bluegills consumed only 3–6% zooplankton compared with 24–54% in those greater than 75 mm SL, the percentage of zooplankton in the diet increasing abruptly at 70–80 mm SL.[379]

Bluegills in one investigation foraged in macrophytes preferentially to the sediments.[380] Orange Lake, Florida, is 4,900 ha with 30% of its surface covered by diverse macrophytes. Henderson Lake, Florida, is 1,000 ha with equal macrophytic cover. Benthic macroinvertebrates in Orange Lake ranged from 287 to 1933/m², and from 88 to 757/m² in Henderson Lake. Ranges of macroinvertebrates associated with plants were 721–17,596/m² in Orange Lake and 1,698–34,379/m² in Henderson Lake. Bluegills larger than 75 mm TL were caught and their stomach contents compared with the food available in each habitat.

Stomach analyses revealed that most macroinvertebrates eaten by bluegills larger than 75 mm TL in Orange and Henderson lakes are epiphytic and not obtained from the benthos.[381] In both lakes there was clear preference for chironomid larvae and pupae, hemipteran (true bug) larvae and adults, and ephemeropterans. Bluegills ate comparatively fewer oligochaetes (anne-

Table 3. Major groups of prey organisms in the vegetation and open water of Lawrence Lake, Michigan. Source: Mittelbach (1981b).

Range in body length (mm)			
Prey in vegetation		22 May	19 July
Genus *Simocephalus*		0.6-2.2	0.6-2.0
Genus *Sida*		0.8-2.8	0.8-2.0
Copepods		0.3-1.7	0.3-1.7
Ostracods		0.3-1.0	0.3-1.0
Genus *Hyalella*		0.6-5.0	0.6-4.0
Chironomids		1.1-12.6	0.5-9.0
Other dipterans		1.0-17.5	1.2-16.3
Trichopterans		1.6-12.8	1.3-9.1
Ephemeropterans		1.8-15.2	0.5-5.9
Odonates		1.4-15.3	1.6-5.4
Gastropods		0.6-6.4	0.6-5.2
Zooplankton			
	19 July	3 August	23 August
Daphnia pulex	0.7-2.1	0.7-2.2	0.8-1.4
D. retrocurva		0.6-2.0	0.6-1.8
D. galeata mendotae		0.6-1.9	0.6-1.3
Genus *Bosmina*		0.3-0.4	
Genus *Ceriodaphnia*		0.3-0.7	0.5-0.8
Genus *Pseudosida*		0.5-1.2	
Copepods	0.3-1.2	0.3-1.3	0.4-1.3

lid worms), hirudineans (leeches), gastropods, pelecypods (mussels), amphipods (*Hyalella azteca*), coleopterans (beetle larvae), and other dipteran larvae (phantom midges). A pattern of consumption was not apparent for odonatan naiads (dragonflies and damselflies), trichopterans, lepidopteran larvae (butterflies and moths), or the natantian shrimp (genus *Palaemonetes*). Of all food organisms only the shrimps were more common in the benthos than on weeds. Large bluegills also consumed tiny crustaceans, mainly cladocerans. Specimens with stomachs containing more than 100 of these were longer than 150 mm TL. Those with more than 1,000 in their stomachs generally exceeded 200 mm TL.

Snags are important attachment sites for macroinvertebrates,[382] and their removal to improve navigation and recreational boating or for esthetic reasons reduces both the food and cover available to fishes, probably lowering their natural production.[383] Snags in the upper Mississippi River contain as many as 16,000 macroinvertebrates/m² of surface area.[384] The Satilla River on the Lower Coastal Plain of Georgia is a subtropical blackwater stream. The biomass and species diversity of its macroinvertebrate fauna is considerably greater on snags than associated with either the sandy bottom of the main channel or the muddy bottoms of its backwaters.[385] Larvae of filter-feeding caddisflies (e.g., genus *Hydropsyche*) and black flies (genus *Simulium*) were major consumers on snags in the Satilla, as were the larvae of some midges, mayflies, and beetles. Principal predators were hellgrammites, dragonflies, and stoneflies. At least 40 genera were found on snags, compared with 20 or fewer in the other habitats, and individuals were, on average, larger.[386] Based on surface area, snags held 20–50× more biomass than the riverbed and 5–10× more than bottom mud of the backwaters. Although snags accounted for only 4% of the available surface area, they contained 60% of the total biomass of macroinvertebrates, accounted for 16% of the production in the section of river investigated, and provided the highest percentage of drift organisms.[387] Resident bluegills obtained 60% of their diet (mainly caddisflies and midges) from snag fauna.

Habitat complexity also affects foraging behavior. A bluegill searching for prey stops swimming and hovers using slight movements of its fins (pectoral, soft dorsal, caudal, soft anal) to maintain position.[388] If prey is not detected it moves a short distance, stops, and hovers again. Foraging rate is most efficient when hovers and time between locations are brief.[389] Longer hovers and slow movements are necessary when foraging in vegetation where prey organisms can easily hide.[390] Short rapid hovers and quick movements to other locations maximize efficiency in open water.

Bluegills in aquarium experiments learned to slow their movements when foraging on damselfly nymphs (genus *Enallagma*) in fake vegetation and to quicken them when feeding on water fleas *Daphnia pulex* in open water.[391] Unlike filter-feeders that sieve suspended particles more or less indiscriminately while moving forward,[392] bluegills stop swimming when encountering planktonic prey items and ingest them individually. Bluegills temporarily extended their initial hover times—long or short—to the other habitat when forced to switch abruptly (Figure 37). The habitat switching described in Chapter 4 is evidence of pliable foraging behavior. However, any capacity for adjusting to new conditions also carries the restrictions imposed by morphology, implying that foraging decisions might not be strictly stimulus-directed, but mediated instead by the capacity to forage more efficiently in a specific habitat.[393]

Morphological variation has been reported in age-0 bluegills segregated along a depth gradient in the littoral zone.[394] Bluegills in certain lakes demonstrate trophic polymorphisms, including variation in dimensions of the pectoral fins and in body depth.[395] Fish with longer fins and deeper bodies forage more efficiently in vegetation; those with shorter fins and more fusiform bodies excel in open water.[396] These relationships correlate with habitat choices and appear to explain the segregation of certain populations into one or the other.[397]

Habitat segregation is also inferred by parasite load and diversity. Bluegills caught in the littoral zone at Holcomb Lake, Michigan, were significantly longer than the open-water form, which had a more extended body and deeper caudal peduncle near the proximal end.[398] Fish from the littoral zone contained 5× more individuals of two digenetic trematodes (genus *Neascus* and *Posthodiplostomum minimum*) that use snails as intermediate hosts. Bluegills caught in the limnos contained nearly twice as many specimens of *Proteocephalus ambloplitis*, a cestode that relies on copepods as intermediate hosts.

Bluegills introduced into Lake Biwa, Japan, demonstrate at least five trophic polymorphisms despite the lake's large diversity (58 species and subspecies of native fishes, 13 introduced fishes).[399] The three largest bluegill morphs are specialized for foraging on zooplankters, aquatic vegetation, and benthic invertebrates. Two smaller ones (barely distinguishable) feed either on calanoid or cyclopoid copepods. As in other locations planktivorous bluegills are more slender, those that feed on vegetation and in the benthos relatively more robust.

Effect on Lake Dynamics

Bluegills influence community dynamics directly by preying on other organisms. In the case of littoral invertebrates the effect of all fishes combined is slight from the standpoint of either species diversity or biomass. Bluegills exert a stronger effect indirectly when they forage on organisms that will someday be predators at higher trophic levels. In pond experiments tadpoles of the gray treefrog *Hyla versicolor* were 9× less abundant when adult bluegills were present.

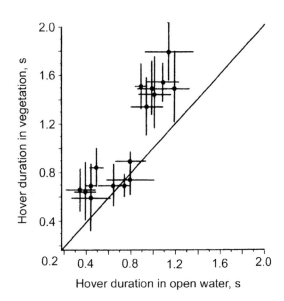

Figure 37. Duration of hovers by individual bluegills while searching for damselfly nymphs in fake vegetation versus that of the same fish foraging for water fleas in open water ($\bar{x} \pm 1$ SE). Diagonal line represents equal durations in the two habitats. Source: Ehlinger (1990).

Adults of the red-spotted newt *Notophthalmus viridescens* were 3× less abundant, probably a consequence of direct predation by bluegills.[400] Bullfrog *Rana catesbeiana* tadpoles, in contrast, showed a positive effect, perhaps because bluegills consume pond insects that prey on anuran larvae.[401] These include odonatans such as damselfly nymphs, coleopterans (diving beetles), and hemipterans (giant water bugs and water scorpions).

Bluegills of sufficient size not to be confined to the vegetation by predators forage preferentially in open water, exerting a direct effect on the zooplankton population.[402] Those in southern Michigan lakes dominate other planktivorous fishes in terms of both abundance and biomass.[403] Success depends largely on zooplankton dynamics. Adult bluegills in these lakes forage extensively on cladocerans, and the diet in open water comprises water fleas (genus *Daphnia*) almost exclusively.[404] Bluegills do not forage in the hypolimnion;[405] most foraging in the epilimnion occurs at dawn before zooplankters start their descent into the fishless hypolimnion below the thermocline[406] or at dusk at the start of the upward migration. Bluegills grew fastest and were most numerous in lakes containing large and abundant water fleas (*D. pulicaria* especially), but differences were more pronounced in May than in August. This was attributed to seasonal changes in migration patterns. In spring the water flea *D. pulicaria* moves vertically between the hypolimnion in daylight into the epilimnion at night, but a smaller species (*D. galeata mendotae*) is epilimniotic at all times. By midsummer, individuals of *D. pulicaria* are spending more time in the hypolimnion, unavailable to bluegills because they do not cross the thermocline.[407] Also in midsummer the population of *D. galeata mendotae* begins a pattern of vertical migration, an activity thought to have adaptive value to zooplankters for avoiding predation.[408]

The effect of bluegills can also be indirect, extending beyond obvious links in the immediate food chain, perhaps even to their own detriment. Rotifers are often the first foods of larval bluegills.[409] Their populations are affected adversely by cladocerans, water fleas in particular. Removal of water fleas, especially large ones (1.2 mm or more), results in substantial increases in the fertility and abundance of rotifers.[410] As adult bluegills crop the largest water fleas preferentially they enhance the environment for smaller conspecifics. Heavy cropping of the zooplankton initiates a top-down trophic effect.[411]

Bluegills forage selectively on large cladocerans, causing their mean size to decline over time.[412] By these choices they alter the size structures within zooplankton populations, sometimes eliminating large size-classes completely.[413] Bluegills in Dynamite Lake, Illinois, cropped nearly all branchiopods of the genus *Diaphanosoma* larger than 0.70 mm, forcing the rest to reproduce at smaller sizes.[414] Cladocerans generally grow bigger if bluegills are absent; in their presence they attain maturity at smaller sizes and produce smaller offspring.[415] Being small at maturity might be an adaptive trait enabling cladocerans to breed before being eaten.[416]

The number of bluegills that a lake can support depends partly on the capacity of its prey to reproduce. However, ontogenetic shifting by bluegills results in separate prey reservoirs available to juveniles and adults (Chapter 4). If, for example, the production of large zooplankters increases substantially, adult bluegills demonstrate enhanced growth and reproduction. Increased numbers of offspring culminate in heightened competition among juveniles in the littoral zone, which eventually keeps the number of adults from increasing enough to deplete the zooplankton population. The result is a larger number of bluegills but one in which juveniles grow slowly and adults rapidly. Variation in the abundance and size of zooplankton—mainly species of large water fleas (genus *Daphnia*)—often accounts for differences among lakes in the growth and numbers of bluegills.[417] Zooplankters are not the only story, of course, just one of several, and a different situation arises in waters dominated by bluegills and largemouth bass (Chapter 4).

Activities of sunfishes accelerate the decomposition of dead leaves on the bottoms of lakes and ponds by delaying their burial in the sediments.[418] The excretory products of bluegills and other fishes influence primary productivity, especially in eutrophic lakes and ponds. Bluegills maintained in fertilized pools significantly increased total phosphorus, turbidity, Secchi depth, the number of chironomid tubes, and the populations of phytoplankton, periphyton, and zooplankton.[419] Individual captive bluegills averaging 50.6 mm TL and fed chironomid larvae excreted ammonia nitrogen at 2.5–3.4 mmol/g/h and soluble reactive phosphorus at 0.04–0.18 mmol/g/h[420] The rate of nitrogen excretion in fishes is size-related, so the following example is strictly an exercise. Based on a report of 4,057 bluegills of 240 total kg recovered from a 4-ha pond,[421] the daily input of nitrogen at 3.0 mmol/g/h by these fish would be 0.72 mol/h, or 17.28 mol/d (4.32 mol/ha/d), a total of 241.92 g N/d. The mean concentration of phosphorus excreted at 0.11 mmol/g/h would be 0.026 mol/h, or 0.63 mol/d (0.16 mol/ha/d), a total of 19.51 g P/d.

Competition

4 Foraging is ultimately energy-driven, and animals are presumed to forage more or less efficiently. For growth and reproduction to occur, the energy value of food consumed must exceed the energy expended to locate, capture, and ingest it. In addition, animals are presumed to control, within certain limits, their own foraging activities, moving to more productive areas as resources become scarce and the effort to obtain them too great. Foraging is always at the mercy of seasonal cycling and population peaks of prey organisms.[422] As shown later, bluegills are in competition for food with fishes that use the same resources, mainly centrarchids and especially other bluegills.

Bluegills of age-0 living in vegetation have wide diets, ingesting mainly invertebrates smaller than predicted by the OFM (Chapter 3).[423] Such size selectivity was evident in stomach analyses of fish from Devil's Lake, Wisconsin, in August.[424] Most prey items ranged from 0.3 to 1.5 mm, and the majority of organisms less than 1 mm were amphipods, cladocerans, copepods, ostracods, snails (hydrobiids), and hydracarinians; larger prey like trichopterans were 1–2 mm (Table 4). The experiments in Lawrence Lake (Chapter 3) indicated that age-0 bluegills stayed in the vegetation in late June foraging on increasingly limited prey while populations of profitable cladocerans were becoming abundant in open water. At Devil's Lake, bluegills averaging 39.4 mm SL displayed a wide diet, foraging on more than a dozen organisms (including zooplankters) among macrophytes having stem concentrations of 352–2,585/m². However, the average mass of prey in the stomachs of these fish declined with increasing stem concentrations of Canadian waterweed *Elodea canadensis* and decreasing submarine illumination.

In some bodies of water a pivotal ontogenetic shift from littoral foraging occurs at 55–85 mm SL and is roughly coincident with maturity (55–85 mm SL)[425] and a new and divergent rate of growth[426] (in an ecological context a bluegill of 20–50 mm SL is considered to be juvenile[427]). These size classes are based on length at the time of annulus formation in early spring,[428] when bluegills of 65 mm SL grow to ~80 mm SL by late June and enter the limnetic zone.[429] But why two shifts, one when very small (~12 mm SL), the other at a size large enough to avoid most predators (> 80 mm SL)? According to a prevalent hypothesis, the first shift of fry might occur because the littoral zone is often crowded with the young of many fishes, including some that are piscivorous. Moreover, largemouth bass patrol the edges of weed beds, often darting in when pursuing prey. The open water above the vegetation might offer greater safety.[430] More importantly, the

Table 4. Diets of juvenile bluegills (presumably counts of individual organisms) foraging at 12 vegetated sites in Devil's Lake, Wisconsin, 1996. Source: Harrel and Dibble (2001).

Habitat sites	1	2	3	4	5	6	7	8	9	10	11	12
Amphipods	0	3	4	4	1	3	0	3	14	0	0	2
Anisopterans	1	1	0	0	0	0	8	0	4	0	0	0
Cladocerans	0	5	3	5	180	7	0	2	0	0	2	1
Coleopterans	0	0	1	0	0	5	2	0	0	0	0	0
Copepods	0	4	0	0	1	5	5	3	3	0	5	0
Dipterans	16	25	23	10	5	16	8	7	40	4	7	15
Ephemeropterans	0	5	2	0	0	1	0	1	2	1	0	0
Gastropods	0	6	1	2	1	11	6	23	2	0	2	0
Hydracarina	0	1	0	0	1	2	2	1	0	0	3	0
Isopods	0	1	0	0	0	0	0	0	0	0	0	0
Ostracods	3	9	8	11	7	16	10	12	15	1	4	6
Trichopterans	9	14	22	14	6	4	7	5	18	4	0	5
Terrestrial	1	0	0	0	0	0	0	0	0	0	0	0
Unknown	1	3	1	0	0	0	0	0	0	0	0	1

event is likely food-driven, with open water offering a more consistent reservoir of prey organisms of appropriate sizes.

Diet shifting is clearly evident in Table 5 for bluegills of First and Second Sister lakes, Michigan. The dominant identifiable food items (by percentage of occurrence) for small bluegills were chironomid larvae and pupae, cladocerans, odonatans, copepods, and isopods. Bluegills in the medium size-class also consumed large numbers of chironomids, cladocerans, and copepods, but also important were trichopterans, amphipods, and plants. Large bluegills diverged substantially after chironomids and cladocerans, consuming many hymenopterans (bees, wasps, ants, and sawflies) and considerably more plant material.

Bluegills and largemouth bass undergo ontogenetic shifts in trophic levels. Age-0 bass fry, like the fry of age-0 bluegills, move into littoral zones where they feed on invertebrates. Their use of resources converge, and the two species are, for a time, competitors.[431] Some bass start to feed on tiny bluegills and other sunfishes at 30–35 mm SL.[432] Probably all largemouths become piscivorous upon reaching 76–100 mm,[433] or by the end of their first summer,[434] and the relationship becomes one of predator and prey until bluegills attain a size too inconvenient to swallow. However, age-0 largemouths are opportunistic, and macroinvertebrates compose most of the diet if suitable fishes are unavailable.[435]

Considerable dietary overlap occurs between juvenile bluegill and largemouth bass during the period when bass feed on invertebrates in the vegetation.[436] Large populations of adult bass, which force bluegills of several size classes into the weed beds, intensify competition among juveniles of both species to the point at which the bass sometimes fail to recruit to piscivorous size because of interspecific competition.[437] Age-0 bass ($\bar{x}$ = 19 mm TL) and bluegills ($\bar{x}$ = 20–70 mm TL) at the size of interspecies spatial overlap[438] were confined in cages of 1 m³ suspended in the littoral zone of Virginia pond, either with conspecifics or the other species.[439] Bluegills ate the same items and grew at the same rate in all cages. Bass, however, ate fewer and larger items when confined with conspecifics and grew more rapidly than when kept with bluegills. These results, consistent with others,[440] imply that bluegills affect the growth of largemouth bass but the effect, at least in this context, is not reciprocal.

Bluegill fry in southern Michigan lakes appear in the littoral zone during July and August at 6–8 weeks old and 12–14 mm SL.[441] Those longer than 20 mm SL fall into two categories based on

Table 5. Organisms eaten by small (29-70 mm FL), medium (71-110 mm FL), and large (111-160 mm FL) bluegills from First and Second Sister lakes, Michigan, 16 June-25 July 1972. Mean vol = average volume in all fish, frequency % = count of item as a percentage of total volume of all items, occurrence % = percentage of stomachs in which the items occurred. L = larvae, P = pupae. Source: After Sadzikowski and Wallace (1976).

	Mean vol, mm³	Frequency %	Occurrence %	Mean vol, mm³	Frequency %	Occurrence %	Mean vol, mm³	Frequency %	Occurrence %
Fish size	Small			Medium			Large		
Sample size	65			71			18		
Chironomids (L)	4.5	29.2	81.5	9.6	32.6	38.0	1.2	0.2	44.4
Chironomids (P)	0.7	1.6	20.0	3.0	10.0	21.1	0.3	0.1	16.7
Other dipterans	0.1	0.6	7.7	0.1	0.1	2.8	0.9	trace	5.6
Coleopterans	1.1	1.1	7.7	1.4	1.0	8.5	4.0	0.1	5.6
Ephemeropterans	0.4	0.5	6.2	0.1	0.1	1.4	0.0	0.0	0.0
Hymenopterans	0.0	0.0	0.0	1.0	1.3	2.8	52.7	3.4	27.8
Odonatans	8.8	2.1	20.0	16.1	1.3	8.5	0.0	0.0	0.0
Trichopterans	1.5	4.6	4.6	0.4	0.9	11.3	0.0	0.0	0.0
Miscellaneous insects	trace	0.1	0.0	0.1	0.1	1.4	0.0	0.0	0.0
Amphipods	0.1	0.4	6.2	4.2	12.5	16.9	0.0	0.0	0.0
Cladocerans	0.9	22.7	58.5	0.1	6.2	12.8	29.6	63.8	27.8
Copepods	0.2	7.0	24.6	0.3	20.9	1.4	0.0	0.0	0.0
Ostracods	0.4	21.1	47.4	0.0	0.0	0.0	0.0	0.0	0.0
Gastropods	0.8	1.9	13.9	1.0	0.9	2.8	3.6	trace	5.6
Pelecypods	0.1	0.2	1.5	0.2	0.4	7.0	0.0	0.0	0.0
Miscellaneous invertebrates	0.1	2.3	13.9	0.2	3.3	16.9	2.8	0.1	5.6
Miscellaneous general	2.5	4.8	3.1	2.5	8.3	7.0	160.5	32.5	44.4
Unidentified animal parts	6.4		83.1	12.5		39.4	26.0		38.9
Unidentified insect parts	2.8		29.2	3.6		23.9	3.8		33.3
Plant material	0.6	16.9	0.1	9.0		18.3	159.5		77.8

switch size, the length at which they switch from a wide limnetic diet to a narrow one consisting almost entirely of zooplankton, or vice versa, when after a time in the limnos they return to the littoral zone.[442] Those slightly below switch size have eaten little or no zooplankton, but for those above it nearly the entire diet is now zooplankton.

Except for age-0 fish, bluegills are unusual among centrarchids by foraging, at times almost exclusively, on zooplankton.[443] As midsummer arrives the limnetic zone sometimes offers more profitable foraging than the littoral vegetation for all size classes of bluegills.[444] Three lines of evidence support this statement. First, the potential for energy gain is greater, as discussed previously. Second, bluegills grow demonstrably faster in the limnos. Small bluegills confined for 45 d in cages hung in the limnetic zone of Lawrence Lake grew an average of 3.3 g compared with an average of 1.1 g for free-ranging fish in the vegetation.[445] Third, the dry mass of food per millimeter of standard length increases sharply in bluegills making the switch out of the littoral zone and into open water (Figure 38).

Size at switching—and whether switching occurs at all—must also depend on habitat factors other than predation pressure. The ontogenetic shifts in diet by bluegills, so well docu-

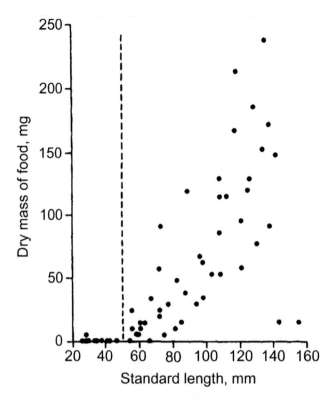

Figure 38. Amount of food in the stomachs of bluegills of different sizes from Lawrence Lake, Michigan, 28 June 1982. The dashed line represents switch size, the point at which bluegills switched from littoral prey to zooplankton and shifted to the limnos. Source: Werner and Hall (1988).

mented in certain lakes and ponds, does not to occur in others[446] and might not hold true generally for large rivers where the water has a shorter retention time.[447] In Lake Onalaska adult and juvenile bluegills stick to the vegetated areas both day and night and feed on the same organisms. They forage almost exclusively in the vegetated littoral zone, shunning open water through summer and autumn. In this situation the open areas are clearly less profitable than the weed beds. Seasonal energy contributed by terrestrial insects from the riparian canopy over streams of the James River drainage system, Virginia, equals that of aquatic macroinvertebrates in other Virginia streams, forming an important addition to the diets of indigenous bluegills.[448] Some lakes support greater zooplankton concentrations in the littoral zones than in the limnos,[449] in which case switching might be superfluous. Logically, the dangers posed by a habitat should apply to all larvae of similar size and activity. Larval green sunfish and pumpkinseeds have been found to undergo ontogenetic shifting in the same Michigan lakes used earlier to model this behavior in bluegills, evidence that such patterns are driven by highly charged exigencies characteristic of some bodies of water but not others.[450]

An example of the polymorphism in age-0 bluegills noted earlier was observed in fish from Lake Rush, Oklahoma.[451] Most of the lake's influent streams dry up in summer, turning the water stagnant and lowering its level by evaporation. Thermal stratification is evident by mid-June when the hypolimnion becomes nearly anoxic. The littoral zones in 1980 were intermittent and widely dispersed, but heavily occupied (19 species of fishes inhabit the lake). Age-0 bluegills found in the shallows were strongly compressiform with long heads. They were more robust

Table 6. Largemouth bass >100 mm SL per 100 m of shoreline for transects in areas of low and high bass concentrations in four southern Michigan lakes, with corresponding switch size of bluegills. Concentrations of bass size-classes were averaged over transects. Bass/m² correlates significantly with switch size of bluegills (R^2 = 0.90, $p < 0.05$). Source: Werner and Hall (1988).

Lake	High-concentration transect	Low-concentration transect	Bass/m²	Mean bluegill switch size (mm SL)
Warner	31.3	17.2	1.22	82.7
Deep	26.7	12.0	0.99	64.4
Three	25.4		0.86	63.0
Lawrence	12.4	4.7	0.82	51.5

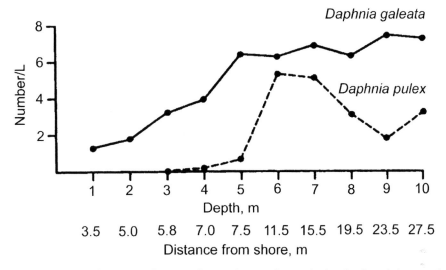

Figure 39. Concentration of the water fleas *Daphnia galeata* and *D. pulex* by depth and distance from shore, Lawrence Lake, Michigan, 30 June 1982. Edge of the littoral zone (maximum depth of rooted vegetation) occurs at 4-5 m. Source: Werner and Hall (1988).

and grew faster than conspecifics in deeper water, which had shorter heads and tended toward fusiform. There was no evidence that the groups intermingled. Lake Rush's fish population was greater than or equal to 3× those of the small Michigan lakes where diet switching has been documented extensively. It was thought that pressure from the more complex fish assemblage, and its far greater numbers, had subsumed any potential value of switching.

Habitat switching apparently does not occur in subtropical Orange Lake, where bluegills less than 8 mm TL occur mainly in panic grass (genus *Panicum*), not in open water, although this habitat composed less than 2% of the lake's area.[452] Few bluegills longer than 12 mm TL occurred in open water, and with growth they moved almost exclusively into thick floating and emergent vegetation, which in 1983–1984 occupied 50–60% of the surface area.

Where switching occurs, differences among lakes are sometimes apparent even in the same region. At Warner Lake, Michigan, mean switch size was 83 mm SL, but only 51.5 mm SL in nearby Lawrence Lake, representing a 2 year delay (Warner Lake bluegills spent 4 years in the littoral zone compared with 2 years in Lawrence Lake).[453] The shift from littoral to limnetic foraging is predicated on reaching a size that negates predation, primarily by largemouth bass

Table 7. Food (vol %) of age-2 bluegills and pumpkin-seeds in Lake Opinicon, Ontario, June 1969-1971. Bluegills were 90-110 mm TL ($n = 63$), pumpkinseeds 95-115 mm TL ($n = 73$). L = larvae, P = pupae, N = nymphs. Source: Adapted from Keast (1978a).

Food organisms	Bluegills	Pumpkinseeds
Amphipods	3	4
Anisopterans	4	6
Chironomids (L)	24	29
Chironomids (P)	1	3
Cladocerans	28	2
Coleopterans (L)	0	1
Dipterans (adult)	3	0
Dipterans (L, P)	5	0
Ephemeropterans (N)	1	10
Hydracarinians	1	0
Isopods	4	8
Mollusks	3	33
Ostracods	2	0
Plant remains	3	0
Trichopterans (L)	14	4
Zygopterans (N)	4	10

(Table 6). This can take several years. As shown, Warner Lake had the highest bass population ($1.22/m^2$), inducing bluegills to delay switching until longer than 80 mm SL.

Switching in small Michigan lakes occurs in two stages.[454] Bluegills first move out of the vegetation to feed on zooplankton immediately overhead. If a predator appears they can retreat into the weeds. The fraction of the typical largemouth bass population capable of swallowing a bluegill longer than 60 mm SL falls off sharply, at least in northern lakes. Having reached ~80 mm SL, and with little fear of predators, bluegills abandon the vegetation and move higher in the water or farther offshore, where in either case the food comprises zooplankters almost exclusively. The water flea *Daphnia pulex*, the most important offshore zooplankter, typically occurs only in the stomachs of bluegills that exceed 80 mm SL.

Smaller bluegills still in the first stage are also starting to feed on zooplankton, and their development parallels a littoral gradient of planktonic species.[455] Concentrations of the water flea *Daphnia galeata* in the littoral zone increase with distance from shore; those of *D. pulex* occur strictly offshore (Figure 39). Stomachs of bluegills feeding in the space above the vegetation during the first stage of switching had eaten comparatively few specimens of *D. pulex* and many of the smaller *D. galeata*, although this pattern varied among lakes. In most lakes the stomachs of bluegills of more than 80 mm SL contained the larger species exclusively, evidence of successful transition to limnetic foraging.

Gill nets set in Lake Opinicon at different depths (offshore to the edge of the littoral zone) revealed the diel distribution of bluegills.[456] By May, one group had congregated near the surface in shallow water, another at 5 m. By July, these aggregations had merged. Proportionately more specimens were caught offshore, and those of 120–180 mm TL dominated the offshore fish assemblage. Bluegills greater than 55 mm TL were relatively safe in open water. Only two large piscivores occupy the lake: largemouth bass rarely consumed bluegills larger than 120 mm TL, and the maximum size eaten by northern pike was 150 mm TL (see below). Bluegills foraged on cladocerans (mainly *Bosmina longirostris*), amphipods, isopods, chironomid larvae, and large ephemeropteran and anisopteran (dragonfly) nymphs.

Fish gillnetted from the surface to 7 m were consuming the same array of organisms, but those caught at the deeper end of the range had fed more heavily on water fleas (genus *Bosmina*). The presence of the other invertebrates, which constituted half the diet, was evidence of movement between the limnetic and littoral zones. Dietary overlap was high between bluegills and black crappies *Pomoxis nigromaculatus* in May, and between bluegills and golden shiners *Notemigonus crysoleucas* in May and July. Bluegills were mainly daytime foragers, but those offshore also fed at dusk when specimens of the genus *Bosmina* were rising to the surface.

As seen in Table 7 for age-2 fish, bluegills and pumpkinseeds are feeding generalists, undergoing diet shifts with age. In the pumpkinseed this means gradually replacing chironomids with mollusks. Pumpkinseeds remain benthic foragers throughout life, as their molarform teeth

Table 8. Monthly variation in dietary overlap (Levin's index) between age-classes of pumpkinseeds and bluegills based on volume fraction of different taxonomic categories of foods in stomachs. In each pair the numerator represents the overlap of pumpkinseeds on bluegills, the denominator the overlap of bluegills on pumpkinseeds. Lake Opinicon, Ontario, May–November 1971–1973. Source: Adapted from Keast (1978a).

Age-class	1	2	3	4-5	6-8
May	0.42/0.37	0.16/0.22	0.66/0.67	0.31/0.37	0.22/0.36
June	0.55/0.25	0.69/0.56	0.47/0.48	0.31/0.51	0.16/0.66
July	0.57/0.72	0.37/0.42	0.44/0.54	0.36/0.33	0.38/0.58
August	0.26/0.13	0.31/0.55	0.53/0.29	0.31/0.52	0.32/0.32
September	0.51/0.23	0.65/0.56	0.20/0.24	0.51/0.52	0.35/0.55
October	0.66/0.43	0.22/0.30	0.54/0.33	0.51/0.51	0.50/0.74
November				0.31/0.75	0.33/0.22

indicate. Young bluegills are limnetic, foraging mainly on cladocerans and switching gradually to a greater percentage of trichopteran larvae, small anisopteran nymphs, and vegetation. As adults, their diet widens to include a variety of soft and mostly small organisms for which their needlelike teeth are adapted.

Pumpkinseeds in northern lakes undergo a dietary shift from soft-bodied littoral organisms to snails at 45–70 mm SL.[457] Juvenile bluegills and pumpkinseeds are restricted to the littoral zone, and their diets overlap.[458] Later, after leaving the protective vegetation and moving to other habitats, their diets diverge and competition is reduced. Meanwhile, as juveniles their mutual growth correlates positively, but negatively with the sum of their concentrations,[459] supporting the hypothesis of interspecific competition for food in the littoral zone.[460] When juvenile bluegills and pumpkinseeds were placed together in cages submerged in littoral areas of Lawrence Lake for 50 d, the growth of both species declined linearly, indicative of competition.[461] Pumpkinseeds in lakes without bluegills respond as expected, being characterized by higher numbers of both juveniles and adults, increased growth rates of juveniles, decreased growth rates of adults, and diminished numbers of snails, the principal food of adults.[462]

Interspecific competition sometimes forces diet shifting. In ponds (29 m diameter, 1.8 m deep) containing vegetation, open sediments, and open water, bluegills, pumpkinseeds, and green sunfish (26–28 mm SL) all preferred to forage in the vegetation when stocked alone or all together.[463] However, when together the more aggressive green sunfish stayed in the energetically profitable vegetation, forcing bluegills to forage in open water and pumpkinseeds in the sediments[464] When green sunfish and bluegills were confined separately to the areas of cattails, green sunfish grew 24% larger over the course of the experiment (June–October). When the two species were confined together, green sunfish outgrew bluegills by 44%. The same competitive relationship is essentially true for pumpkinseeds and green sunfish, with pumpkinseeds being less efficient at foraging in vegetation.[465] The foraging abilities of bluegills and pumpkinseeds are similar in vegetation.[466] Although all these species prefer foraging in vegetation, they differ in efficiency.

Pumpkinseeds confined in similar ponds from which the vegetation had been removed continued using the sediments.[467] So did the bluegills and green sunfish, but here the pumpkinseed was the most efficient. Bluegills versus green sunfish was not tested. Bluegills appear to be the least rigid in their diet shifting, green sunfish the most rigid, and pumpkinseeds intermediate.

Pumpkinseeds had begun to forage more often in the sediments by the end of June. They were joined a month later by bluegills, although bluegills also foraged occasionally in the vegetation throughout the experiment. The green sunfish fed almost exclusively in vegetation. Dietary overlap between bluegills and pumpkinseeds was 0.50–0.55. However, relative growth

Table 9. Fraction similarity of diet by dry mass for small and large bluegills and pumpkinseeds calculated in three Michigan lakes using Schoener's index of overlap. Sample sizes were 3–13 fish per species per month ($\bar{x} = 8.2$ fish/month). Prey were classified into 55 categories. Source: Mittelbach (1984).

Month	Lawrence Lake	Three Lakes II	Three Lakes III
		Small fishes (< 75 mm SL)	
May		0.492	0.373
June	0.313	0.436	
July	0.623	0.431	0.353
August	0.411	0.670	0.749
Seasonal average	0.449	0.507	0.492
		Large fishes (> 75 mm SL)	
May		0.030	0.493
June	0.060	0.040	0.233
July	0.008	0.025	0.049
August	0.136	0.040	0.318
Seasonal average	0.080	0.025	0.273

differed substantially according to the resource. Pumpkinseeds grew fastest when foraging in sediments; in vegetation it was the bluegill.

Levins' Index, which ordinarily ranges from 0.0 to 1.0 or slightly greater, paints the outline of dietary width, its value increasing as foraging becomes more generalized and attaining values of 1.0 and greater if all food types are exploited equally (wide diet). An overlap of 0.3 or less is insignificant; a value of 0.7 or more is high. The overlap, or impact, of a generalist forager on a specialist is greater than if the situation were reversed. Pumpkinseeds are the bluegill's closest dietary competitor,[468] although in Lake Opinicon the overlap is usually not extensive (Table 8). The greater overlap of pumpkinseeds on bluegills in age-1 fish (June and September) is attributable to more specialized foraging by bluegills (cladocerans composing 61% and 52% of the diet). Similarly, in age-3 fish (October) isopods make up 36% of the bluegill's diet. Age-classes 4–5 (June) and 6–8 (July) show the reverse: pumpkinseeds become more specialized and mollusks are, respectively, 69% and 34% of their diet.

The occasional high Levin's index values occur when the diet of one pair member abruptly narrows, giving it the appearance of a temporary foraging specialist.[469] Cyclical changes in the food base are partly responsible, but so is serendipity. Bluegills are particularly resourceful, even stuffing themselves with flying ants during brief periods when these are abundant.[470] Overlap values increase when (1) a food resource appears and becomes abundant, attracting both species (e.g., cladocerans, amphipods); (2) disparate groups of aquatic insects emerge simultaneously, leaving the sediments and weed beds impoverished;[471] and (3) prey organisms of appropriate size must be shared by all early age-0 fish inhabiting the limnetic zone (e.g., specimens of the genus *Bosmina*).[472]

Schoener's index has been a popular tool for assessing dietary overlap.[473] As mentioned, bluegills and pumpkinseeds shorter than 75 mm SL in three southern Michigan lakes obtain 80–90% of their diet from organisms associated with vegetation. Percentage similarity was calculated from stomach contents (dry mass of 55 prey categories, half of them classified to genus or species).[474] Monthly similarities (May–August) were 31–75% and comparable for the three lakes

(Table 9). Major groups of prey eaten by small size-classes of bluegills and pumpkinseeds were chironomids, an amphipod (genus *Hyalella*), caenids, and trichopterans. These made up 44–81% of the total diet from May–August. Mean prey size was significantly larger for pumpkinseeds. The average diets of the larger fishes overlapped very little in Lawrence Lake (8%) and Three Lakes II (2.5%), but 27% in Three Lakes III. This lake does not have a well defined limnetic zone, which reduces the availability of zooplankton to bluegills and forces them to forage with pumpkinseeds in littoral areas. According to Schoener's index, dietary overlap in all lakes was minimal: only three values in the table exceed 0.60, the level ordinarily considered significant.

Nonetheless, foraging efficiency of juvenile bluegills and pumpkinseeds in vegetation might be similar, as indicated by aquarium experiments devised using organisms from these lakes (a macrophyte, genus *Chara*, the amphipod *Hyalella azteca*).[475] The capture rate of amphipods at concentrations of 185 and 550/m² did not differ significantly between bluegills and pumpkinseeds of 37–39 mm SL, and the same was true when larger fishes (57–59 mm SL) were tested at the amphipod concentration of 550/m².

If foraging efficiencies of these species as juveniles are indeed comparable, their diets could overlap depending on available resources. However, bluegills often dominate in many lakes and ponds. In Lawrence Lake the ratio of bluegills to pumpkinseeds was 25, but 9 in Three Lakes II, and only 1 in Three Lakes III.[476] These differences were attributed to variation in "adult" resources (snails and zooplankters) among lakes. Bluegills and pumpkinseeds become more specialized with age. If adult food resources are inadequate, reproduction and ultimately recruitment will be affected.

The mean dry mass of gastropods (genera *Amnicola*, *Physa*, *Valvata*) differed significantly among lakes: Lawrence Lake (59.8 mg/m²), Three Lakes II (300.5 mg/m²), Three Lakes III (183.2 mg/m²).[477] These three genera accounted for greater than 90% of the total biomass of snails consumed by pumpkinseeds (snails of the genera *Gyraulus* and *Helisoma* were seldom eaten). Three Lakes II was clearly most profitable for adult pumpkinseeds and Lawrence Lake least profitable.

Bluegills greater than 75 mm SL foraging on zooplankton in these lakes selected large water fleas, 75% of which exceeded 1.2 mm.[478] Seasonal abundance of large water fleas was 4.06/L (Lawrence Lake), 1.95/L (Three Lakes II), and 1.29/L (Three Lakes III). Lawrence Lake was the most profitable for adult bluegills and Three Lakes III the least profitable. Not surprisingly, 44% of stomachs of adult bluegills collected in Lawrence Lake contained at least 80% water fleas, those from Three Lakes II 27%, and those of Three Lakes III 7%. As to habitat, the surface areas of Lawrence Lake and Three Lakes II are divided equally between limnetic and littoral zones; Three Lakes III is 75% littoral and 25% limnetic.

Sunfishes demonstrate obvious dietary plasticity, enabling them to exist on different foods or shift and choose specific items when competing with congeners. The bluegill might be the most adaptable member of the genus *Lepomis*, and diet shifts often result from such competition. This was shown when bluegills, green sunfish, and pumpkinseeds were stocked alone or together in four Michigan ponds of the group described previously (29 m in diameter and 1.8 m deep) between June and October.[479] All contained stands of cattails (genus *Typha*) extending out 2 m. Beyond the cattails the habitat comprised exposed sediments interrupted by patches of submerged vegetation (genera *Chara* and *Potamogeton*) growing to within 0.5 m of the surface. To one pond were added 900 fish of each species measuring 26–28 mm (SL?). The other ponds separately held 900 of each species. Fishes were removed periodically for stomach analyses and replaced with new ones. Natural mortality in the ponds was similar. All species grew fastest when isolated with conspecifics, bluegills the most (179% of initial dry weight) followed by green sunfish (30%), then pumpkinseeds (14%). Food organisms sorted from the stomachs were assigned to three categories: (1) restricted to stems and leaves, (2) open-water zooplankton, and

Table 10. Percentage contribution of prey categories based on dry weight from June-October 1973 when sunfishes were confined in ponds alone or with the other species. The "other" category represents prey items presumed to have been eaten in habitats isolated in the first three categories. Source: Werner and Hall (1976).

Prey category	Bluegill	Pumpkinseed	Green sunfish
		With conspecifics	
Fauna on vegetation	61	41	43
Open-water zooplankton	8	0.1	0.1
Benthic fauna	10	12	23
Other	21	47	33
		With congeners	
Fauna on vegetation	15	5	40
Open-water zooplankton	33	6	4
Benthic fauna	15	34	12
Other	37	55	44

(3) living on or in the sediments. Use of prey was similar when species were stocked separately (Table 10). However, when stocked with congeners the diet of the green sunfish changed little, but bluegills shifted to midwater zooplankton, and pumpkinseeds focused on the sediments. As in the other experiment, all species preferred foraging in vegetation, presumably because the prey organisms there are larger, offering greater potential return per unit of effort.

Repeating the experiment with only bluegills and green sunfish in one of the same ponds refined the distinctions (Table 11).[480] This time the cattails were separated from open water by Nylon fences (3.2 mm mesh), dividing the area into three spaces of ~50 m^3 each and containing cattails at stem concentrations of 32–40/m^2. The spaces were stocked with (1) 250 of both species, (2) 500 bluegills, and (3) 500 green sunfish. All fishes were 24–37 mm SL. Stomach analyses were performed as before and the contents enumerated. Zooplankters are not an important dietary item in the shallow littoral zone. Proportionately, bluegills consumed twice the benthic fauna of green sunfish when the two species were confined together, and half as much fauna from the vegetation. The same pattern prevailed when the species were kept separately. Dietary overlap assessed using Schoener's index was 0.72 when the species were confined together, 0.70 when separated. The value had been 0.44 in the earlier experiment in which both had been free to segregate. Forced integration raised the overlap value by 0.39.

More green sunfish survived (85% in the combined section, 80% in the section with conspecifics) than bluegills (75% compared with 70%). The green sunfish also grew faster and ate a greater size range of prey items. When stocked only with conspecifics they were 24% larger by

Table 11. Percentage contribution of prey categories based on dry weight from July-October 1974 when bluegills and green sunfishes were confined in ponds together or alone. The "other" category represents prey items presumed to have been eaten in habitats isolated in the first three categories. Source: After Werner and Hall (1977).

	Fauna on vegetation	Open-water zooplankton	Benthic fauna	Other
Together				
Bluegills	19.2	4.2	36.8	40.0
Green sunfish	38.6	1.4	18.0	42.0
Alone				
Bluegills	19.4	3.9	33.2	43.5
Green sunfish	31.8	2.4	17.9	47.9

October. In the combined space the effect was even greater: green sunfish were 44% larger than the bluegills.

One of these ponds was used in tests of habitat profitability for 10 weeks in 1979.[481] It was again divided with a net, this time in half, and each part was stocked with bluegills of three size-classes: small (35.5 mm SL); medium (52.9 mm SL), and large (73.0 mm SL) representing the first three age-classes in local lakes.[482] Bluegills of each size-class were removed periodically for stomach analysis and measurement and replaced with similar specimens. Prey items in the stomachs corresponded with one of the three habitats: open water, bottom sediment, or vegetation.

Two species of cladocerans appeared naturally in the open water, followed by cyclopoid copepods. Water fleas were abundant at first, then declined nearly to zero. The bluegills showed clear size selection when feeding on them, and the pattern differed significantly from expected random encounters with prey. Furthermore, water fleas in the stomachs were significantly larger than in the water, and bigger fish ate bigger water fleas. As water fleas became scarce the bluegills switched to midge larvae in the sediment, mainly specimens of *Chironomus plumosus*, choosing midges (< 2–20 mm long) smaller than predicted by the OFM (Chapter 3). The small bluegills ate few bigger than 12 mm; medium and large bluegills ate few that exceeded 14 mm. Only 9–14% of prey from all size-classes of bluegills came from the vegetation. The prey there ranged from less than 0.25 to 20 mm; the minimum size range consumed was 0.25–1.75 mm. How profitable was this foraging in terms of energy intake per unit time?

Bluegills of all size-classes displayed the same pattern, although absolute energy increased with increasing fish size because big fish ate more. Water fleas were abundant at first, and foraging profitability was high in open water for all size-classes, but their numbers fell quickly, forcing a shift in late July to the sediments as chironomids increased in both numbers and size. Chironomids then composed 80% of the diet. The medium and large size-classes continued to forage on them through September, but small bluegills again switched to foraging in open water as zooplankton increased. In northern lakes the greatest diversity and abundance of food organisms occurs in May; thereafter, some organisms are still abundant, but diversity declines abruptly beginning in July.[483]

Intraspecific competition for a bluegill begins the moment it leaves the nest and enters the limnos. Large numbers of larvae (e.g., 280 and 360/m^3 in two Alabama ponds) can alter the abundance of zooplankters, their taxonomic composition, and their size structure.[484] At ~5 mm TL and just starting to feed,[485] bluegills are gape-limited, able to consume only small zooplankters.[486] Meanwhile, heavy consumption by older fish selectively depletes the large zooplankters. By the time age-0 bluegills attain 13.5 mm TL, their gape has increased enough to permit capture of the big cladocerans (1.2 mm),[487] further diminishing the zooplankton population.[488]

Larval bluegills eat more and grow faster when foraging on large zooplankters.[489] Through competition for the same organisms (e.g., phantom midges, large water fleas) adults exert a negative effect on survival of their own larvae and early juveniles.[490] In a pond experiment, newly hatched bluegills were stocked at 16.55/m^3 with adults in adjoining wedge-shaped areas of 90.6 m^3. Adult concentrations inside the different wedges were zero (larvae only), low (0.033/m^3), medium (0.66/m^3), and high (0.132/m^3).[491] Control larvae survived poorly in the absence of adults, most mortality being caused by predatory insects (mainly damselfly larvae and giant water bugs). However, mean body mass was greatest in this group, which experienced no adult competition. Predatory insects were reduced 80% when adults were present. Decreased survival at the high adult concentration was attributed to competition for food and to cannibalism. The best balance of growth and survival of age-0 bluegills was achieved at the medium adult concentration.

Bluegills are flexible, aggressive foragers in a variety of habitats. In aquarium experiments,

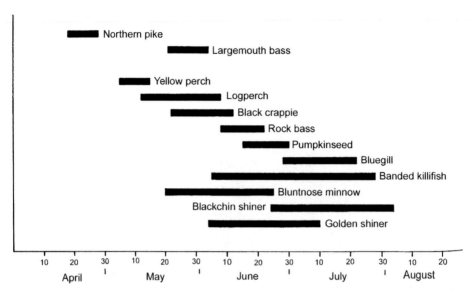

Figure 40. Time at which early juvenile fishes appear in Lake Opinicon, Ontario, 1969-1970. Source: Keast (1985a).

specimens of 46–55 mm TL out-competed more specialized golden shiners measuring 54–59 mm TL for flour beetle larvae (genus *Tribolium*) offered in situations arranged to mimic benthic, midwater, vegetation, and surface locations.[492] The bluegills' performance improved with experience both in intra- and interspecific trials; that of the shiners did not.

Much of the foraging competition in lacustrine environments involves fishes preying on each other.[493] The primary piscivores commence this behavior at age-0 and quickly rely on prey fishes as their principal foods. At Lake Opinicon the two primary piscivores are largemouth bass and northern pike. As mentioned, age-0 largemouths feed first on zooplankton, competing in the limnos with age-0 bluegills and other planktivores. They quickly outgrow this phase and switch to a diet of small invertebrates and then small fishes, ceasing to compete with age-0 bluegills and preying on them instead. Piscivory commences at ~23 mm TL and targets fishes of 4.5–6.0 mm TL. Stomachs of juvenile bass (28–35 mm TL) commonly contained fishes this size. Fish composed 50% of the diet by volume at the end of the first summer, 70% at the end of age-1, and 85% at the end of age-2. The northern pike is also a piscivore in its first summer, probably attaining this status at ~35 mm TL.[494]

Secondary piscivores at Lake Opinicon delay eating fishes until age-3 or older, and fishes seldom compose more than 40% of the diet.[495] Black crappies rely mainly on zooplankton through age-1 before switching to small invertebrates, principally phantom midges (genus *Chaoborus*) and other larval chironomids. Piscivory commences gradually, eventually reaching 30% of the diet in older specimens. Progression in the rock bass is similar except for skipping small invertebrates and moving directly to larger ones (e.g., anisopteran nymphs, crayfishes). Fishes become regular dietary items at age-4, stabilizing at 20% thereafter. Yellow bullheads *Ameiurus natalis* skip the zooplankton-feeding stage, foraging on small invertebrates like chironomid larvae. Beyond age-2 the main foods are large invertebrates (e.g., odonatan nymphs, crayfishes) with fishes constituting 45%. Yellow perch forage on zooplankton and small invertebrates through age-1 and large invertebrates (ephemeropteran nymphs and crayfishes) at age-2. Large invertebrates are the principal prey, with fishes composing 25% starting at age-5.

Predation at Lake Opinicon is diverse and extensive. Mean total lengths of late age-0 fishes are: black crappie (43 mm),[496] rock bass (45 mm),[497] bluegill (42 mm) and pumpkinseed (48 mm),[498] largemouth bass (62 mm),[499] and yellow perch (54 mm).[500] These, in sum, are 64% of the prey fishes eaten by black crappies, 66% by rock bass, and 67% by yellow perch.[501] At some point in their lives all 18 species in the lake are prey for other fishes. Of these, centrarchids (genus *Lepomis*) are the most prevalent prey, especially when small. Adult largemouth bass capture bluegills and other fishes up to 100 mm TL and rarely to 120 mm TL. Northern pike longer than 300 mm TL forage on fishes up to 150 mm TL, including sunfishes (genus *Lepomis*), although incidences of compressiform species constituting more than 30% of a pike's total length are unusual.[502] Yellow bullheads were thought to prey on centrarchids at night while they rest on the bottom. Black crappies and rock bass are also nocturnal foragers.[503]

Competition is intense over a short growing season in northern latitudes. Small Michigan lakes often support 25 species of fishes, including eight centrarchids, of which the bluegill commonly exceeds 80% of the biomass.[504] The OFM predicts ontogenetic diet shifts to maximize energy consumption in these cyclical environments (Chapter 3). Primary piscivores grow fast, and the size of their prey increases proportionately. Diet shifts must benefit from plentiful prey of the right size. One hypothesis posits that early spawning of largemouth bass and northern pike in Lake Opinicon is an adaptation to gain advantage on their eventual prey (Figure 40).[505] Note that pumpkinseeds and bluegills have spawning times extending well beyond those of northern pike and largemouth bass, perhaps evolutionary assurance that if the earliest age-class does not survive there will be others to take its place (Chapter 7). As described above, age-0 young of the secondary piscivores do not forage on fishes, and their spawning times are later.

Invertebrates also compete directly with bluegills for food resources. In aquarium experiments the predatory effects of bluegills ($\bar{x}$ = 52.2 mm TL) and dragonfly larvae *Erythemis simplicicollis* ($\bar{x}$ = 4.7 mm head width) foraging on mayfly larvae *Cloeon cognatum* were tested for additivity using fake vegetation at concentrations of 292, 583, and 875 stems/m².[506] Predation was greater with bluegills and dragonflies together than when dragonflies foraged alone. Their combined predation exceeded an additive model at the lowest stem concentration, and the presence of bluegills did not inhibit prey capture by dragonfly larvae, indicating direct competition.

Competitive interaction can disrupt ontogenetic diet shifts, but so can a lack of competition. The severe winter of 1977–1978 destroyed the entire bluegill population of Wintergreen Lake, Michigan, leaving pumpkinseeds largely unaffected.[507] Previously, bluegills had outnumbered pumpkinseeds by a ratio of 4. In 1988, bluegills were still absent from Wintergreen Lake and present in nearby Three Lakes II and III.[508] Pumpkinseeds inhabited all three lakes but were an order of magnitude more numerous in Wintergreen Lake. Juvenile pumpkinseeds (those < 45 mm SL) grew rapidly without competition from bluegills for littoral invertebrates. From this length to 75 mm SL, when they begin the transition to snails and bluegills to zooplankton, the pumpkinseeds in Wintergreen Lake hit a trophic wall: their excessive numbers had diminished the snail populations to 10% of the other lakes, forcing them to continue feeding on soft-bodied invertebrates such as amphipods (genus *Hyalella*), chironomids, caenids, and trichopterans. Instead of a diet consisting of more than 70% snails by mass, as in Three Lakes II and III, adult pumpkinseeds (those > 75 mm SL) in Wintergreen Lake survived on 2% by dry mass. They grew slowly, and their stomachs contained less than the expected mass of prey. Juveniles collected in 1988 grew at twice the rate of specimens collected in 1935, when bluegills had also inhabited the lake. However, age-4 and age-5 adults that had reached 204 and 229 g in 1935 barely reached 50 g in 1988. Without competition from bluegills the pumpkinseed population of Wintergreen Lake exploded, causing increased growth rates of small fish and functional destruction of the snail population, which consequently depressed the growth of adults.

In a mere 10 years since bluegills had been eliminated from Wintergreen Lake, the pumpkinseeds had undergone a trophic polymorphism.[509] This took the form of reduced crushing muscles in the jaws: the levator posteriors of these fish were less than half as massive as those of Three Lakes pumpkinseeds and generated less than half the crushing force.[510] Aquarium experiments showed handling time (the time to crush and consume a snail) to be 3× longer in Wintergreen Lake pumpkinseeds, although efficacy in consuming soft-bodied prey was not significantly different.[511]

Bluegills, redspotted sunfish *Lepomis miniatus*, and redear sunfish *L. microlophus* demonstrated overlapping diets in an estuarine bayou in southeastern Mississippi.[512] Size-classes were small (< 30 mm SL), medium (30 to < 60 mm SL), and large (60–100 mm SL). Zooplankton (mainly calanoid copepods) and cladocerans composed most of the diet of small sunfishes during all seasons, bluegills consuming the highest proportion and readear sunfish the lowest. In autumn and winter the principal prey organisms were gammarid amphipods, which were more abundant in submerged vegetation (*Vallisneria americana* and *Ruppia maritima*) than in sediments. Redspotted sunfish consumed the highest proportion and bluegills the lowest. During warmer months there was a shift to chironomids, ceratopogonids, and caenids by all three species.

Bluegills of medium size foraged heavily on gammarid amphipods with redspotted sunfish again consuming the proportionately greatest number and bluegills the least.[513] All sunfishes, but especially bluegills, continued to consume zooplankton and gammarids. Redspotted and redear sunfish also foraged on polychaetes in the sediments; chironomids were important to all three species from autumn through spring. Diets showed the most divergence in large sunfishes (60–100 mm SL). All species continued to feed seasonally on gammarids, which were most abundant in the vegetation during autumn and winter. Redears then relied consistently on hard-shelled prey (e.g., ostracods, hydrobiid snails, mussels) and were restricted to the vegetation and sediments. Large bluegills continued to forage on zooplankton but in spring showed a partial shift to chironomid larvae, ephemeropteran nymphs, and gammarids.

Dietary overlap was measured using Horn's index,[514] which provides a range of 0.0–1.0 with 1.0 representing 100% overlap.[515] Intraspecific overlap was high in the two smallest size-classes: bluegills (0.90), readear sunfish (0.87), redspotted (0.84), and also between medium and large redears (0.86). The highest interspecific overlap involving the bluegill was 0.87 (small redears, medium bluegills).

The exotic zebra mussel *Dreissena polymorpha* is now a fixture in the Great Lakes region, Mississippi River drainage system, and numerous lakes throughout eastern and middle America.[516] When larval bluegills enter the limnos, zebra mussels compete with them on at least two levels. During enclosure experiments bluegill larvae of 5.5 mm SL grew 24% more slowly than controls by competing directly for smaller zooplankters (e.g., copepod nauplii, rotifers).[517] Zebra mussels are potential indirect competitors when they consume phytoplankton, creating starvation conditions for zooplankters[518] and theoretically lessening their availability to larval fishes.

Competition from bluegills that alters the behavior or survival of other species generates ripple effects through aquatic communities. The influence on prey organisms can be finely nuanced and indirect, manifested in avoidance behaviors and intricate methods of detecting predators. Bluegills and other fishes are thought to release chemical compounds into the environment that modify the behavior of prey organisms in the vicinity. These substances, which have yet to be identified, are nonrefractory, degrading in a few days.[519] Forces controlling feedback and subsequent responses are plastic and probably involve rudimentary memory retention at the species level. However, damselflies that ordinarily reproduce in fishless lakes or ponds are unable to distinguish those containing fishes.[520]

When bluegills in cages were submerged in outdoor wading pools, counts of mosquito *Anopheles punctipennis* and phantom midge *Chaoborus albatus* larvae and pupae were significantly less numerous than in control pools containing only empty cages.[521] In tub experiments the presence of bluegills indirectly inhibited feeding of the two damselflies tested (*Enallagma aspersum* and *E. traviatum*) by lowering the zooplankton population.[522] In aquarium experiments, bluegills and an insect predator (genus *Anax*) inhibited crawling by specimens of *E. aspersum*, forcing them to increase these movements at night. Overall, bluegills substantially lowered the numbers of predaceous invertebrates, shifting the insect community to fewer, cryptic species. In experiments conducted using cattle watering tanks the invisible presence of bluegills (50–60 g) significantly reduced colonization by an aquatic beetle *Tropisternus lateralis*.[523] Activities of beetles that did colonize were sharply reduced. To avoid sham predation, adults even left the water and clung to the sides of the containers.

Bluegills affect amphibian populations directly by predation and indirectly by competing with them for food. In aquarium experiments, juvenile bluegills averaging 43.7 mm SL ate tadpoles of leopard frogs *Rana sphenocephala* and crawfish frogs *R. areolata*, but not the eggs.[524] During experiments using cattle watering tanks, bluegills affected the growth and survival of salamander larvae (mole salamanders *Ambystoma talpoideum* and spotted salamanders *A. maculatum*).[525] The presence of bluegills reduced body size at 76 d posthatch by 18% (*A. talpoideum*) and 16% (*A. maculatum*) compared with controls (larvae reared alone). Survival was reduced 61% (*A. talpoideum*) and 97% (*A. maculatum*) compared with controls. Food competition was apparent. Salamanders reared without bluegills fed mainly on chydorids (81%), but these composed only 9% of the diets of salamanders reared with bluegills. When bluegills were present, 51% of the diet was ostracods, with ostracods accounting for 4% in larvae reared alone. The mean number of prey eaten by salamander larvae placed with bluegills was lowered 70% below that of the controls, from 188.5 to 56.5 items per salamander. In plastic wading pool experiments, bluegills disrupted the normal activities of spotted salamander larvae, causing them to take refuge in leaf litter instead of foraging in open water.[526] By heavily exploiting the zooplankters, bluegills reduced the food available to salamander larvae, suppressing their growth.

Bullfrogs typically increase in ponds containing adult bluegills, for two apparent reasons. First, bluegills find their tadpoles unpalatable; second, bluegills forage on aquatic insect larvae that constitute the principal predators of bullfrog tadpoles.[527] These courtesies are not extended to tadpoles of the gray treefrog *Hyla versicolor* on which adult bluegills prey, nor to adult redspotted newts *Notophthalmus viridescens* with which bluegills compete for zooplankton.[528] The numbers of both species decline when bluegills are present.

Predation

5 Bluegills are most susceptible to predation as eggs and fry (Chapter 6), becoming less vulnerable as they grow. Their behavior shows it. Fear of predators, especially other fishes, diminishes upon reaching a certain size, enabling large specimens to wander freely among different habitats. A bluegill's body depth, not its length, is the factor that determines whether it can be swallowed by another fish.[529] In the bluegill, however, body length and depth show nearly perfect correlation (Figure 41), making them statistically redundant and therefore equally useful for predictive purposes.

The natural mortality of bluegills greater than 125 mm FL can be near 50%, little of it caused by predation.[530] For example, predation on bluegills this size by spotted gars *Lepisosteus oculatus* in Indiana lakes was reported to be rare, although dead specimens less than 150 mm FL were sometimes eaten. A bowfin *Amia calva* of 740 mm TL and 4.3 kg from an Indiana lake contained two bluegills of 92 and 115 g (length unstated).[531] Bowfins prefer soft-rayed fishes and crayfishes and are ineffective predators of bluegills.[532]

A predator's gape limits the size of a bluegill it can swallow. Walleyes *Sander vitreum* can swallow bluegills of 127 mm TL,[533] the limit for the largest northern pike is 160 mm TL, and for largemouth bass the maximum size is 150 mm TL[534] or 160 mm TL,[535] although other reports claim that larger sizes are vulnerable,[536] including specimens to 192 mm TL.[537] Centrarchids are not a preferred prey of pike.[538] Bluegills, even small ones, are rejected because of their body morphology and evasiveness, and pike growth correlates negatively with the abundance of small bluegills.[539] Information to calculate the gapes of largemouth bass based on their total lengths is given in Figure 42. A bluegill greater than 200 mm TL would likely be safe from all but the very largest piscine predators, the true "lunkers." Even bluegills of 125 mm FL would constitute unlikely prey for all but the largest bass, and then the effort would be difficult.[540] Estimating the vulnerability of bluegills of known size to predation by largemouth bass is a simple calculation. To swallow a bluegill of 200 mm TL, for example, would require a bass of 491 mm TL (Figure 43 and regression equation). In American anglers parlance this would be a 19-in fish weighing about 8 lb. Not many bass this big exist except in the southeast and certain California reservoirs.[541]

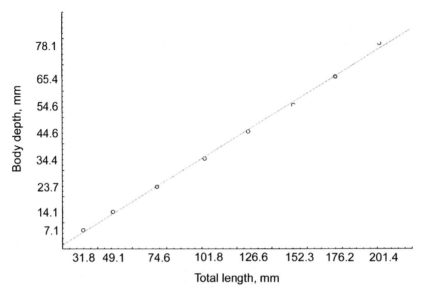

Figure 41. Body depth of bluegills regressed against their total lengths: pooled means of length categories ($n =$ 21, raw n unknown), $R^2 = 0.98$, SE = ±0.91, $F_{(1,6)} = 3306.28$, $p < 0.0001$, total length (ß) is significant at 0.99. The data best fit a linear curve in which body depth is predicted by $y = -6.77 + 0.41x$. Source: Plotted from data in Lawrence (1958).

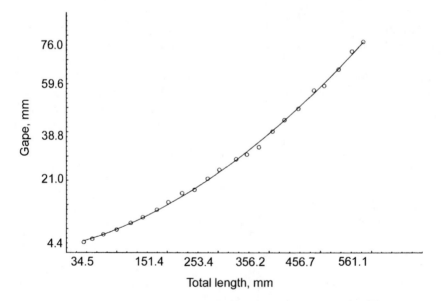

Figure 42. Gapes of largemouth bass regressed against their total lengths: pooled means of length categories (n = 21, raw n unknown), $R^2 = 0.98$, SE = ±1.79, $F_{(1,21)} = 845.14$, $p < 0.0001$; intercept = –7.30, length (ß) is significant at 0.99. The data best fit a polynomial curve in which maximum gape is predicted by $y = 2.85 + 0.5x$ $+ 0.0002x^2$. Source: Plotted from data in Lawrence (1958).

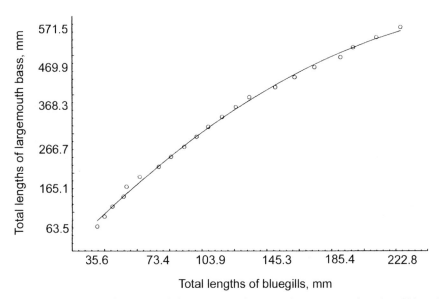

Figure 43. Minimum lengths of largemouth bass regressed against the maximum lengths of bluegills they can swallow: pooled means by length category: ($n = 21$, raw n unknown), $R^2 = 0.98$, SE = ±11.57, $F_{(1,19)} = 850.81$, $p < 0.0001$; intercept = 16.28, total length of bluegills (ß) is significant at 0.99. The data best fit a polynomial curve in which minimum lengths of bass are predicted by $y = -72.35 + 4.49x - 0.0074x^2$. Source: Plotted from data in Lawrence (1958).

The majority of bluegills (young age-0 fish excepted) are in little danger of being swallowed, as evaluated using relative vulnerability.

$$V_d = 1 - \sum_{w=0}^{d} W$$

in which V = relative vulnerability of prey based on body depth, d = body depth in a prey fish population, W = frequency of mouth widths in the predator population, and ΣW = the cumulative frequency of predator mouth widths.[542] Prey species with body depths less than or equal to the smallest piscivore mouth width can be swallowed by any member of the piscivore population ($V = 1$). Fishes having body depths that exceed the largest piscivore mouth width are invulnerable ($V = 0$), and those of intermediate size are vulnerable to some piscine predators but not others (relative vulnerability of $0 < V < 1$). When Patten Lake, a 7.7-ha lake in Texas, was drained in 1979, 85% of the forage fishes (including bluegills) had body depths that exceeded the mouth widths of 75% of the largemouth bass. Less than 5% had relative vulnerabilities greater than or equal to 0.5.

Young northern pike and yellow perch forage actively in weed beds.[543] Perch are not ordinarily considered piscivores until reaching ~150 mm TL, although specimens of 70 mm have been captured in thick inshore weed beds, their stomachs filled with sunfishes of 20–30 mm TL.[544] In northern Mississippi River backwaters the principal predators of age-0 bluegills are age-0 largemouth bass, and they share the same vegetated areas during the first summer.[545] The vulnerability of the bluegills declines over summer as their mean body depth begins to exceed the mean gape of the bass (Figure 44). In June and July 71% are susceptible to predation, but the percentages fall to 40% in August and 6% in September. At Ridge Lake, Illinois, age-0 bluegills were eaten only by largemouths of age-3 or younger (< 350 mm TL). Bluegills in general became

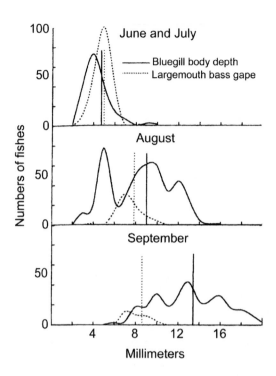

Figure 44. Frequency distributions of body depth of age-0 bluegills and gape of age-0 largemouth bass over June-September 1992 in a vegetated Mississippi River backwater lake (Lake Onalaska, Wisconsin). Source: Dewey et al. (1997).

less important as the bass grew. Those of age-0 composed 89% of the diet of age-0 bass, 25% for bass of age-1, and less than 9% for bigger bass.[546] However, more bluegills of age-1 or older were consumed by larger bass.

Three characteristics of a prey fish influence the outcome when a predator attacks: its body depth, whether it has soft or spiny fin rays, and its locomotor performance during avoidance (acceleration and speed).[547] Prey fishes that are small with shallow body depths are the most vulnerable,[548] and they become even less safe if soft-rayed. Tub experiments were designed to test the limiting effects of these variables using largemouth bass as predators and smaller largemouth bass, bluegills, fathead minnows, and tiger muskellunge (northern pike *Esox lucius* × muskellunge *E. masquinongy* sterile hybrid) as prey.[549] The predator's target, defined as the intersection of its strike path and the prey's body, differed only in the bluegill, which had a mean target significantly posterior to its center of mass.[550] However, targets were distributed over a substantial part of its length. Strike targets on largemouth bass were not significantly different from those of the minnow or muskellunge, both soft-rayed species, meaning that the spiny fin rays did not influence the outcome of attacks. The large body depth of the bluegill compared with the other species, perhaps in combination with its spines, affected how it was targeted by predators. That bluegills were struck off center demonstrated a lesser vulnerability.

Swimming speed affected outcome in these experiments.[551] Maximum average speeds during chases were: fathead minnow (80.7 cm/s); largemouth bass (96.4 cm/s); bluegill (100.6 cm/s); tiger muskellunge (136 cm/s). Swimming speed of the bass (~3.5 km/h) is far slower than reported previously (19.2 km/h).[552] Body form (e.g., compressiform, sagittiform) and shape of the fins affect predator–prey outcome only if the prey fish is moving at maximum speed and rate of acceleration.[553] Acceleration performance in the species tested differed by body form. High rates of acceleration correlated positively with number of aborted strikes and negatively with frequency of prey chases. Therefore, high locomotor performance reduces a prey fish's vulnerability by causing a predator to give up the chase sooner.

Some effort is required for a fish to locate, pursue, capture, manipulate, and finally swallow its prey. Handling time (the interval between capture and swallowing of prey) has been used as one measure of optimal foraging (Chapter 3). However, its tenets might better apply to planktivores than piscivores for which encounter rate is probably more limiting.[554] Experiments using largemouth bass and redfin pickerel *Esox americanus* showed handling time to increase steeply with size of the prey.[555] The maximum time in these experiments was less than 6 min. Meanwhile, the predator would seem to have expended little energy except to breathe and move its jaw and pharyngeal muscles. As to pursuit and capture, both distance to the prey and time needed to catch it ordinarily are short, whether the prey is stalked or ambushed. Captive largemouth bass waited to attack bluegills until ~0.3 m away, northern pike until half that distance.[556] Regardless of its size, the velocity of a captive largemouth bass attacking another fish in midwater is fast, 3.1 L/s.[557] Most hunts begin and end abruptly with little time elapsed. The whole sequence can occur before an observer reacts with a stopwatch.[558] Time expended in location, pursuit, and capture is probably negligible and changes little even with increasing size of the prey.[559]

Assuming that small and large prey require similar effort by a predator, differences in handling time over the size range of the prey is a few minutes at most. The total time necessary to locate, pursue, capture, manipulate, and swallow the prey is doubtfully long enough to have a significant impact on a predator's energy balance.

Bluegills encounter two kinds of piscine predators, those like largemouth bass that actively hunt, and others such as bowfins, gars, and esocids that wait in ambush. Bluegills of vulnerable size counteract predators by hiding in complex structures and altering their behavior. Some of the same techniques that might give them an edge are also available to their attackers. However, habitat selection by adults should logically be based on foraging possibilities, not shelter. This seems to have been the case at Pelican Lake, Nebraska, where foraging was apparently similar everywhere, and adult bluegills roamed at will both day and night.[560]

Bluegills can maneuver adroitly in tight spaces, in part because of their compressiform shape. But the largemouth bass, the bluegill's principal predator in North American lakes and ponds, is also compressiform and maneuvers well too. Many ambush predators have sagittiform shapes, excellent for crypsis and stealth, and most are masters of immobility. Esocids use the lateral line to detect moving prey in the near-field (Chapter 2). Northern pike typically attack only prey moving in their visual field,[561] which implies that for a predator to define another organism as prey it must possess certain characteristics. Perhaps a bluegill stops all motion in the presence of a northern pike to avoid detection, but this is speculation. A bluegill that remains absolutely still lacks visual relevance to a pike, becoming just another object. By not moving it also disappears from near-field mechanosensory detection (Chapter 2). The bluegill, in other words, has evaded detection by vanishing before the pike's eyes and mechanoreceptors.

Bluegills are preyed on by many other fishes. Warmouth *Lepomis gulosus* in Lake Pontchartrain, Louisiana, sometimes feed on them exclusively.[562] Nonetheless, larger juvenile and adult bluegills are seldom the prey of choice. The reasons are unclear, although postulates blame their deep-bodied form, spiny-rayed fins, and facile evasiveness. Esocids and largemouth bass are the main piscine predators of bluegills. All esocids grow slowly and survive less well in ponds where bluegills dominate other prey fishes[563] or are the only prey.[564] Growth and survival of esocids are superior if fathead minnows or gizzard shad *Dorosoma cepedianum* constitute a principal source of food.[565] Given options, no esocid preys heavily on bluegills.[566] One reason might be because bluegills, like other sunfishes, erect their spines when attacked,[567] perhaps as a means of protection, making them more difficult to ingest than soft-rayed fishes.[568]

As just described, body depth and not spines appears to be the principal deterrent when the predator is a largemouth bass, but this apparently is not true of all predatory fishes. During aquarium and pool experiments, juvenile walleyes of 100–210 mm TL captured and swallowed gizzard shad and bluegills of similar size (to 41% and 38% of their own body lengths).[569] The gizzard shad, like the bluegill, is deep-bodied, but its fins are soft-rayed instead of spiny. Walleyes could swallow golden shiners, another soft-rayed species, up to 55% of their own total length. Handling times increased with length of the prey, but were highest for bluegills; times for gizzard shad and golden shiners were similar. Bluegills captured near the tail had higher mean handling times (375 s) than specimens of similar size caught by the head (171 s). A walleye could swallow a small bluegill tail first, but bigger ones (> 35% of its own length) had to be turned and swallowed head first. As a result, small and large bluegills often had similar handling times, and these were always higher than the times for shad and shiners. Here the bluegill's spiny fin rays clearly increased handling time or prevented ingestion because shad were no more difficult to swallow than the more sagittiform shiners.

Bluegills required significantly more effort to capture than shad and shiners.[570] Walleyes of 185–210 mm TL made more strikes at bluegills. Capture efficiencies for bluegills (13%) were substantially lower than for shad (41%) and shiners (32%). Walleyes, like other piscine predators, are limited in their prey selection by gape, and body depth was a better predictor than length for size selection across species of prey.

Northern pike in 19 small Wisconsin lakes dominated by sunfishes (mainly bluegills) preferred to feed on yellow perch.[571] Captive northern pike chose goldfish and common carp, both soft-rayed, over green sunfish and bluegills.[572] Pike held in pools and ponds and presented with 17 species of potential prey selected bluegills, channel catfish Ictalurus punctatus, and black bullheads Ameiurus melas least often.[573] Green sunfish were intermediate in vulnerability when presented along with more favored prey, but became unpopular when offered alone. Catfishes, like sunfishes, erect strong spines when attacked. Black bullheads became more vulnerable if their dorsal and pectoral spines were clipped. Of 455 black bullheads offered, only 18 were eaten, including those with the abbreviated spines.

Centrarchids are not just deep-bodied and spiny; esocids find them more difficult to capture than other fishes. In tub experiments, pellet-reared tiger muskellunge needed more strikes to capture bluegills compared with fathead minnows.[574] The minnows schooled continuously in open water, but bluegills dispersed to the corners and edges, often remaining motionless. Another experiment documented the comparative vulnerability of captive bluegills, fathead minnows, and gizzard shad to northern pike, muskellunge, and tiger muskellunge.[575] The ability to capture prey was similar among the esocids, which ranged from 150 to 225 mm TL. No refuge was provided in the pools and ponds. Bluegills were attacked the most often. Nonetheless, mean captures per strike were higher for fathead minnows (67%) and gizzard shad (78%) than for bluegills (14%). As the numbers show, bluegills required 5× more attack attempts before a successful capture, and after having caught a bluegill the handling time was significantly longer. In container experiments, the time needed for a largemouth bass of 240 g to ingest and swallow a green sunfish of 33.5 g was the same as for bluegills of 2.5 and 2.7 g.[576] A largemouth bass of 527 g ingested green sunfish of all sizes tested (6.0–38.5 g) more efficiently than even the smallest bluegills (2.5 g).

Evasive behavior seems more highly developed in sunfishes than in most sympatric soft-rayed species. Captive bluegills evaded esocids using maneuverability; fathead minnows and gizzard shad relied solely on speed, and fewer escaped.[577] As shown in similar experiments, bluegills also maintained greater distance from predators.[578] Evasive behaviors recorded in these and other investigations included "back-peddling," darting forward and stopping abruptly, and assuming a perpendicular orientation.[579] The apparent functions of the first two behaviors is to maintain maximum distance from danger, that of the third to exaggerate size by increasing a predator's gape requirement. All three prey species schooled, but bluegills were attacked least frequently. Bluegills in other experiments stopped schooling in the presence of northern pike,[580] perhaps to avoid detection.

Where more than one species of *Lepomis* is present, competition can result in morphological variation (character displacement) and differences in the use of food and other resources (niche shifts). On occasion, bluegills have been reported as having distinct limnetic and littoral forms, one feeding in open water, the other in vegetation and sediments. A study at Forbes Lake, Illinois, compared age-1 bluegills from open water ($\bar{x}$ = 41.7 mm SL) with others from stands of sub-merged and floating vegetation ($\bar{x}$ = 44.4 mm SL).[581] Mean body depth and pectoral fin length were significantly greater for "littoral" bluegills, but caudal peduncle length was greater in limnetic fish. These differences were thought to be adaptations for avoiding predation. The hypothesis was tested in 1.14-m^3 circular pools with largemouth bass (178–220 mm TL) and fake vegetation at ~1,430 stems/m^2. Fish of both morphologies were exposed to bass in open water and vegetation. Limnetic bluegills in open water swam in a tighter school than littoral bluegills and maintained greater distance from the bass. Littoral bluegills in open water were captured ~10× more quickly. Time to capture the first bluegill was similar in vegetation, although more limnetic bluegills were captured overall, and bass spent significantly more time pursuing lit-toral bluegills while catching fewer.

As mentioned previously, the body depth of a prey fish can barely exceed the gape of a largemouth bass trying to swallow it.[582] Given a choice, however, captive largemouths consis-tently select fishes smaller than this.[583] Handling time by a bass increases with size of the prey, but size is not the only factor: crayfishes take more time to manipulate and swallow than fishes of similar size.[584] A test of several common fishes and a larval amphibian eaten by bass ranked bluegills as the most difficult, followed in descending order by the yellow perch, brook stickle-back *Culaea inconstans*, bluntnose minnow *Pimephales notatus*, and bullfrog tadpole.[585]

Relative size is also a factor. For captive largemouths of 280 mm TL (240 g) the time required to swallow bluegills correlated positively with their body masses (2.5–36.2 g, lengths unstated), but green sunfish (6.0–38.5 g, length unstated) were ingested at nearly the same rate across all body masses tested.[586] A larger bass (340 mm TL, 527 g) ingested all sizes of both prey species with the same ease. Stomach analyses of predators at Spirit Lake, Iowa, found that the majority of prey fishes recovered were 10–30% of the body lengths of fishes that ate them.[587] Incidences of prey exceeding 40% of a predator's length occurred in less than 3% of the cases. Gape evidently was not limiting. Of 19 identified prey fishes, the bluegill was the most deep-bodied, yet it was the most frequent fish eaten by black crappies and yellow perch, the piscivores with the smallest mouths.

Living in thick stands of macrophytes, as bluegills of certain ages and at certain locations are sometimes forced to do (Chapter 4), presents the hypothetical dilemma of enhanced survival at the expense of lower foraging efficiency,[588] an effect not unlike locking yourself safely inside your house and then not being able to get to a grocery store. In a pond experiment, small bluegills averaging 35.5 mm SL under threat of predation by largemouth bass passed up abundant zooplankton in open water, remaining instead among stands of less productive cattails (*Typha augustifolia* and *T. latifolia*) where the mean stem concentration of 176/m^2 (maximum 400/m^2) offered adequate protection.[589] In the absence of bass, control bluegills of the same size foraged in open water, outgrowing those relegated to the vegetation. Captive bluegills (35–50 mm SL) placed in tanks containing fake plant stems of concentrations 100, 250, and 500/m^2 foraged least effi-ciently on damselfly larvae at the highest stem concentration, which was also the safest.[590]

Previous experiments had shown that in the presence of largemouth bass, bluegills of 35–50 mm SL escaped into plots having a stem concentration of 1,000/m², ignoring those of 50, 100, and 250/m².[591]

In another experiment, captive bluegills (35–50 mm SL) were offered two plots seeded with damselfly larvae. The small plot contained 100 stems/m², the large one 500/m².[592] In the absence of a largemouth bass, bluegills preferred whichever plot had more food. In the company of a bass (200–300 mm SL) they selected the large plot even if the smaller one contained more food, but spent less time in both plots and more time moving along the farthest wall of the pool or leaning against it.

When stocked with six largemouth bass (165, 167, 170, 200, 215, and 245 mm SL) in an open pond (29 m diameter, 1.8 m deep) without cover, bluegills of 30, 40, and 60 mm SL had mortality rates that were similar and heavy, but all fish of 75 mm SL survived.[593] Predation was low in a pond the same size with thick vegetation. When bluegills of all size classes were placed together with six largemouth bass, only those in the 30- and 40-mm size classes experienced any predation, and the mortality was considerably less than in open water. The same was true of bluegills of 30 mm SL stocked alone with bass. When the two smaller size classes were stocked with larger bluegills and bass the daily mortality rate of the two smallest size classes was 40–50× less than in open water, and 30-mm bluegills were 80× less likely to be attacked. The risk curve probably declines monotonically, and a bluegill's relative risk should be proportional with that fraction of the bass population capable of swallowing it.[594]

Bluegills and their predators coexist in many shallow, nutrient-rich lakes where macrophytes are either absent or nearly so.[595] Complex structures are strong attractants for prey species like small bluegills, but also the predators that hunt them.[596] Largemouth bass in Florida canals hunt in groups and in locations with structures, often accompanied by bluegills of similar size.[597] The spotted gar *Lepisosteus oculatus* is a sagittiform ambush predator. Spotted gars in the laboratory take cover among plots of artificial plant stems along with their bluegill prey.[598] Within 24 h gars captured significantly fewer bluegills at high stem concentrations (250 and 1,000/m²) than at low ones (≤ 50/m²). The gars spent most of the time lying motionless in the top half of the water column at high stem concentrations, but switched to the bottom half if stem concentrations were low. When gars were at the surface, bluegills moved down in the water column; when gars were near the bottom they moved up. Schooling behavior by bluegills diminished with increasing stem concentration, but was never extinguished. The ambush mode of gars remained unchanged at all stem concentrations, unlike the situation with largemouth bass, which switch from active hunters to ambushers upon entering thick vegetation.[599]

Despite the increased probability of encountering each other, prey species are still safer than they would be in the open.[600] Given a choice of open water or thick cover provided by fake vegetation, captive bluegills (35–45 mm TL) dispersed among the polypropylene stems, but so did largemouth bass and northern pike placed with them.[601] Bass hunted the bluegills actively in both open and planted areas; the pike mostly waited in ambush among the stems. Bluegills that strayed from protective cover could better avoid being preyed on by pike but were quickly eaten by bass.

Largemouth bass become less effective predators in structurally complex habitats.[602] Bass successfully captured bluegills among fake plants at stem concentrations of 0 and 50/m², but at 250 and 1,000/m² their success fell nearly to zero.[603] These higher concentrations are reminiscent of stem numbers in natural macrophyte stands,[604] but without comparable variation in architecture. With a bass among them bluegills adapted their activities to the amount of cover.[605]

In the same experiment, bluegills altered their behavior around both bass and pike, in part by taking advantage of any cover, but also by their movements.[606] Left without predators, 50% schooled at all stem concentrations. In the presence of largemouth bass this proportion increased to 50–80% at the low concentration (50/m²) but fell to less than 20% at medium (250/m²) and high (1,000/m²) concentrations. At zero concentration they schooled less in the presence of pike than with bass; 60% schooled at low concentration in the presence of both predators. At medium concentration the percentage of schooling bluegills was higher with pike than with bass, and at high concentration more schooled when predators were absent, becoming lowest when a bass was the predator. Bluegills are facultative schoolers, and the evasive behaviors mentioned previously are probably more important in nature than in captivity.

These results conflict in some ways with a different investigation in which the same experimental apparatus was used, except that stems at high concentration covered half the pool.[607] Bluegills schooled at distances greater than 1 m from both predators. In the absence of a predator ~30% schooled, and this percentage stayed the same when bass were present but declined nearly to zero in the presence of pike. Schooling offered no protection from pike, as also confirmed by still another study,[608] but bass were more likely to attack milling bluegills. As mentioned in Chapter 2, esocids rely on the lateral line to locate prey nearby, and schooling, which involves constant movement, might be a poor evasive tactic.

At low stem concentrations and in the presence of bass, bluegills schooled near the edges of the pool, dispersing into the center when stem concentrations were high. Dispersed bluegills remained motionless if predators were close. Bluegills occupied every part of the pool in the absence of predators. When bass were added they stayed near the top or bottom edges if the available cover was useless (low concentration), moving to the bottom and near the center at high concentrations.

Bluegills given access to high-concentration habitats were nearly immune to predators, large and small. A predator's size had no influence on its foraging efficacy, and the intraspecific behaviors of large and small predators did not differ noticeably. In other words, the ability of smaller predatory fishes to maneuver through habitats of the complexity described offers no apparent benefit. In nature, however, size is ultimately limiting in heavy cover.[609] Assuming these results are at least partly applicable to natural situations, it appears that evasive adaptations of bluegills are flexible, capable of mitigating either predatory mode—active hunting or waiting in ambush—in structurally complex habitats. In such situations the advantage is to the prey.

Given a choice, captive bluegills select the heaviest cover when predators are present.[610] Stem concentrations in plots of 50, 100, 250, and 1,000/m² were tested using bluegills of 35–50 mm SL and largemouth bass. Without bass present, bluegills left cover at all concentrations, but their movements were reduced substantially upon addition of a bass. Stem concentrations were tested in pairs, and bluegills always took shelter preferentially in 1,000/m² plots when provided. If this was not one of the choices they formed groups and spent most of the time at the surface, usually in a corner of the container, and remained motionless.

The same behavior was expressed when bluegills in the presence of a bass left a plot regardless of its stem concentration. Normal activity resumed within 2–3 min after removal of the bass, including swimming in and out of any available 1,000/m² plot. Combinations of 250:100 and 100:50 were avoided even after the bass was gone. When attacked, bluegills chose 1,000/m² plots significantly more often than any other. At combinations of 1,000 and 100, and 1,000 and 50, they selectively reentered the 1,000/m² plots even after a bass had chased them out. Bluegills occasionally swam through thinner plots without stopping on their way to one of 1,000/m². If chased out of plot combinations of 1,000 and 250 they reentered either instead of going to the surface, but picked the more concentrated plot most often. Bluegills that occasionally left the 1,000/m² plot stayed nearby, darting into it quickly if a bass approached. Bass attacked bluegills more frequently in 1,000/m² plots, but the number caught was not significantly different from the others. Although 250 stems/m² had been shown previously to offer protection from predation,[611] bluegills in this later study treated this plot as an unsafe refuge.

To some extent the behaviors described here were compromises made by bluegills in captivity where ultimate escape was impossible. Maintenance of distance is different in the wild. Gathering in groups at the surface, remaining motionless in the close company of a predator, and leaning against the walls of the container are certainly artifacts of captivity. Schooling behavior was inconsistent across similar experiments with the same predators. My own experience is that many species of facultative schoolers either abandon this behavior in confinement or display it less often. Whether bluegills preferentially school, mill about, or hide in the presence predators is impossible to ascertain in restricted spaces. Data obtained under these conditions are likely to misrepresent nature, and interpreting them out of context is risky.

Information obtained using captive animals requires duplication in nature before the results can be presented with confidence in a broader context. An experiment on predation risk similar to these was done in a 5-ha Ohio pond and also replicated in pools.[612] Sections of vegetation were replaced with mats of 1 m^2 containing buoyant polypropylene ribbons. Four stem concentrations were tested: zero, low (400/m^2), medium (961/m^2), and high (3,844/m^2). For predation trials the mats were enclosed. Age-0 bluegills (< 50 mm TL) gathered rapidly, and after 6 weeks the high-concentration mats held the greatest numbers. Mean counts rose with increasing stem concentration, a trend continuing through the experiment (June–October).

No pattern was apparent for bluegills larger than 50 mm TL, and observations with scuba indicated that they seldom used the cover at any stem concentration. More largemouth bass were counted near the high-concentration mats, but they seldom entered. Zero-concentration mats attracted very few age-0 bluegills, and the low- and medium-concentration mats were only slightly more effective. Stem concentration affected predation significantly, both in the field and when the experiment was replicated in pools (Figure 45), but with different patterns.

In Halverson Lake, Wisconsin, a 4.2-ha pond, bluegills and largemouth bass less than 120 mm TL sheltered among the weeds; those larger dispersed offshore.[613] Bass longer than 180 mm rarely entered the foilage. By late August the openings left by senescing plants allowed predators to enter, diminishing the shelter available to small fishes, and they appeared increasingly in the diet of bass.

Foraging of largemouth bass on bluegills (both age-0) was tested in aquariums containing plants of different levels of complexity (alive or plastic) at varying plant and bluegill concentrations.[614] Growth forms comprised monospecific canopies (mono) and polyspecific stands (diverse). Categories for stem concentrations were moderate and high: mono 58/m^2 and 115/m^2; diverse 329/m^2 and 707/m^2. Bluegills were tested in groups of two and four. Each trial involved one bass. When tested in aquariums with diverse, bass hunted bluegills throughout the entire volume, but in mono trials they restricted searches to areas underneath the overhanging canopy. Search times per prey capture did not vary with bluegill concentration, took longer at high than at moderate plant concentrations, and was unaffected by plant architecture. Attack rates were the same at both bluegill concentrations, but higher at moderate plant concentrations (both architectures) and diverse (both concentrations). Capture success did not vary. Results showed more bluegills being eaten when their numbers were high and plant concentration moderate and diverse, but the patterns were generally weak. A finding unrelated to the results was that plant complexity regressed against plant volume was proportional, demonstrating significant correlation. Plant volume therefore predicted complexity.[615]

The aquarium and pool investigations described above undoubtedly overestimate the actual danger a bluegill faces in nature, where habitat complexity and ample space make escape easier. The notion of predation risk as observed in restricted spaces exposes a minefield of potential type I errors. Seldom mentioned is the possibility that comparable situations are unlikely in natural waters. At Dog Lake, Florida, the proportion of foraging bluegills was unrelated

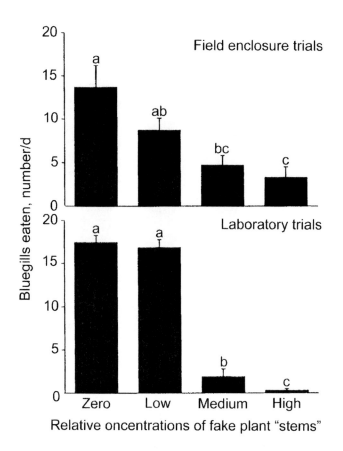

Figure 45. Mean numbers of age-0 captive bluegills eaten in 24 hours by largemouth bass at different stem concentrations of fake vegetation. Vertical lines = ±SE. Within a graph, bar values without a letter in common differ significantly (Tukey's HSD test, $p < 0.05$). Source: Hayse and Wissing (1996).

either to thickness of the vegetation or the presence of largemouth bass, which were distributed equally at all plant concentrations.[616] If a bass appeared, some bluegills moved away or slipped into thicker vegetation, but others occupying places of thin vegetation usually stayed. This behavior is not evidence either of the absence of risk or of ignoring risk. That bluegills take refuge from predators in thick vegetation is well documented. The picture presented in nature is simply that evolution has smoothed the wrinkles of conflict, allowing bluegills and largemouth to live in mostly peaceful coexistence.

Reproduction

6 The age at which bluegills mature varies depending on latitude, food resources, predation pressure (including angling), and competition. The optimal reproductive age of any teleost depends only on natural mortality and growth rate.[617] Bluegills start to breed at age-4 (females) and 7 (males), or longer than 160 mm TL, in Lake Opinicon,[618] but commonly at age-1 and 75–125 mm TL for both sexes in the southeastern United States,[619] although breeding occurs at larger size and greater age in unfished waters (see Chapter 8). Bluegills at Par Pond, South Carolina, for example, mature at 75–215 mm TL (ages 3–4), or 1–2 years later and ~80 mm TL larger than those at comparable latitude where angling is permitted.[620] Alabama bluegills can spawn at 4 months and 28–56 g, although most activity is seen at 1 year.[621] Michigan bluegills spawned at age-1 in ponds with sufficient food and little competition.[622] Utah bluegills mature at about age-4 under conditions of low predation.[623]

Maturity can also be delayed until ages 3–4 and 180–200 mm TL in southern populations experiencing a history of intensive predation.[624] Delayed maturation is thought to enhance fitness by increasing mating success of males and the fecundity of females.[625] Fishes demonstrate indeterminate growth, and fecundity is related to body size.[626] Female bluegills in South Carolina can be 40× more fecund at age-3 than at age-1.[627] A territorial male that is 6% larger than its cohorts can produce 50% more fry.[628] Stunting is common in the absence of effective predators (Chapter 8), and there would be little to gain from delaying reproduction.[629] Mortality rates might remain the same, and the increased fecundity that comes with large size would not alleviate growth suppression.

Gonadal enlargement at northern latitudes is evident just after feeding begins in mid-May.[630] With the onset of spawning in mid-June (water temperature ~22°C), mature females have ovaries ~10% of their body masses. For example, from 1939 to 1942 spawning at Fork Lake, Illinois, commenced in late May at 24°C, at which time ovaries were a maximum of 8% of body mass.[631] Bluegill ovaries vary in size over the ensuing 3 weeks as eggs are produced successively and spawned. Gonadal maturation in central Tennessee accelerates from March–May with spawning occurring mostly from May–July.[632] Spawning begins in April[633] and early May[634] in South Carolina; April in Arkansas[635] and North Carolina north through Maryland and Delaware;[636] late May and early June in New York;[637] March and April in Florida;[638] late May in Missouri;[639] May and June in Minnesota,[640] Oklahoma,[641] and Wyoming;[642] May in Illinois[643] and South Da-

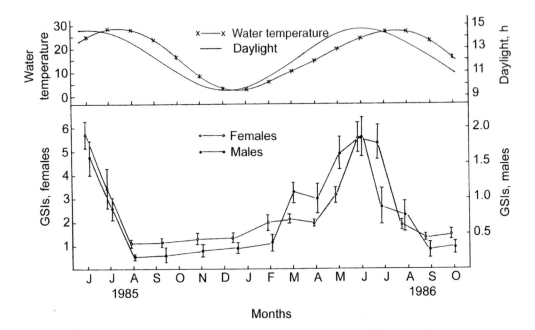

Figure 46. Annual changes in water temperature and daylength in Korean wild adult bluegills and corresponding changes in the gonadosomatic index (GSI), defined as the gonad mass relative to body mass, or 100 x gonad mass/total body mass ($\bar{x}$ ±SE). Source: Lee and Kim (1987).

kota;[644] June in Iowa[645] and Nevada;[646] late April into early June in central California;[647] late May in Idaho;[648] April and May in Arizona;[649] and late May into early June in Colorado.[650] Alabama bluegills can spawn from April through September[651] and into October,[652] and those from other parts of the country and Canada also undergo multiple bouts of spawning that often extend past midsummer (see below).

Bluegills become active in northern lakes and ponds as soon as the ice melts, often schooling with other sunfishes in deep water.[653] If pumpkinseeds are also present, mature males of this species are the first to move into the shallows, staying inshore for several days before commencing nest-building activities.[654] In southern Ontario the shoreward movement of male pumpkinseeds starts early in May, and the incidence of nest building, which correlates positively with rising water temperature, continues into mid-June, at which time it diminishes rapidly.[655] I include information about the pumpkinseed in this chapter because its life is intertwined with the bluegill's: the two species breed concurrently,[656] behave similarly,[657] and hybridize frequently.[658]

Gonadal recrudescens starts early in spring in conjunction with increasing water temperature and lengthening hours of daylight (Figure 46). The gonads reach maturation in late spring or early summer, start to degenerate in early autumn, and enter a winter resting stage until the cycle is repeated beginning the following spring.

The breeding seasons of bluegills and pumpkinseeds are slightly offset. Adult male bluegills in Ontario and many other locations in North America become active about 3 weeks later than male pumpkinseeds, and nest building sometimes continues into late July.[659] Higher absolute temperature, a more rapid increase in temperature, or both affect bluegills more than pumpkinseeds. At one location pumpkinseeds commenced nesting at 13–17°C,[660] bluegills at 17–23°C.[661]

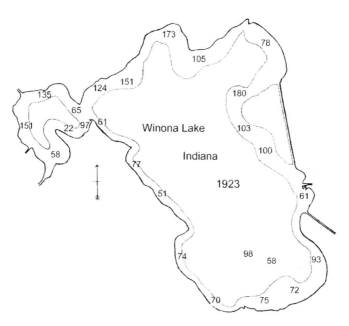

Figure 47. Number of bluegill nests per colony in 222-ha Winona Lake, Indiana, in 1923. Source: Coggeshall (1924).

Nest Site Selection

Important factors in selecting nest sites include level of illumination, water depth, composition and features of the substratum, availability of large submerged objects, and proximity to the nests of conspecifics. This last factor is particularly important to bluegills, which nest in colonies. The closely packed nests of a typical colony range from a few to hundreds,[662] the nests packed rim to rim.[663] An old report from Winona Lake, Indiana, describes 120 nests in a space measuring 35.5 × 4.5 m, and the lake contained many such colonies, some even larger (Figure 47).[664]

Stationary breeding aggregations of any species are properly called colonies if parental care takes place and the mutual attraction among the occupants is social and not caused by a shortage of suitable habitats.[665] Colonial nesting in the case of bluegills is defined by five features.[666]

(1) Bluegills nest in clumped patterns even when surrounded by unoccupied, continuous space of similar water depth, temperature, and substratum features.
(2) When colonies expand they do so despite any differences in the adjacent habitat.
(3) Coloniality is typical, and fewer than 7% of the nests are solitary.
(4) Breeding within colonies is synchronous to a greater extent than it is between colonies.
(5) Initial aggression among males during nest building subsides into mutual acceptance.[667]

Other sunfishes are not so gregarious. Pumpkinseeds nest singly or in loose aggregations, sometimes between bluegill colonies, although they can also nest as close as 8–15 cm.[668] Bluegills and pumpkinseeds nest predictably each year at the same sites.[669] Often no obvious relationship is apparent between nest sites and physical characteristics of the habitat.[670] This is perhaps an artifact of lakes and ponds where choices or space might be limiting.

Space partitioning is common where bluegills and pumpkinseeds share locations, the bluegills nesting farther from shore and in deeper water. Bluegills are reported to prefer shady sites under overhanging trees,[671] although they apparently nest just as often in sunny locations.[672] At White and Blackburn ponds, Ontario, pumpkinseeds seemed unperturbed about nesting in the shade.[673] At Pines and Llewellyn lakes, New Jersey, pumpkinseeds always nested in full sunlight, abandoning their posts temporarily if a cloud passed overhead.[674] At such times they formed loose schools near the nesting areas, returning only when the sun reappeared. Most activity stopped on overcast days, and the males remained quietly in their nests.

Both species prefer hard bottoms of sand, gravel, or mud in locations of little vegetation or debris, but breeding continues regardless of the substratum.[675] At White and Blackburn ponds there was no consistent correlation between where nests were located and the presence of aquatic vegetation or composition of the bottom.[676] In the absence of ideal places to nest, bluegills settle for submerged branches, plant roots, or any substratum that can be cleaned of debris and silt.[677] At Orange Lake, for example, they routinely nest on extensive networks of roots produced by the emergent aquatic plants spadderdock *Nuphar luteum* and maidencane *Panicum hemitomon*.[678] In desperate situations even the flat concrete floor of an ornamental pond suffices.[679]

A few territorial male bluegills excavate nests apart from colonies. Such fish are rarer in some locations than others. Only one solitary male, for example, was seen among hundreds of colonies at Winona Lake in the early 1920s,[680] and the behavior of another in a Colorado pond was described in the 1970s.[681] Solitary nesters at Lake Opinicon are more common. Although similar in size and age to colonial males, those examined were in better condition as determined using Fulton's condition factor (body mass/total length^3).[682] As the ratio demonstrates this is actually a measure of stoutness. Solitary Lake Opinicon males accumulated as many eggs as males occupying the choice central locations of colonies (see below) and significantly more than males nesting on the peripheries. This indicates that females actually have no preference for large colonies (see below), perhaps because the incidence of aggression among males increases significantly from the periphery to central sites.[683] Nonetheless, the presumed preference of females for central nests because of lower egg predation and greater survival of eggs and fry[684] has not proved valid for Wisconsin lakes,[685] nor have the putative disadvantages of solitary nesting been affirmed.

Of 901 territorial males tagged in May and June at Lake Opinicon, 119 (13%) nested again. Seven colonial nesters relinquished urban life and became solitary the second time, and the original solitary nesters (4.5%) remained so. The Lake Opinicon findings conflict with an earlier investigation in Lake Cazenovia in which males nesting away from colonies failed to receive any eggs, or if they did too few to justify parental care.[686]

Size of the dark opercular, or ear, tabs of territorial males is presumably a sexually selected character.[687] Earlier writers had attributed size differences in this character to represent intraspecific variation.[688] Aggressive displays by territorial males include flaring the opercular flaps to show the tabs.[689] In captive males the dominance rank order correlates with size of the ear tabs after effects of body size have been removed, and males with larger ear tabs obtain more central locations when establishing territories.[690] Solitary males had smaller ear tabs than colonial males[691] but presumably were capable of colonial nesting had they so chosen. The fitness consequences of a male bluegill living successfully on its own might offset the disadvantages. Incidences of cuckoldry (described later) are lower for solitary males, giving them more opportunity to fertilize the eggs deposited in their nests.[692]

Nest Building

Nest sites are generally shallow (0.4–1.4 m deep).[693] All sunfishes make nests by sweeping the substratum clean of debris. The behavior is mostly diurnal, but also occurs at night in captive specimens.[694] Nest sweeping starts when the resident male, in a normal horizontal and stationary position, begins moving his caudal fin side to side.[695] As the undulations strengthen he assumes a nearly vertical position with head up and tail down, all the while fanning the bottom vigorously with his tail. The number of caudal sweeps in an episode ranges from 2 to 15, and an episode lasts 3–10 s.[696] When sweeping stops the fish once again assumes a horizontal position. Because sweeping propels the fish forward, braking action by the pectorals is important (Chapter 1). Forward motion is dampened further by turning in all directions. Sweeping behavior is ritualized, occurring even when no obvious purpose is served. For example, a captive male pumpkinseed will sweep vigorously at the clean glass floor of its container.[697] Sweeping is also linked with aggression. The sweeping tempo in captive pumpkinseeds quickens when males hold adjacent territories, a neighboring male spawns, or a female indicating a willingness to spawn enters the nest.[698] Sweeping behavior ceases immediately after spawning, but resumes when larvae leave the nest.

The finished pumpkinseed nest is a circular dished depression 20–100 cm across, the larger ones constructed in deeper water.[699] A finished bluegill nest is 20–45 cm in diameter.[700] Depth of the nest in both species depends on the substratum, varying in the bluegill from little more than a centimeter on a suitable location to at least 40 cm on a soft, silty bottom.[701] Pumpkinseed nests excavated to 60 cm below the substratum were reported in the 1930s at Wampus Pond, New Jersey, on bottom covered by a deep layer of silt.[702]

Courtship and Spawning

After a bluegill colony consisting solely of males becomes established, females arrive in schools and mill above the nests until spawning commences.[703] At the onset of courtship activity they enter the nests singly to spawn.[704] Colonies spawn synchronously in a single day.[705] Some territorial males in Lake Opinicon participate in up to four spawning sessions, or bouts, in a season and can survive to spawn up to 3 years.[706] Multiple bouts are also common elsewhere.[707] At Ridge Lake, Illinois, protracted spawning lasted from 87 to 108 d starting in mid-May and extending into mid-August.[708] Territorial males guarding ova or fry sometimes miss participating in the next spawning bout.[709] Nesting males of both species demonstrate initial aggression toward conspecific females.[710] Afterward, the female's behavior determines whether she is driven away or stays and mates with the male.[711] If a female bluegill refuses to flee, the male courts her. Male pumpkinseeds chase all females, those of their own species the most vigorously.[712]

A female bluegill ready to spawn drops out of the water and into the nest below, initiating courtship by approaching the resident male and displaying dark coloration, dark eyes, and dark vertical bars.[713] Male bluegills often began circling (see below) when approached by a conspecific female, and she often stays nearby.[714] Upon entering a nest a female spawns in a series of dips, during which her ventrum touches the substratum. With each dip she releases ~10–30 eggs. Some observers have not mentioned dips, describing instead the male remaining parallel with the substratum while the female tilts sideways to press her ventrum against his (see below). I shall treat dip and tilt as synonyms.

The female might remain in the nest until several thousand eggs have been released.[715] One female can dip hundreds of times in a single spawning session[716] that extends 6–12 h.[717] At the onset of courtship the male begins to swim in tight circles, the female following. Every few seconds, as they turn, the female tilts to one side, presses her genital pore against the male's, quivers, and releases a few eggs that the male fertilizes with a simultaneous release of milt.[718] While in this act the male's anterior ventral surface darkens.[719] Spawning is mainly a daytime activity, but spawning pairs been observed at midnight at Lake Cazenovia.[720] Courtship details are described below.

Males of both species recognize females by a change in behavior when she seems prepared to spawn.[721] These signs evidently are not subtle. Territorial male pumpkinseeds can be fooled by a cardboard silhouette cut roughly in the shape of a sunfish and attached to the end of a stick. Holding the model over the nest, dipping it slightly, and making it quiver elicits a spawning response.[722] Whether the female's appearance is a factor in sex recognition has not been determined, but male bluegills, as described later, are often fooled by cuckolding males mimicking females and duped into courting them. Territorial male bluegills have a blue sheen, two intense blue streaks along the cheek, and dark yellow-rusty breasts.[723] Others state that bluegills have no blue streaks on the cheeks, but without mentioning the time of year.[724] The male's bright coloration, if used to make himself conspicuous and attractive to females, has no demonstrated element of sexual selection.[725]

The number of eggs deposited in bluegill nests varies within wide limits. Individual females produce thousands of eggs, although whether all or most are exhausted in one extended spawn at a single nest or several is unclear. A female caught in Mississippi measured 155 mm (TL?) and contained 12,000 eggs.[726] Another from Minnesota had 67,000 eggs; 27 others weighing 226.4–228.3 g had egg counts of 15,000–58,000.[727] A territorial male sometimes spawns with more than one female in succession, and the eggs in a nest might represent the maximum effort of one female or the partial contributions of several.[728] Egg counts in three of four nests collected in the same colony at Winona Lake, Indiana: 11,257, 30,374, 80,000, and 224,900.[729] That the higher counts came from single females seems unlikely. The lake, which was 222 ha in the early 1920s, held an estimated 86,000 eggs per nest, a total production of 207×10^6 over one breeding season.[730] The average bluegill nest at Lake Opinicon holds 15,000 eggs.[731]

The sequence of courtship behaviors in bluegills and pumpkinseeds has been described several times. Some publications were written by some of the same authors working at the same location, but the descriptions are nonetheless inconsistent. Among the reasons are apparent disagreements on standard terminology, occasional failure to state which species is being described, combining or partitioning behaviors already described by others, and not distinguishing between observations made on wild and captive fishes. The behavior of resident males involves territorial defense, courtship, spawning, and parental care, that of the females only courtship and spawning. Five reports give detailed observations,[732] but the problems listed above render a synthesis parlous and in the end might confuse matters further. My recounting of various elements of territorial and reproductive behavior are therefore representative, based generally on the two most detailed studies.

Table 12 defines the terms used in Figure 48, which summarizes courtship behavior in bluegills and pumpkinseeds observed in Lake Opinicon and in captive specimens kept in pools erected on the shore. Wild males of both species approached females arriving at the nest (Ap), swam parallel to them (Pa), and nudged them toward the nest (Cy). Captivity extended the sequence by eliminating the many disruptions inherent in wild colonies and aggregations. For example, confining the female in a pool eliminated any chance of escape, and she was therefore pursued (Pu). Captive male bluegills still swam parallel to females entering their nests (Pa), but male pumpkinseeds swam in circles to the female and back to the nest (Ci).

When approached, a wild female became stationary on the substratum (Sd) then swam parallel to the male in a tight circle (Cy), tilted on her side (Ti), and raised her genital opening to the male's. A captive female avoided (Av) the male and attempted to swim away or became stationary on the substratum, eventually swimming parallel with him (Pa). She then pivoted in a circle with the male, side by side (Cy), tilted onto one side, and raised her genital opening. There is no specific mention of dipping behavior (see below), which features prominently in other reports.

Courtship and agonistic behavior expressed in territorial defense are conflicting. Selection

Table 12. Terminology describing courtship behavior of bluegills and pumpkinseeds. Sex of the instigating fish is in the middle column. Source: After Clarke et al. (1984).

Stationary (St)	M, F	Stationary on nest or in water above nest.
Approach (Ap)	M	Approaches female.
Pursue (Pu)	M	Chases female
Circle (Ci)	M	Swims in a circle from nest to female and back again.
Parallel (Pa)	M, F	Swims beside other fish maintaining even distance.
Cycle (Cy)	M, F	Male swims beside female, nudging her toward nest with head; female pivots in tight circle side by side with male.
Avoid (Av)	F	Avoids male and might swim abruptly away.
Stationary down (Sd)	F	Stationary on substratum, usually the nest.
Tilt (Ti)	F	Female tilts on her side prior to releasing eggs.

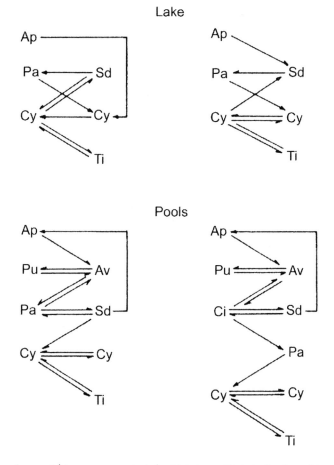

Figure 48. Diagrammatic courtship sequences in Lake Opinicon, Ontario (*top*), and in pools erected on the shore (*bottom*) that result in spawning of bluegills (left) and pumpkinseeds (right). Within individual diagrams the male's behaviors are on the left, the female's on the right. Arrows show the most frequent transitions between behaviors. Source: Clarke et al. (1984).

Table 13. Repertoires initiated by male bluegills, pumpkinseeds, and their hybrids during territorial defense, courtship, and spawning. Source: Information in Ballantyne and Colgan (1978a).

Nears (Ne)	Includes approaches, rushes, swipes, and so forth, all bringing male closer to stationary recipient.
Opercular spread (OS)	Male spreads opercula and displays ear tabs to recipient.
Chase (C)	Male follows retreating recipient, whether or not distance between them increases.
Lateral Display (La)	Performer orients side toward head or side of recipient, spreads and beats caudal fin. Corresponds to Miller's (1963) lateral threat display.
Nudge (Nu)	Contact made between snout of male and body of recipient.
Biting movements (BM)	Jaws open and close quickly; often accompanied by nudges; also occurs in absence of body contact, as during chases.
Leap (Le)	Male stationary in territory, swims quickly toward female with dorsal fin raised and veers sharply beside or above her, then returns to territory; breaks the surface when performed vigorously; corresponds to Miller's (1963) courtship circle.
Circle (Cir) path	Male swims in circle around stationary recipient; similar to leap but is elliptical instead of circular, during leap recipient is outside the path, Leap executed faster than circle, plane of path during leap tipped instead of horizontal in circle, dorsal fin not raised so high as in leap.
Spawn formation (SF)	Male positioned laterally beside female and pivots body forcing female into same movements; both fish circle tightly with male on outside; female breaks formation unless sexually responsive, and in spawning dips ventral surface to touch substratum, presumably to deposit eggs.
Pharyngeal sound production (PSP)	Sound made by resident males during attacks on intruders.
Territorial maintenance (TM)	Behaviors contributing to defense of territory.
Gap (G)	Interval >10 seconds when none of the other behaviors is performed.

requires a male to defend his territory successfully. To this end he must remain aggressive enough to expel intruders set on usurping him, interrupting him in the middle of spawning, or eating his eggs and larvae, behaviors not always observed in pools and aquariums. At the same time such comminatory activities must be tempered sufficiently to allow females into the nest, and males often attack females before courting them. Pharyngeal sounds produced by male bluegills and pumpkinseeds are believed to signal both aggression and sexual arousal, serving as a pivotal point in the transition from agonistic behavior to courtship.[733] According to one report, a single repertoire of behaviors labeled leap (Table 13) is sufficient to recognize courtship in a string of agonistic behaviors. The absence of leap signals aggression but without a sexual component. I define a repertoire as a suite of discrete sequential behaviors having an identifiable beginning and end. Here it substitutes for act, the undefined term used in the original report.[734]

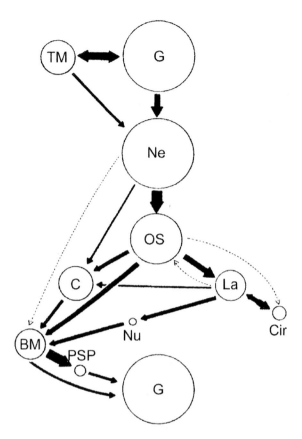

Figure 49. Statistically significant transactions between suites of discrete behaviors (repertoires) for noncourting male pumpkinseeds defending territories in captivity. See Table 13 for definitions of the abbreviations. Source: Ballantyne and Colgan (1978a).

Repertoires in the flow diagrams (Figures 49–54) thought to be exclusively agonistic are placed to the left, those that are agonistic but include a sexual component are to the right, and those of indeterminate intent are intermediate. Note that for each pair of behaviors the width of the solid arrow represents the relative positive z value, the minimum being $z = 1.96$ (CI = 95%). A transitional pair involving leap or spawn has a solid arrow if the behavior immediately before led in 20% or more of the cases to the repertoire immediately after. Width of one of these arrows represents the relative percentage. Dotted arrows show transitions between infrequent repertoires that were not significant. Relative sizes of the circles pertain to numbers of each repertoire observed for all fish in a category (e.g., courting, noncourting). The main sequence of repertoires can be followed by tracing the widest solid arrows between the largest circles. All sequences are for captive fishes.

As seen in Figure 49, the skeleton of the main sequence for noncourting pumpkinseeds was Ne-Os-BM-PSP-G (consult Table 13). Chase and biting movements are indicative of aggression and appear to the left. The transition between lateral display and circle was reversible. Circle was displayed more often to females than males and therefore has a weak sexual connotation. Consequently, these two repertoires appear to the right. Opercular spread was seen in several situations, but in the absence of a link to any one of them specifically it was placed in the middle. When courtship is not the intent, pharyngeal sound production is unusual but preceded by

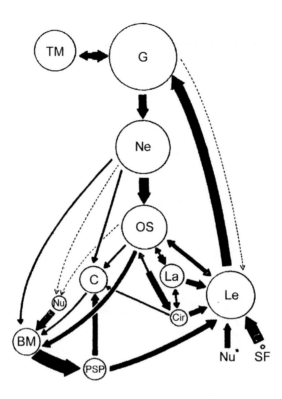

Figure 50. Statistically significant transactions between suites of discrete behaviors (repertoires) for courting male pumpkinseeds defending territories in captivity. See Table 13 for definitions of the abbreviations. Source: Ballantyne and Colgan (1978a).

biting movements when it occurs. Note, however, that some biting movements led to gap.

As shown in Figure 50, the main sequence for courting pumpkinseeds was Ne-OS-BM-PSP-Le-G. The principal difference between this sequence and the one before is leap, which alone defines it as courtship and not simply territorial aggression. As before, chase and biting movements, being signs of aggression, appear to the left. The transition between lateral display and circle was again reversible, possessing a weak sexual connotation. Both repertoires subsequently appear to the right. Opercular spread, as seen by its central location, was not linked to any repertoire specifically. In this sequence courtship is the intent, and the incidence of pharyngeal sound production has increased, preceded by an increased incidence of biting movements. None of the biting movements led to gap, dismissing any element of hesitancy and tightening the link among pharyngeal sound production, biting movements, and leap. Only leap itself flowed to gap, but it also led in a minority of the cases to opercular spread. Meanwhile, lateral display was a one-way transition to leap, as were nudge and spawn formation, the final overtly sexual repertoire. Spawn formation is probably what an older publication described as "a nuptial gyration over the redd...."[735]

The main sequence for noncourting bluegills was Ne-C-G (Figure 51). Another sequence, Ne-Nu-BM-PSP-G, was common too. The difference between them probably depended on the female's behavior. In the bluegill chase did not lead to nudge, perhaps because the female did not move away. The position of nears was therefore uncertain. Compared with the pumpkinseed opercular spread was infrequent; consequently, the transition from nears to opercular spread

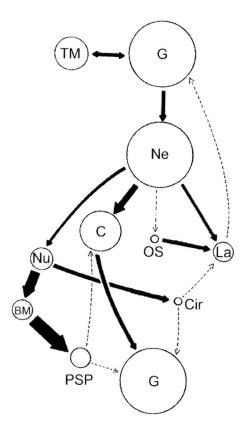

Figure 51. Statistically significant transactions between suites of discrete behaviors (repertoires) for noncourting male bluegills defending territories in captivity. See Table 13 for definitions of the abbreviations. Source: Ballantyne and Colgan (1978a).

was not significant (dotted arrow). Nonetheless, the main sequences between the species (particularly Nu-BM-PSP-G) were not very different.

The main sequence for courting bluegills (Ne-Nu-BM-PSP-C-La-Cir) shows clearly the transition from strictly aggressive repertoires to those emphasizing courtship (Figure 52). The left side indicates heavy aggression (Nu–PSP) culminating in chase, lateral display, and circle, the transition between these last two repertoires being reversible but stronger in the direction of circle. Leap led to circle, but just as often circle was bypassed in favor of lateral display. Many other transitions were not significant (dotted arrows). Opercular spread once again was reduced compared with pumpkinseeds, but occurred in significant transitions with nears and nudge. In both species opercular spread was more involved with courtship than with isolated aggression.

Unlike pumpkinseeds, courting bluegills performed lateral display and circle more often than in purely agonistic situations, and both repertoires involved frequent transitions with leap and spawn formation. It was postulated that lateral display in bluegills has a function in communication comparable with opercular spread in pumpkinseeds. The opercular flaps in male pumpkinseeds are bright and colorful, those of male bluegills drab in comparison. The coloration of the body and dorsal fins of male bluegills is more visible from the sides,[736] and lateral display might have greater importance. The authors wrote: "In the pumpkinseeds, opercular spread formed transitions with act categories that led to increasingly aggressive or sexual be-

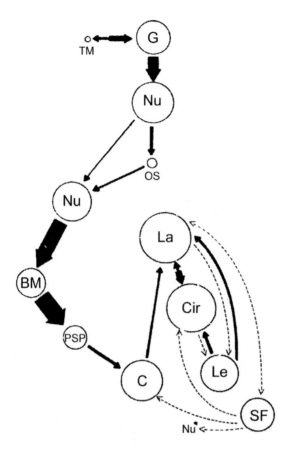

Figure 52. Statistically significant transactions between suites of discrete behaviors (repertoires) for courting male bluegills defending territories in captivity. See Table 13 for definitions of the abbreviations. Source: Ballantyne and Colgan (1978a).

haviors. Similarly the bluegill's lateral display formed transitions between chase and circle, leap, or spawn formation."[737]

The skeletal sequence in strictly territorial hybrid males was variable, one being Ne-C-OS-BM-PSP (Figure 53). Bluegill-pumpkinseed hybrids resembled bluegills in the reduced importance of opercular spread and increased incidence of chase. In the sequence Nu-BM-PSP-C the hybrids resembled both parental species, except for performing lateral display following pharyngeal sound production.

The courting sequence in male bluegill-pumpkinseed hybrids contained elements of both parental species, although it more closely resembled that of pumpkinseed males (Figure 54). In its main sequence of Ne-OS-C-BM-PSP-Le the two were identical. Male hybrids courted female pumpkinseeds in preference to female bluegills.[738] Nonetheless, there were patterns of transition between repertoires that did not match either parent's. The conjecture was that these anomalies prevented viable backcrossing in Lake Opinicon.

Parental Care

The female departs after depositing her eggs, leaving the resident male responsible for their care. Territorial male bluegills guard the nests for ~10 d, at which time the fry swim up and disappear into

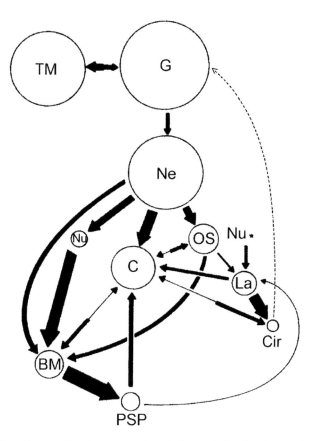

Figure 53. Statistically significant transactions between suites of discrete behaviors (repertoires) for noncourting male bluegill-pumpkinseed hybrids defending territories in captivity. See Table 13 for definitions of the abbreviations. Source: Ballantyne and Colgan (1978a).

the limnos.[739] During this period the males dispatch their duties with vigor and stamina. Males in the spawning phase maintain high serum concentrations of two androgens, the steroid hormones 11-ketotestosterone and testosterone, but these decrease rapidly postspawn to undetectable levels during the parental care phase.[740] Parental care is probably not sustained by androgenic effects. More likely, the process is driven by prolactin mediated through dopamine action.[741]

Nest defense by bluegills against another territorial male consists mostly of swimming at the intruder, although if contact is made occasional prolonged fighting ensues.[742] Large size is beneficial in gaining and keeping a territory.[743] Sometimes a resident male is displaced, and in ~11% of the cases the victorious male is larger.[744] However, such deracinations seldom happen gracefully: nearly all such incidents involve vigorous and often extended fighting.[745]

In addition to guarding the nest a territorial male fans the eggs with his pectoral fins, probably not to aerate them (sunfish eggs hatch well in aquariums without aeration) but to reduce siltation.[746] When the suspended silt load is excessive, bluegills often do not spawn.[747] Actually, the space occupied by the nest is being fanned, not the eggs. Male pumpkinseeds in captivity continue fanning even after plastic has been placed over the nest, and associated behaviors (e.g., periodically biting the substratum) occur with the usual frequency.[748] Fanning is a nonshareable investment by the male. That is, the oxygen consumed by an egg is unavailable to other eggs, and total oxygen consumption therefore increases with egg number.[749] Male blue-

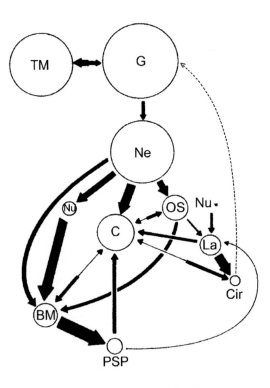

Figure 54. Statistically significant transactions between suites of discrete behaviors (repertoires) for courting male bluegill-pumpkinseed hybrids defending territories in captivity. See Table 13 for definitions of the abbreviations. Source: Ballantyne and Colgan (1978a).

gills tending large clutches of eggs ($\bar{x}$ = 5,797) spent 66% of their time fanning compared with those guarding smaller clutches ($\bar{x}$ = 3,459), which fanned 56% of the time.[750] The frequency of fanning changed, but not its intensity.

Sometimes a male pumpkinseeds picks up sand or detritus and spits it out or expels it through the gills.[751] Feeding pumpkinseeds process the substratum in the same way: they "methodically search the bottom, characteristically either sucking in mouthfuls of sediments and spitting everything out in a cloud from which the prey is selected, or separating the prey in the buccal cavity and exhausting the sediments from the mouth and opercular openings."[752] Similar activities on the nest probably represent displaced feeding behavior. It is not reported for male bluegills, which feed less often in the sediments (Chapter 3).

Male pumpkinseeds at two small ponds in Ontario guarded their nests an average of 18.5 d in succession; for male bluegills the duration was 8.7 d.[753] For territorial bluegill males at Lake Cazenovia the duration was 8–10 d.[754] Some male pumpkinseeds deserted their posts when the water temperature dropped suddenly; others stayed on empty nests for more than 3 weeks even when temperatures did not vary appreciably.[755] Bluegills seemed more motivated to remain on nests containing eggs or fry, whether or not the water temperature changed.[756] Tagged males of both species occupied more than one nest built by conspecifics, and bluegills sometimes took up residence in previously owned pumpkinseed nests. Nests were occasionally occupied by males of both species. Similarly, pumpkinseeds at Llewellyn Lake, New Jersey, frequently usurped nests constructed by other species of *Lepomis*.[757] These incidences of "musical nests" could be artifacts of small ponds or angling pressure, which removes resident male sunfishes and leaves their nests available for occupancy.[758]

A bluegill guarding its territory contends with constant threats of nest predation (see below). The most persistent intruders are other bluegills, and yet bluegills occupy the adjacent nests. How does a resident male decide which conspecifics are potential nest predators and which are trustworthy? Faced with the same problem, his neighbors are not major threats to eat his eggs and larvae, and he is unlikely to eat theirs. Colonial species find mutual tolerance to be necessary, even during antagonistic situations. You might intensely dislike your next-door neighbor, even to the point of shouting at him across the property line. Nonetheless, you still leave the garage door open, not worrying that he might steal your lawnmower.

Territorial bluegills packed tightly together can distinguish neighbors from intruders by habituation, defined as "the relatively permanent waning of a response as a result of repeated stimulation which is not followed by any kind of reinforcement."[759] The practical effect? "In an almost literal sense, the neighbors 'tame' one another."[760] Habituation of another male bluegill occupying the adjacent nest involves recognition, either as an individual or by his location. The neighbor, in other words, signals who he is through a system of visual cues. Something about the appearance or suite of behaviors of an intruding bluegill is recognizably different, triggering the agonistic response. The defining elements of habituation have been tested using rim circling (circling the rim of the nest by the resident male)[761] as the dependent variable. Results of a test of the individual clues hypothesis based partly on rim circling are summarized here.[762]

As 16 groups composed of four neighboring males were observed, aggressive and comminatory episodes (e.g., nips, swipes, chases) and number of complete rim circles (RC) were recorded for each of four 30-min periods (baseline 1, B_1). Each group was labeled central or peripheral depending on whether the nests were completely surrounded by other nests or one of the four was partly exposed at the perimeter. The neighboring males were then captured by group, anesthetized, and three were manipulated by placing red metal tags over the opercular ear tabs of one, cutting off the ear tabs of a second, and sewing red sequins over the dark spot on the dorsal fin of a third. The fourth fish in each group was not manipulated and served as a control. This procedure was termed after disturbance and manipulation (ADM). The fish were subsequently returned to their nests, observed, and the data recorded (second observation period). In the third observation period (baseline 2, B_2) all fish were left undisturbed, and data were recorded as in B_1. In the fourth observation period the fish were captured and anesthetized but not manipulated. They were returned to their nests and observational data recorded. This procedure was termed after disturbance (AD). Nine experimental fish deserted their nests after manipulation or disturbance, leaving 55.

Table 14 shows that aggressive behavior of the control fish did not vary significantly ($p > 0.05$). The significance of B_1 versus ADM in the test fish indicates increased aggression after manipulation. However, the number of aggressive incidents diminished with time (2 h) to original baseline (B_1) levels (i.e., B_1 and B_2 are not significantly different). Disturbance without manipulation—that is, no additional change in appearance—also culminated in significantly more aggression (B_2 versus AD), but less than the increase following manipulation (ADM versus AD). If the quantitative difference between these procedures is caused by a decline in responsiveness then the same effect would also have been apparent in the controls. Therefore, disturbance caused an increase in aggression, but disturbance combined with manipulation made the effect more pronounced.

What effect did altering the appearance (ADM) of the experimental fish have on the controls? The answer is in Table 15. Significance between B_1 versus ADM and ADM versus AD shows that control fish initiated more aggressive episodes after manipulation of the test fish. Moreover, significance of B_1 versus ADM and of B_2 versus AD (test fish) combined with the nonsignificance of ADM versus AD points to a disturbance effect, but no effect of altered appearance (i.e., ADM). In conclusion: "Therefore, an altered appearance did not cause the [test] fish to

Table 14. Statistical results of the mean number of aggressive episodes between control and test fish over four observation periods (Wilcoxon matched-pairs test). Source: Colgan et al. (1979).

	Neighboring Fish	
Manipulation	Control	Test
B_1 vs. B_2	12	25
	24	150
	> 0.10	> 0.10
B_1 vs. AMD	12	33
	23	47.5
	> 0.10	< 0.01
B_2 vs. AD	9	26
	13	90
	> 0.10	< 0.05
AMD vs. AD	12	32
	29	95.5
	> 0.10	< 0.01

Table 15. Statistical results of the mean number of aggressive episodes between control and test fish over four observation periods (Wilcoxon matched-pairs test). Source: Colgan et al. (1979).

	Fish initiating aggressive episode	
Manipulation	Control	Test
B_1 vs. B_2	22	22
	116	72
	> 0.10	> 0.05
B_1 vs. AMD	32	19
	72.5	39.5
	< 0.01	< 0.05
B_2 vs. AD	25	17
	101.5	35
	> 0.10	0.05
AMD vs. AD	29	24
	90	81.5
	< 0.01	< 0.05

initiate more aggressive episodes, but disturbing them did."[763]

However, data in Table 14 show more than a disturbance effect. Test males (those with their appearance changed) were more aggressive toward their neighbors, and the increased aggression following ADM was caused mostly by the controls. Did the appearance of the test fish trigger it or was it their behavior? The answer is found in B_1 versus ADM (Table 14). Differences in the mean number of aggressive episodes are much larger for the test fish. The null hypothesis would project no disparity. Changing the appearance of the test fish stimulated the controls to be more aggressive, but with habituation the number of interactions attenuated to baseline levels. The controls had grown accustomed to the changes. Visual appearance is therefore an important cue in habituation. Despite a mutual dislike, peace eventually reigns, one of the conditions of colonial living. That is, until an intruder appears determined to feast on eggs and larvae.

Predation on Eggs and Larvae

Development from fertilized egg to yolk sac fry is a matter of survival. Nest predation guarantees that not all eggs culminate in larval bluegills. Predation is reduced by males standing guard,[764] although losses are inevitable. Juvenile bluegills (30–120 mm TL) are often major predators, cannibalizing both eggs and larvae,[765] but so is the snail *Viviparous georgianus*, which in some locations accounts for more than 50% of the estimated mortality.[766] Other demonstrated predators are large male and female bluegills and pumpkinseeds, their hybrids, juvenile pumpkinseeds (70–110 mm TL), smallmouth bass *Micropterus dolomieu*, yellow bullheads, and brown bullheads *A. nebulosus*;[767] rusty crayfish *Orconectes rusticus* and virile crayfish *O. virilis*;[768] and juvenile largemouth bass (40–50 mm TL) and whitefin shiners *Cyprinella nivea* of 50–60 mm TL.[769] Other bluegills at one location accounted for 94% of nest predation;[770] at another, foraging bluegills were responsible for 72% of the diurnal attacks on nests.[771] In Indiana the common carp spawns at the height of the bluegill breeding season, and its rooting can destroy nests.[772] Being omnivores,[773] carp probably eat many eggs and larvae too.

Nest predators impinge relentlessly on a colony's defenses both day and night. Snails and bullheads follow the contour of the substratum to colonies. The rest, comprising mainly centrarchids, sometimes attack from nest level, but over deeper nests they also lurk high in the water and attack from above. For the week or so that active defense by resident males is necessary, pressure can be intense and losses of eggs and larvae substantial. The cnidarian *Hydra canadensis* sometimes blankets macrophytes (up to 30,000/m²) and rocky bottoms and preys heavily on age-0 bluegills.[774] At one location, concentrations of fry just leaving the nests were ~22.5/750 mL, but the hydras were even more numerous (25.5/750 mL) and killed an estimated 20% of fry from the colony.

In a study conducted at Lake Opinicon, pumpkinseeds and smallmouth bass accounted for small fractions of the predatory attempts, although other fishes preyed actively on nests.[775] Marauding centrarchids swam singly or in groups past colonies strung out along a bar, attacking nests from all angles. Fishes approaching along the substratum swam rapidly to the edge of a nest and began biting at it before being driven away by the resident male. Sometimes they lingered near the peripheries of colonies waiting for a male's attention to be diverted. If positioned higher in the water a centrarchid might bask motionless for a time before diving to the nest. Attacks from predators were more common from low elevations just above the bottom.

When the predator was a large bluegill the average mortality per attack was 17.9 eggs and larvae.[776] The intensity of a resident male's response was greatest when directed at large conspecifics and hybrids, and when an attacker was intercepted a vigorous chase ensued. A predator caught in the act of robbing a nest endured fierce bites to its sides and usually made a rapid retreat with the resident male giving chase for a meter or so. Territorial male bluegills at Lake Cazenovia defended their nests against other adult males (presumably territorial males) an average of 3× per observation period of 10 min.[777] Pumpkinseeds attack intruders when they stray within 1 m of the nest perimeter; bluegills ordinarily defend a more limited space beyond the perimeter.[778] At Lake Opinicon only ~53% of attacks were intercepted.[779] After watching a sunfish ferociously defend its territory against larger fishes one early observer described what he saw as "a truly remarkable performance."[780]

Tagging studies have shown that some fishes rob nests repeatedly, becoming more proficient with practice.[781] Nest defense proved ineffective when several large bluegills or hybrids simultaneously attacked a peripheral nest (Figure 55), and the result was loss of the brood. Adult females—ostensibly partners in procreation—caused much of the predation, either directly by eating eggs and fry or inadvertently by diverting the attention of resident males and allowing other predators to slip through the defenses. Predation by female conspecifics was most intense during the act of spawning. Being recognized as female proved an open invitation to prey on the eggs and fry of a resident male's earlier paramours, and upon entering a nest most adult females began biting at the substratum. The resident males subsequently chased them away unless they showed interest in spawning. Of 20 gravid females examined, 13 had eggs in their stomachs. Spawning females distributed through the colony caused considerable disruption among resident males. The difficulty of protecting the perimeter became greater still when a male took time off to spawn. Adding further confusion were the "teases," females that entered nests on the pretense of spawning only to gobble eggs instead. Fortunately, predation pressure (the frequency of attacks and their success) by species of the genus *Lepomis* and their hybrids declined over 7 d.

The site of a colony seldom affects the amount of predation it endures, although the positions of individual nests within a colony can make a difference.[782] For descriptive purposes a colony's nests are either solitary, peripheral (positioned around the outside of the colony and at least partly exposed on the periphery), or central (shielded by at least one peripheral nest and not having any exposed edges), as shown in Figure 56.[783]

To bluegills the principal advantage of colonial nesting seems to be reduced predation on eggs and fry. Isolated nests are exposed to considerably more potential predators. The number of

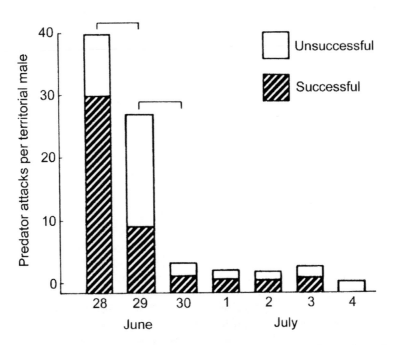

Figure 55. Daily predation pressure exerted by species of the genus *Lepomis* during the 7-d post-spawning period at Lake Opinicon, Ontario. Upside-down brackets indicate significant differences between days in successful and unsuccessful attempts at predation (two-tailed ANOVA, $p < 0.05$). Source: Gross and MacMillan (1981).

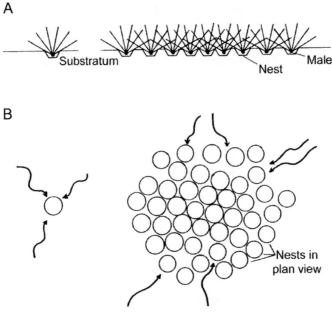

Figure 56. Schematic representation of nest defense by territorial male bluegills at Lake Opinicon, Ontario. A: Cross section through a colony and a solitary nest where radiating lines represent the defended zone of a resident male. The lines overlap, indicating group defense. Peripheral nests are on the colony's edges; the rest are central. A solitary nest is on the left. B: Arrows indicate approaches of predators. Nests of solitary males are confronted by predators arriving from all directions. Peripheral males must fend off attacks on sides facing the perimeter. Central males are shielded on all sides. Source: Gross and MacMillan (1981).

predators at Lake Opinicon correlated negatively with the number of nests in a colony.[784] Predation attempts were highest at the lowest nest concentrations, at least for predators attacking from above the substratum. Colonies also benefit from group defense against brood predators.[785] Position was also important. Predation pressure was significantly less in central than in peripheral nests, and centrally located males repelled fewer attacks. Overall, the loss of broods in peripheral nests was 3× greater than in central nests, and loss in colonial nests (peripheral and central combined) was less than in solitary nests. Two explanations were offered: (1) the overlapping territories of central nests resulted in more group responses to attacks (central-nest predators were chased by neighboring males 3.5× more than peripheral-nest predators), and (2) with the periphery guarded, fewer predators penetrated to a colony's interior. The clustered arrangement of nests is considered adaptive: eggs placed in locations with several territorial males adds extra protection,[786] and nests located centrally would then be best of all.

Bullhead catfishes and snails are important predators in Lake Opinicon and no doubt in other lakes . Bullheads attacked nests at night, often in groups, and their large individual sizes made them difficult to repel.[787] One bullhead examined had consumed 400 bluegill eggs in 5 min, oblivious to the resident male's vigorous attacks. Most attacks (84%) were on peripheral nests. Successful repulsion of attacking bullheads took place at central locations where the combined defense efforts of resident males were often effective. Despite their being solitary, bullheads seldom raided pumpkinseed nests and were promptly repelled when they did.

Nest-building activity dislodges many snails from the substratum, temporarily reducing their numbers.[788] However, the effect on the benthic invertebrate fauna is short-lived, so long as the disturbed areas are not extensive and are close to undisturbed areas that can serve as reservoirs for recolonization.[789] At Lake Opinicon the snails rebounded quickly, their numbers increasing by 10× within 2 d. One colony contained an average of 23.7 snails per nest, enough to cover 20–50% of the bottom of a typical nest and in 4 d consume nearly 20% of the broods. At peak density the stomachs of these snails contained an average of 4.1 yolk sac larvae, although 3 d later, when the fry became agile, the number had fallen to 0.16. Because spawning within a colony is synchronous, the snails left soon after.

Snails are seldom recognized by bluegills as nest predators and subsequently repelled.[790] Nonetheless, snail predation was greater in peripheral nests. If equal egg distribution is assumed then central nests lost 4.3% to snails and peripheral nests 13.4%. Overall, snails accounted for more than 50% of nest predation in bluegills, but they barely affected pumpkinseed nests. Pumpkinseeds possess a behavioral repertoire lacking in bluegills: they routinely pick up stray objects dropped into their nests, carry them to the perimeter, and expel them.[791] Unlike the bluegills, these pumpkinseeds removed the invading snails. The snails had shell dimensions of 19 × 16 mm. They were probably too large to be picked up by bluegills even were they so inclined. As discussed in Chapter 3, mouth width is similar in pumpkinseeds and bluegills, but prey size differs. Pumpkinseeds consume prey greater than 50% of mouth width compared with less than 25% of mouth width in bluegills.[792]

Colonial nesting seems to offer few advantages to pumpkinseeds, but its evolution in bluegills has probably reduced nest predation. To the bluegill these advantages, at least to territorial males on central nests, amount to decreased encounters with predators and the opportunity for cumulative defense. Distinctions in nesting pattern with the pumpkinseed might depend as well on differences in gape and morphology (Chapter 3).

An added benefit of colonial nesting is reduced egg loss to fungal infections (Figure 57). A parasitic fungus of the genus *Saprolegnia* was demonstrated to be more common in solitary bluegill nests, and the incidence of infection correlated negatively with nest concentration, perhaps because males are able to spend more time fanning their eggs than defending them.[793]

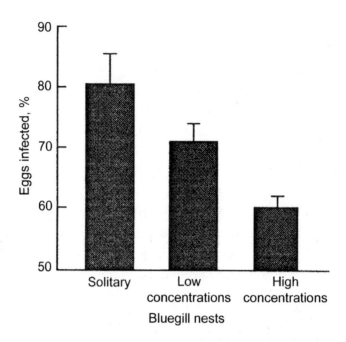

Figure 57. Mean proportion (±SE) of bluegill eggs infected by a fungus of the genus *Saprolegnia* in solitary nests and in colonies of high and low nest concentrations. Source: Côté and Gross (1993).

Hybridization

Bluegills hybridize naturally with the warmouth, longear *Lepomis megalotis*, orangespotted *L. humilis*, green, redbreast, redear, and pumpkinseed sunfishes.[794] Anglers in the Florida panhandle call bluegill × warmouth hybrids "mongrel perch."[795] A bluegill × largemouth bass hybrid, called a "bluebass," has been reported from Puu Ka Ele and Morita reservoirs at Kauai, Hawaii.[796] Viable hatches have been produced from the stripped gametes of bluegills and other sunfishes (Table 16), several classified previously as distinct species.[797] Hybridization has been thought to occur when two sunfishes compete for spawning locations or are present in dissimilar numbers (e.g., one of the species is introduced where it did not exist previously).[798] Reproductive isolation can be maintained in bluegills and pumpkinseeds when they are present in equal number and sex ratios.[799] Aquarium experiments show that male pumpkinseeds and bluegills preferentially court conspecific females.[800]

The genetics of hybridizing sunfishes were studied at Hall's Pond, Connecticut. The pond contained bluegills, pumpkinseeds, and green sunfish. Hybrids were common: between 1964 and 1977 pumpkinseed × green sunfish hybrids dominated the sunfish population, then declined abruptly. The first bluegills were discovered in 1974. By 1983 they composed 90% or more of the centrarchid phenotypes, and pumpkinseed × green sunfish hybrids had declined from 35% to less than 1%.[801] These hybrids were first thought to be reproducing because males were seen guarding nests. But they were not. All were F_1. Female hybrids in the laboratory produced diploid eggs without recombination.[802] When backcrossed to males of parental species the young were triploid containing the female's diploid genome and the male's haploid. Male F_1 hybrids were 100× more numerous than females.[803] Triploids also occurred naturally in the pond: pumpkinseed × green sunfish × green sunfish, and pumpkinseed × green sunfish × bluegill.

Table 16. Hatch viability of stripped gametes of bluegills combined with those of other sunfishes. Percentages are compared against a standard of 100% hatch for bluegill x bluegill crosses. Females of each pairing are listed on the left, males on the right. Source: Hester (1970).

Interspecific Crosses, female (left) × male (right)		
Common names	Scientific names	Hatch, %
Bluegill × bluegill	*L. macrochirus × L. macrochirus*	100
Bluegill × green sunfish	*L. macrochirus × L. cyanellus*	79
Bluegill × redear sunfish	*L. macrochirus × L. microlophus*	68
Bluegill × redbreast sunfish	*L. macrochirus × L. auritus*	122
Redear sunfish × bluegill	*L. microlophus × L. macrochirus*	110
Bluegill × warmouth	*L. macrochirus × L. gulosus*	25
Intergeneric crosses, female (left) × male (right)		
Bluegill × bluegill	*L. macrochirus × L. macrochirus*	100
Bluegill × flier	*L. macrochirus × Centrarchus macropterus*	12
Bluegill × blackbanded sunfish	*L. macrochirus × Enneacanthus chaetodon*	22
Bluegill × largemouth bass	*L. macrochirus × Micropterus salmoides*	9
Bluegill × black crappie	*L. macrochirus × Pomoxis nigromaculatus*	11
Bluegill × rockbass	*L. macrochirus × Ambloplites rupestris*	5
Warmouth × bluegill	*L. gulosus × L. macrochirus*	65
Largemouth bass × bluegill	*M. salmoides × L. macrochirus*	66
Black crappie × bluegill	*P. nigromaculatus × bluegill*	39

Cuckoldry and Fitness

Cuckoldry among bluegills is contingent in the sense that not all ponds and lakes contain cuckolding populations. In those that do, male bluegills that mate with females are not always territorial. Depending on body size, males can conform with one of two contingent reproductive strategies by either defending territories (territorial males) or invading a territorial male's nest and attempting to mate with visiting females (cuckolders).[804] The contingency derives from a proposed combination of genetic and environmental factors impinging on the choice of developmental trajectories.[805] In either case three polymorphisms (two of them expressed in cuckolders) are involved,[806] each analogous to an individual courtship signal.[807] Unknown cues trigger an ontogenetic and irreversible switch at a critical time during maturation when one or the other of these paths is taken.[808] Evolution then sums them,[809] distributing equal fitness through frequency-dependent selection and differentiating the resultant phenotypes by status (social rank) and state (body size).[810] For male bluegills in a hypothetical group 1, for example, A = 10 cm and invades, and B = 15 cm and is territorial. For those in a hypothetical group 2, C = 5 cm and invades, and D = 10 cm and is territorial. Bluegills A and D have similar states (10 cm) but different status within their respective groups.[811]

The situation with male bluegills and their mating strategies is this. Territorial males establish territories to attract females and procure their eggs. These fish invest their capital (reproductive potential as energy) in real estate and become property owners, hoping to gain primary access to females visiting for one-day stands. Based on this and related reasons some researchers refer to them as bourgeois males,[812] although the traditional terms (territorial, or resident, males) seem adequate. Maturation in territorial males is delayed and upon attaining maturity they construct nests and defend them, court females, and care for the eggs and young.[813]

Figure 58. Cuckoldry by a satellite (female mimic). Territorial male (left), satellite (middle), female (right) spawning simultaneously. Source: After Dominey (1980). Also see Gross (1982: 5).

Cuckolders, as practitioners of the alternative strategy, assume none of these responsibilities, although their capital outlay is still substantial (see below). They mature early and enter the nests of territory holders to steal fertilizations with visiting females. Cuckolders are of two types. Sneakers mature at age 2 or 3. One report gives the size range in Lake Opinicon as 64–81.8 mm TL,[814] another as 74.1–90.4 mm TL.[815] Sneakers in five Minnesota lakes ranged from 59.0 to 82.7 mm TL, assuming only those of at least age-3 warranted inclusion (Table 3, original report).[816] Sneakers are light in color, similar to territorial males, but they lack the yellow-orange breasts.[817] Those from Lake Opinicon stock are distinguished from territorial males by being deeper bodied posterior of the abdomen, shorter along the dorsal surface, longer on the ventral margins, and in having shorter pelvic fins and longer caudal peduncles.[818] Sneakers hide among plants or debris near a nest waiting for opportunities to dart across its boundary and spawn underneath the female and territorial male,[819] ordinarily spending less than 10 s in the nest.[820] Their timing often coincides with the female's dipping behavior.[821] Central nests lack hiding places, making them less vulnerable to sneakers. However, sneakers often follow the rims of nests to gain access to internal locations, thereby reducing attacks from territorial males.[822]

Lake Opinicon sneakers change into satellites upon reaching age-4 and 86.2–103.4 mm TL, at which time they exceed the size of most sneakers and function as female mimics.[823] Satellites in five Minnesota lakes ranged from 81.5 at age-4 to 112.0 mm TL at age-7, assuming that all cuckolders age-4 or younger were satellites (Table 3, original report).[824] Like mature females, satellites are darker than either territorial males or sneakers and show pronounced vertical bars.[825] Their behavior also resembles that of females except for failure to master fully the dip associated with egg release.[826] Satellites are smaller than territorial males and most adult females and progress no further; that is, they never grow substantially larger or become territorial.[827] Those at Lake Opinicon (ages 4–5) are similar in size to mature females (ages 4–8).[828] Those at Lake Cazenovia average 126 mm TL(?), territorial males 190 mm, and adult females 156 mm.[829] Satellites mill about with adult females in schools above the colonies.[830] Sometimes several enter a nest and begin turning in spawn formation with the mating pair.[831] Reports of multiple females in nests are probably based on misidentified satellites.[832]

A satellite often enters a nest brazenly, wedges itself between the female and territorial male, and spawns with them (Figure 58).[833] The typical *ménage a trois* involves two males; the presence of two females simultaneously occurs in less than 10% of simultaneous matings at Lake Opinicon.[834] Territorial males commonly misidentify satellites, assuming them to be females.[835] At Lake Cazenovia ~6% of the nests contained a satellite.[836] Satellites might let themselves be courted if no female is available, probably a delaying tactic until one appears. Sometimes this continues for more than 10 min.

The territory owners recognize sneakers and chase them away, but satellites are seldom detected. Territorial males gain some measure of revenge by outgrowing cuckolders,[837] and by outliving them.[838] At Lake Opinicon the proportion of cuckolders in a cohort diminishes rapidly over time (21% at age-2, 3% at age-6);[839] most cuckolders are dead by age-5, but some territorial males survive to age-11.[840] Mean longevity of territorial males in a sample colony was 8.5 years, that of satellites 4.2 years, and sneakers 2.7 years.[841]

Cuckolders are often called parasites.[842] This seems to me a misnomer. If a territory holder is analogous to a bourgeois city dweller secure in its community of nests, then a cuckolder, which actually exploits the other fish's territory and not its body, invades only the space, like a burglar. It could be argued that the cuckolder's sperm survives functionally at the expense of the territorial male's, but this stretches analogy past the breaking point. In fact, nothing is actually parasitized; rather, the burglar steals some of a visiting female's eggs by fertilizing them, often while the distracted territorial male chases away other hopeful burglars. Furthermore, if a cuckolder is a parasite, then a territorial male should properly be a host. However, this too seems out of place, in part because 8.8% of territorial males cuckold a neighbor occupying the adjacent nest.[843] Socially, cuckolders (sneakers especially), like any burglars, are uninvited and unwelcome. Biologically, eponymous sneakers arrive intent on fertilizing eggs without detection, leaving the territory owner's state and status uncompromised. Even the eggs, although fertilized by the cuckolder, are not actually subtracted from the clutch but only devalued by the territorial male if he perceives them as not his own (see below). Parental is another term used for territorial male,[844] but its inclusive meaning dilutes any descriptive value: the parenthood of cuckolders is undiminished just because they decline to stick around and fan the nest.

The relative numbers of male participants in an actively breeding colony vary considerably. A colony at Lake Opinicon contained 99 territorial males (including one bluegill–pumpkinseed hybrid), 44 adult females, and 58 cuckolders (32 sneakers, 26 satellites).[845] Pairing success among cuckolders varies negatively with the number present, evidence of competition among themselves and not just with the resident males.[846] In one colony the average spawning success peaked at 17% of female dips with one cuckolder in the nest but declined to 4% of dips when 11 were there. Aggression among cuckolders also increased with their numbers. In such situations the territorial male also became more aggressive, chasing both the cuckolders and any females that stopped to spawn and biting the females to slow their dips. This behavior likely increased his own successful spawns, but some females were driven from the nests before they could release eggs. As the male's aggression intensified, the cuckolders dispersed to nests with fewer other cuckolders.

The relative pairing success of territorial males and cuckolders is therefore frequency dependent. Sixty percent of egg releases at Lake Opinicon were coincident with cuckolding attempts, of which 16.9% of the intruders successfully breached the nest.[847] The amount of available cover correlates positively with the number of cuckolders, increasing competition among them, and each colony has an optimal concentration of cuckolders at which pairing is maximized.[848] For territorial males, constraints on pairing success are imposed not just by cuckolders but by (1) the short duration of synchronous spawning (1 d), (2) other territorial males competing for females on adjacent nests, (3) impatience of the females to spawn and leave, and (4) the distractions imposed by everything happening simultaneously. A resident male can relinquish some dips to competitors and allow a female to spawn rapidly or, through aggression, slow her dipping to better control fertilization but with fewer eggs and the risk of her abrupt departure.[849] When competition in the nest becomes too intense the territorial male gains advantage by driving away the female instead of surrendering all fertilizations to cuckolders.[850]

Equal fitness between territorial males and cuckolders occurs when the percentage of cuckolders, q, equals the fraction of eggs, h, they fertilize.[851] Most cuckolders at Lake Opinicon mature at age-2, and $q = 11$–31%. This is the frequency at which early maturity of cuckolders and declining survivorship of territorial males culminates in a ratio of 6 favoring cuckolders. Considering that h rises relative to q at lower frequencies of cuckolders, and h decreases relative to q

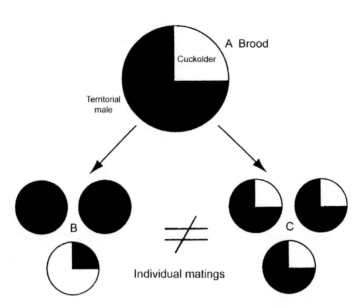

Figure 59. Behavioral data on differential matings and genetic data on the relative contribution of the competitors are required before a winner can be declared in a sperm competition. In this hypothetical brood of bluegills the females batch-release eggs in multiple dips (black = territorial male, white = cuckolder). A: According to genetic analysis the territorial male fertilized 75% of the eggs, the cuckolder 25%. Paternities could result from either B or C. In B, 33% of dips involved sperm competition, and the cuckolder fertilized 75% of the eggs per dip. In C, 100% of dips involved sperm competition, and the cuckolder fertilized only 25% of the eggs. Although B and C are not equivalent events, either could result in the same overall paternities by both males. Behavioral information on the frequency of sperm competition (i.e., number of intrusions) must be available to calculate which male is the superior sperm competitor before a cuckolder-territorial male model can be tested. Source: Fu et al. (2001).

at the higher frequencies, frequency-dependent sexual selection in this lake maintains the two strategies in approximate equilibrium.[852] Such ratios vary widely. During a study of five Minnesota lakes and Lake Opinicon, 4,315 bluegills were caught, of which 58% (2,730) were males.[853] The relative proportions: 1,837 (48.6%) immature, 576 (31.4%) cuckolders, and 317 (17.2%) territorial males, or a cuckolder–territorial male ratio of ~2.

Such factors as fecundity, age at maturation, and longevity affect individual fitness.[854] Growth rate and maximum body size are reduced when energy is shunted to service reproductive functions.[855] Longevity is ultimately affected too. The maturation of gonads, gamete production, behaviors associated with nesting and spawning, and defense of the fertilized eggs and fry all subtract from somatic growth. But the toll on cuckolders is more severe still. Growth of mature cuckolders at Lake Opinicon is 70% the rate of future territorial males of the same age with 15% comparable survivorship. Growth of all males in Lake Opinicon is similar to age-2[856] and probably similar in males of other populations before onset of maturation.[857]

All the aggression, posturing, skullduggery, and subterfuge described so far is window dressing for the real issue: which male's sperm gets to the eggs first. Sperm competition (Figure 59) is a race between sperm cells from at least two males for the fertilization of eggs.[858] The contest is over quickly: fish sperm is immobile until activated by dilution, then it remains viable for only a minute or so.[859] Osmotic stress, unfavorable pH, dispersion in currents, and other factors combine to hasten the end.[860] Cuckolders must release a volume of milt ~1.7× greater than a territorial male's to achieve equal the paternity[861] despite sperm cells that are more concentrated (50% more in sneakers, 16.5×10^6 versus 11.5×10^6 cells/mL of milt).[862] Nonetheless, because of

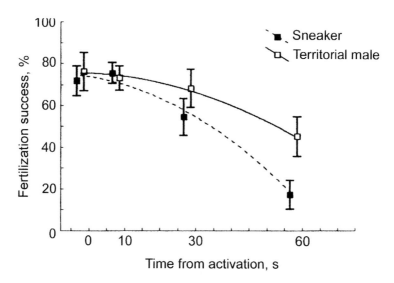

Figure 60. Mean (±SE) fertilization success declines more quickly in sneakers than in territorial males. Quadratic curves are fitted to the data. Source: Schulte-Hostedde and Burness (2005).

their smaller size sneakers contain nearly 400 million fewer sperm cells, or 32% fewer than territorial males, and their ejaculate volumes are 81% less.[863] In another investigation the mean concentration of satellite sperm cells (2.0×10^6) exceeded that of sneakers (1.4×10^6), and both were greater than the mean of territorial males (0.9×10^6).[864] The number of eggs fertilized by cuckolders increased with sperm number, meaning that high sperm numbers leveraged a competitive edge.

Cuckolder sperm cells swim faster than those of territorial males, and a greater proportion are motile immediately after ejaculation.[865] However, these advantages might be offset by the longevity of a territorial male's sperm (Figure 60), which can exceed that of cuckolders by 40%.[866] Perhaps the milt contains mucins or other compounds that extend cell life, providing added time to fertilize the eggs and offering a competitive edge.[867] To keep pace a sneaker must close the distance with a spawning female or release more sperm than the territorial male during one of her dips.

Sperm competition can only occur when a cuckolder invades a nest during a spawning incident, and cuckolders ordinarily participate in less than 25% of the dips.[868] Because a territorial male rarely misses a dip, most of his sperm has no competition, but the cuckolder's sperm, in contrast, is nearly always competing against the another male's. Painted broadly, a cuckolder's paternity is the product of the percentage of eggs fertilized and the number of intrusions.[869]

During experiments at Lake Opinicon and in pools on the shore, 8,625 female dips were recorded in 20 h 18 min of observations at 44 nests from seven colonies (lake and pools combined).[870] Of these, 10.3% of dips included competing sperm from territorial males and cuckolders (8.4% sneakers, 1.9% satellites). Paternities were 81% territorial males, 19% cuckolders. Females released ~3× more eggs per dip when a cuckolder was present than when the territorial male was alone. During a typical threesome the cuckolder fertilized 78% of eggs in a dip with the territorial male fertilizing the remaining 22%. Sneakers were especially effective, fertilizing 89% of the eggs compared with 67% by satellites. If cuckolder intrusions occur in 10–20% of dips, and if females release 3× more eggs when a cuckolder is present, then cuckolders have access to 25–43% of the total eggs from a spawning bout.[871] Cuckolders were 4× more numerous than territorial males, giving an individual cuckolder relative access to only 6–11% of the eggs.[872] Satellites spawn 3× more often than sneakers, making their access 4–8% and leaving sneakers with 2–3%.[873] In sperm competition among bluegills the underdogs (or underfish) are often winners. The reason could be preferential female choice or the cuckolder's choice by recognizing which dips are likely to result in the most eggs released.[874] If, in fact, the proportion of cuckolders in a population matches the number of eggs they fertilize,[875] then the lifetime payoff is the same for both cuckolders and territorial males, resulting in evolutionary equilibrium.[876]

When comparable volumes of milt are equidistant from the eggs, percentage fertilization is proportional to the relative number of sperm cells.[877] Satellites have a more favorable position than sneakers, which are underneath the spawning pair instead of between them. This suggests that, compared with satellites, sneakers release more sperm per ejaculate.[878] In addition, satellites have greater success than sneakers by mating more often,[879] which might reduce the number of sperm cells in proportion to the number of eggs released by a female per dip.[880]

Large sneakers and small satellites are less successful than their counterparts, and large satellites are the most successful, spawning ~4× more often than small sneakers.[881] The testes mass of sneakers increases with body mass, although large sneakers have fewer spawning opportunities. Testis size in a sneaker seems unrelated to either its chances of spawning or its risk of sperm competition. Small sneakers are perhaps more stealthy than large ones and less visible, giving their sperm certain advantages. The "loaded raffle" analogy also extends to larger satellites if they prove themselves superior female mimics.

An increase in testes size relative to body size, and the concomitant increase in sperm number, might subtract energy available for male–male competition.[882] Conversely, energy needed to defend a territory perhaps restricts testes size and sperm numbers. Growth slows after maturation, but the effect is more pronounced in males than in females.[883] Future territorial males continue to grow, reaching larger size than mature cuckolders while still immature.[884] However, because growth to maturity of territorial males correlates negatively with the relative abundance of cuckolders, male fitness seems strongly frequency dependent.[885]

Testes masses in bluegills from Lake Opinicon differed significantly among territorial males, sneakers, and satellites.[886] Mean satellite testes were 34%, and sneaker testes 11%, of the testes masses from territorial males. The gonadosomatic index (GSI) is a measure of the gonad mass relative to body mass and expressed as 100 × gonad mass/total body mass (Figure 46). The GSIs of satellites (3.74) and sneakers (3.66) did not differ significantly, but significantly exceeded the mean GSI of territorial males (1.32). Testes and GSIs of territorial males correlated positively with body mass, and this held true for testes mass and body mass of sneakers and satellites. However, GSI and body mass in sneakers were unrelated, and the correlation in satellites was negative. Sperm concentration and testes mass were unrelated in territorial males but positively related in cuckolders. In another investigation, F_1 male bluegills from Lake Opinicon stock raised to 11 months in Illinois had GSIs of 5.27 (sneakers) and 1.24 (territorial males),[887] values comparable with the older and larger males mentioned above. This disparity in testes size has been called "an evolutionary arms race between reproductive competitors."[888]

Are territorial males actually competitive? Approximately 20% of juvenile males can mature early as cuckolders, but differential survivorship to maturity results in cuckolders representing ~80% of the breeding males at Lake Opinicon.[889] Nonetheless, by mating with females during 89.7% of his dips the risk of a territorial male losing a sperm competition is low.[890] Territorial males have larger testes than cuckolders. Additionally, testes mass and spawning chances both increase with body size, giving bigger fish absolute advantages.[891] Any reduction in cuckolder intrusions raises a territorial male's odds of winning the competition. Larger territorial males experience lower rates of intrusion, tilting the game even more in their favor.[892] Intrusions are reduced still further if a male's nest is near the center of a colony.[893] Genetic analysis has shown that territorial males at Lake Opinicon fertilize 41–100% of eggs in their own nests, depending

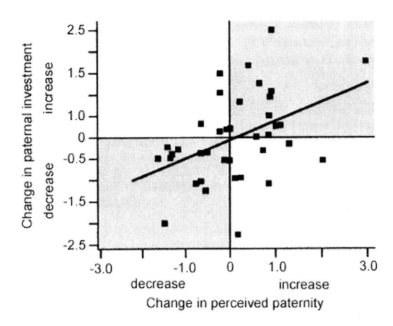

Figure 61. Changes in parental investment by territorial male bluegills in response to the change in perceived paternity between eggs and fry. The relationship is positive (note slope of the curve). Males with large negative changes in perceived paternity were more heavily cuckolded by satellites than expected relative to cuckoldry by sneakers (see text). These males might detect the additional loss in paternity to satellites only after the eggs hatch (see text), subsequently lowering their investment. Shaded areas represent evolutionarily adaptive changes in parental investment in response to available information on the change in perceived paternity. Source: Neff and Gross (2001).

on the numbers of cuckolders.[894]

Territorial males—5–80% in some colonies—cannibalize their eggs or fry or abandon them to predators.[895] Both behaviors seem inconsistent for a species that provides complex parental care. However, their underlying causes are well grounded theoretically. A male that consumes all its eggs or fry can be viewed as conserving energy to invest in the future, whereas partial consumption represents investment both now (those that survive) and later.[896] The fraction eaten should therefore correlate negatively with degree of relatedness to the male, degree of independence of the young (how prepared they are to survive), or the male's own physical condition.

The care period has two phases, eggs and larvae. Through the combined phases males are reported to fast and lose body mass.[897] Actually, they stop searching for food but will feed on insects and other items that float past.[898] Territorial males at Lake Cazenovia have been seen feeding late at night.[899] Nesting males are notoriously easy to catch by hook and line, and their removal rapidly destroys the extended size structure of stable populations (Chapter 8). In any case, fasting causes territorial males to lose ~75% of the energy they will have ultimately invested in parental care, as determined by changes in body mass.[900] Care after hatching involves defense of the nest, but fanning stops. During the 7–10 d while the nest is defended, a territorial male loses 10–15% of its body mass,[901] apparently none of it from fanning.[902] After the fry leave, these males move into deeper water to feed and reconstitute their energy reserves before nesting again and preparing for the next spawning bout.[903]

A territorial male makes the equivalent of financial investment decisions during both care phases (Figure 61). As capital he uses his own energy stores. Equity is his fractional share of ownership in the brood minus that of any cuckolders. Every egg or fry represents a share of stock, and the male's decision about whether to accept ownership of it means assessing it for relatedness to himself. His choices are to (1) keep that share and hope its value rises (i.e., survives and passes on his genes), (2) dispose of it (and perhaps all the others) and replenish his personal capital (gain energy through cannibalism), or (3) dump everything on the open market (abandon the nest to predators) and take a loss. Unless the investment is worthy, the first choice is an example of the Concorde fallacy: the smart move would be to cut losses (everything invested previously has been lost anyway) and not invest more assets in a losing proposition (choices 2 and 3). In the last two choices the male might recognize some eggs or fry as his own but also knows many of them are not. Instead of continuing to guard them he dumps all present progeny, loses some equity (those eggs or fry that are actually his), but retains what capital remains for a future investment. Having done this, he slinks off to deeper water to feed and replenish the bank account, perhaps in time for another spawning bout.

Empirical evidence exists for all three choices. Evidence for the first is obvious: the resident male stays and guards the nest. During the second choice—and in the fanning stage—a territorial male notices intrusions by sneakers and somehow recognizes them as presumably diluting his own paternity.[904] Intrusion by satellites is evidently not considered at the egg phase. Heavily cuckolded males are more likely to abandon their nests.[905] In one investigation those that remained had fertilized ~79% of their own young (26–100%), sneakers ~10% (range 0–31%), and satellites ~11% (range 0–45%).[906] The third choice comes into play at hatching. Olfactory cues alert a male to his actual paternity,[907] although supporting evidence is largely indirect and therefore inferential. Care is adjusted accordingly, taking into account the activities of both sneakers and satellites. Cuckolder paternity correlates positively with cannibalism by territorial males, cannibalism and body condition of territorial males correlate negatively, and paternity and body condition exert independent effects on cannibalism.[908]

It seems to me that a territorial male choosing not to cannibalize all fry after recognizing some as not his own commits the Concorde fallacy. Eating just the cuckolder's fry reduces the size of the brood, compromising both its fitness and his own. Considering the cost of reproduction and all its attendant functions, guarding and fanning unrelated eggs makes for a losing investment. Cuckoldry reduces the duration of fanning,[909] compromising the quality of the brood. The loss, which was already accumulating during the fanning stage, now compounds rapidly with every minute devoted to care of the fry. And with each moment the male sticks around the value of his future broods drops proportionately.

Capital allocated to the present subtracts from the future. In an optimal situation a territorial male might balance the two. In other words, he could consider the value of the present brood relative to his prospects for later reproduction.[910] The probability of a male's gain in fitness through the brood he now guards depends on their number, probability of surviving to reproduce, and degree of relatedness to him.[911] On the other hand, his future reproduction is largely undefined and therefore less well framed.

To optimize present reproductive success requires the largest possible sum of present and future.[912] This is logically based on present status, which is known. Because reproduction is expensive, a male heavily invested in the present can expect lower future returns (think of interest paid on a big loan that subtracts from gains). However, a large past investment raises the prospect of today's being successful. (Here, past refers the time interval spanning the brood's first day to the present.) The optimal decision by a territorial male involves knowing when to cut losses by abandoning the nest or cannibalizing the eggs or fry and when to stay and see the process through. Having seen his dream of colonial living shattered by nest predators, unruly neighbors, fickle females, and lurking cuckolds, a prudent territorial male must know when to sell his stocks.

Hybrids might lack the capacity for shrewd investing. Male pumpkinseed × green sunfish hybrids at Hall's Pond had deformed sperm with multiple tails and reduced fertility, but still guarded nests.[913] The fry, which represented all three sunfishes in the pond (bluegill, pumpkinseed, green sunfish) and three diploid hybrid combinations, were doubtfully the progeny of the males guarding them. Nest counts of fry varied from ~50 to thousands, often with many decaying eggs. These males, obviously cuckolded and incapable of normal spawning, trudged on despite the unlikely prospect of improved fitness.

The accepted view that females of species subjected to alternative male reproductive tactics prefer territorial males[914] and avoid cuckolders appears to work in the opposite way for bluegills: females sometimes release more eggs when a cuckolder is present.[915] Moreover, females spawn preferentially in nests adjacent to other nests where spawning is occurring, and the presence of satellites could be an attractant.[916] Comparison of maternal half-siblings raised in captivity demonstrated significant differences in mean total length upon leaving the nest. The predicted size of the territorial male's fry was 4.37 mm, that of the cuckolder's 5.29 mm, a difference of 21%. The greater size of the cuckolder's fry conferred 3× higher survivorship against predation by hydras and an expected 30% lower risk of starvation. These, at least, were the predictions through age-0. The choices for females might be increased genetic advantages to their young from mating with cuckolders or the security of having their brood fanned and defended by a diligent territorial male. Any additional survivorship of the fry—which is only potential—is valueless if the eggs are eaten or abandoned before they can hatch.

In a colony of 98 territorial males breeding in Lake Opinicon in June 1996, 60 abandoned their nests immediately after spawning.[917] The eggs perished without care and protection. Genotypes were obtained from the 39 males that stayed (including a sterile bluegill-pumpkinseed hybrid) and their fry. From these, more than 18,000 genotypes were identified using at least 11 loci. Mean paternity by the territorial males was 78.9% (range 26–100%), or 76.9% including the hybrid. Cuckoldry by neighboring territorial males was infrequent (1.8% of the total eggs fertilized). Cuckolders therefore fertilized 21.3% of the fry (including those raised by the hybrid). If Lake Opinicon is representative, roughly a fourth of a colony's eggs are fertilized by cuckolders. About 21% of males of age-2 are cuckolders, thus equating the mean fitness of the two lifestyles.[918] After extensive study one investigator wrote: "These data indicate that *approximately 85% of the reproductively active* [males] *in the population are attempting to cuckold the 15% that build nests and provide care.* This is a striking result for a fish whose male reproductive behavior has previously been characterized solely by 'parental care'!"[919]

Cuckolding has been well described in the literature, but whether its occurrence is unique to crowded waters has not been assessed. Lakes and ponds with highly structured populations of bluegills (Chapter 8) might be less vulnerable. Either limited spawning sites, low numbers of males, and high-intensity predation by other fishes might produce only large territorial males and not the bimodal size distribution characteristic of waters containing cuckolders. Male bluegills at Par Pond, South Carolina, for example, show such a unimodal size distribution.[920]

Development, Growth, and Mortality

7 Development of the eggs and larvae of bluegills (Figure 62) has been described several times.[921] Identifying larvae of the genus *Lepomis* to species is difficult. Two reports offer advice based on observational comparisons,[922] and another describes an allozyme technique.[923] Bluegills develop vertical bars that become visible on the lateral surfaces at ~20 mm TL and increasingly distinct by ~24 mm.[924] The lateral bars of pumpkinseed are similar, becoming visible at ~21.5 mm TL, but by 26 mm spots have appeared between them. Bluegill eggs are adhesive and demersal,[925] ranging in diameter from 1.16 to 1.37 mm.[926] Egg diameter in fishes limits the size of the hatched larva according to

$$TL = 1.96 + 1.89D$$

in which TL = total length (mm) at hatching and D = egg diameter (mm).[927]

Bluegill eggs ordinarily hatch ~40 h postfertilization at 24.3–25.4°C,[928] but higher and lower temperatures prolong it: 28.5°C (27–29 h) and 18.5°C (75–85 h).[929] Eggs can hatch at temperatures of 18–36°C, and the range of thermal tolerance is eggs < fry < juveniles.[930] Maximum normal hatch (45%) reportedly occurs at 28°C, although percentages at temperatures ranging from 22–32°C are not significantly lower.[931] The hatch was 24.5% at 34°C, 2.5% at 20°C and 36°C, and zero at temperatures not bracketed by this range. Bluegill eggs in Alabama hatch at ~27°C.[932] Annual variation in seasonal temperature, especially in the upper Midwest and Canada, can accelerate or delay hatching by 2 weeks or more.[933]

Newly hatched larvae are 3.75–4.05 mm TL with a yolk sac, 29–30 myotomes, and numerous melanophores distributed evenly over the body.[934] Another description puts the average at 3.23 mm TL with a yolk sac of 1.13 × 0.9 mm and no pigmentation on the body.[935] Newly hatched bluegills reflect a bright golden color, which fades as the yolk sac is gradually absorbed.[936] Within 5 d the fry are swimming.[937] Others have reported the yolk sac being absorbed by 10 d and 6.05–6.35 mm TL.[938] Yolk sac larvae are sedentary, occupying interstices in the substratum.[939] The mortality of larvae is greater over muddy and silty bottoms that lack a system of such cracks and crevices, and in unguarded nests the death rate correlates negatively with increasing proportions of coarse particles.[940]

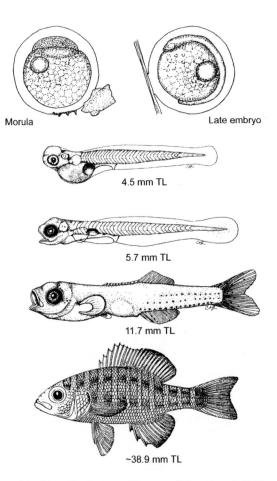

Morula

Late embryo

4.5 mm TL

5.7 mm TL

11.7 mm TL

~38.9 mm TL

Figure 62. Development of the bluegill. Source: Wang and Kernehan (1977).

The "golden-eye" stage, when the yolk sac has been nearly depleted and sedentary development is finished, represents the final larval stage in the nest.[941] Larvae become free swimming ~3–12 d posthatch, depending on temperature, after inflation of the swim bladder.[942] The first scales form at 11.9 mm SL,[943] and scale formation is complete by 14–15 mm TL.[944] Fin spines and fin rays have appeared by 13 mm TL.[945]

Feeding begins at ~5 mm TL.[946] Nauplii and small cyclopoids,[947] but also rotifers,[948] are among the first foods of larval bluegills. However, captive specimens grew fastest when fed small cladocerans (genus *Morina*).[949] Other captive larvae (10–26 mm FL) demonstrated no taxonomic preference, foraging on water fleas (genera *Ceriodaphnia* and *Daphnia*) and calanoid and cyclopoid copepods at total zooplankton concentrations of 125/L.[950] Larvae smaller than 9 mm TL in Alabama ponds fed on ostracods, cyclopoids, small water fleas (genus *Ceriodaphnia*) and phantom midges (genus *Chaoborus*).[951]

The time of yolk absorption in fishes depends on yolk volume (an exponential function of yolk sac diameter), and duration of yolk absorption increases with length of the larva.[952] Larger size at hatching confers undeniable benefits, including greater allotted time to first feeding before starvation ensues. For each incremental increase of 0.1 mm TL at hatching, larvae gain ~6 h to find food, and for each increase of 1 mm the gain is ~2.5 d.[953] These relationships are generally true, although as discussed below starvation in early bluegill larvae during the puta-

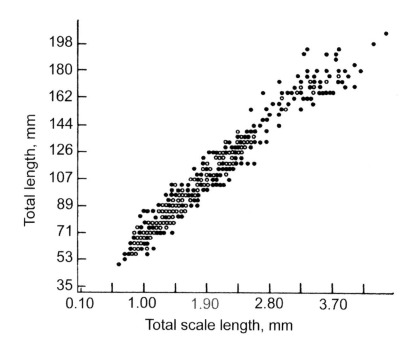

Figure 63. Total length regressed against scale length for male bluegills at Lake Opinicon, Ontario. ● = individual fish, o = mean of 2–8 fish. $y = 30.63 + 40.89x$; $n = 446$. Source: Gross and Charnov (1980).

tive critical period[954] to first feeding is evidently an artifact of captivity and seldom seen in nature. Both sustained and burst swimming speeds increase with length, offering advantages for capturing food and avoiding predators. Bigger larvae might be more adept at avoiding predators because of their better visual acuity.[955] Nonetheless, size-selective mortality is not a universal trait in bluegills, and under some conditions the process not only is variable but reversible.[956]

Age is typically assessed using otoliths or scales.[957] Daily otolith rings form for at least the first 125 d.[958] On scales, the anterior field and distance from the focus to each annulus is measured.[959] Length of the fish is proportional to the anterior radius of the scale. Scale readings are sometimes problematic,[960] but age can usually be back-calculated accurately (Figure 63).[961]

Growth

The length–mass relationship of age-0 bluegills of 4.4–31.2 mm TL is shown by

$$\log_{10}W = -5.430 + 3.345 \log_{10}L$$

in which W = body mass (g) and L = total length (mm).[962] The early growth of age-0 bluegills occurs in two phases, rapid for the first 30–40 d and afterward much slower.[963] The increase in size during the first phase is nearly linear, ~0.6 mm TL/d. Onset of the slow phase of growth is precipitated by the depletion of large zooplankters as a result of heavy predation by juveniles,[964] but also by adults. With the big cladocerans gone, age-0 fish turn to less profitable small ones (e.g., genus *Bosmina*) and to copepods, ostracods, and midge larvae.[965]

Individual-based modeling indicates that final length at 120 d posthatch is concentration-dependent at stocking levels greater than 2.5 fish/m³.[966] Above this concentration rapid growth ended sooner and final lengths were shorter. Mortality during this phase was ~28% and independent of concentration. However, in the simulation using 25.8 fish/m³ the whole natal cohort starved and died. Like mortality, growth appears to be strongly dependent on concentration. Based on a combination of simulated and empirical data, raising the fish concentration one order of magnitude (1.42–14.2 fish/m³) yielded a decrease in final length of 47% at 120 d. The rapid growth phase is strongly affected. Multiplying the number of fish 10× reduced the duration of rapid growth 2.8×. Mean and maximum lengths attained were greatest at 1.1 and 1.4 fish/m³, a range adequate in this model to deplete limnetic prey at 30–35 d posthatch but not demersal organisms. Rapid first-phase growth at diet switch then continues. Age-0 bluegills attain 65 mm TL at concentrations of 1.4/m³. Larger actual sizes have been reported. Yolk sac fry of 5 mm TL stocked at 0.6 fish/m³ in a fertilized Michigan pond 31 May 1941 reached a mean of 99 mm TL by the third week of October, or after ~146 d; mortality was 60.7%.[967]

Because age-0 bluegills have a lower percentage dry mass than adults, a unit of energy consumed yields proportionately greater increases in both length and mass.[968] Rapid increase in length is necessary for increased gape and the capacity to eat bigger organisms. Successful captures undoubtedly increase too. Having grown 15–17× larger than its prey, 100% capture success is assured.[969] Fish of at 10–14 d posthatch start consuming more diversified prey, including larger specimens of the genera *Cyclops*, *Bosmina*, *Sida*, *Polyphemus*, *Diaphanosoma*, and *Ceriodaphnia*.[970] An age-0 bluegill that grows from 5 to 25 mm TL experiences a concomitant increase in mass of ~200×. The above regression equation shows that a bluegill of 5 mm TL = 0.81 mg; a fish of 25 mm TL = 180 mg.

Protracted spawning, or spawning by a population of bluegills over an extended period (Chapter 6), results in continuous streams of larvae entering the plankton and perhaps is an adaptation to life in unstable habitats.[971] Early reproduction gives larvae extra time to grow. They enter autumn larger that those hatched later, improving their chances of overwintering successfully and surviving to age-1. However, more of them also die from cold spring temperatures and other causes. Earlier hatches are larger. Mean production at Ridge Lake from 1987 to 1989 in terms of larvae/m³ was: May (11–275), June (7–89), July (5–37), and August (1–10).[972] Overwintering juveniles experienced high mortality. The mean concentration of age-1 fish in early May (3.5/m³) was far below the number from the previous September (22.7/m³). Losses from overwintering were 75–88% across the 3 years. Size-selective mortality, however, was small, and the size structure between autumn and spring was similar. Larvae were more numerous in May and June, but most were dead by autumn. Conversely, those spawned later in the summer had the highest survival entering autumn.

Bluegills typically start moving offshore into deeper water with falling temperatures.[973] Little growth occurs in winter at Lake Opinicon, and these size disparities correlating with hatch date continue into the next spring. Recruits from 1993 ranged from 35 to 53 mm TL in May 1994, otolith rings confirming that larger fish were also older.[974] In addition, each successively later spawning bout from 1993 pushed back the age-1 length further. By May 1994, bluegills hatched in early spring 1993 were 7.4% bigger than midseason hatchlings and 13.5% bigger than those hatched in late summer (Figure 64). Nonetheless, all recruits from 1993 grew at similar rates into autumn.

As seen above, most larvae hatched at Lake Opinicon prior to mid-June die before reaching the juvenile stage, a pattern also observed in 1998. Larvae resulting from late reproduction were smaller by autumn, having grown at rates similar to earlier hatches but over fewer days. However, higher numbers survived because of warm summer temperatures. During 1998, spawning extended from 22 May until 20 July, again resulting in natal cohorts entering the plankton sequentially. Although length diminished with hatch date, growth rates for all hatch dates were similar between 21 September and 6 October, discounting any significant size-selective mortal-

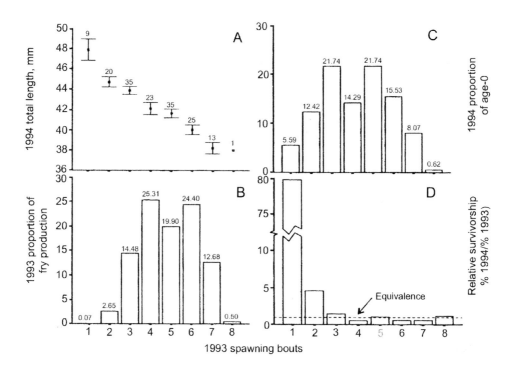

Figure 64. Data from 1993 spawning bouts at Lake Opinicon, Ontario. A: Lengths of age-1 bluegills from the 1993 hatches ($\bar{x}$= mm TL ±SE) from each of 8 bouts. Numbers represent sample sizes. B: Proportion of fry from each 1993 bout. C: Proportion of 1993 recruits from each bout in spring 1994. Numbers represent actual proportions. D: Relative proportional survivorship in spring 1994 for each 1993 bout calculated by dividing the proportion of 1993 fry (B) into the proportion of recruits in 1994 (C). Broken line represents a survival value of 1.0. Above it is increased representation, below it a decrease. Source: Cargnelli and Gross (1996).

ity in autumn. Overwintering produced higher mortalities for small fish, and some growth of the survivors was evident.

Assessing aspects of growth in terms of size rather than age is more realistic,[975] especially when comparing juvenile bluegills with adults.[976] (Ordinarily, size and length are terms used interchangeably.[977]) However, growth-length relationships mask any effect of physiological changes, such as protein use, that are specific to age. Age-specific growth is also useful for determining survivorship. The problem with it arises when length-frequency distributions of age-classes overlap,[978] as they often do. Then assigning ages based on length alone is unreliable, especially in fish from growth-suppressed populations.

For example, mean back-calculated total lengths of age-3 bluegills from 1,146 Minnesota lakes ranged from 57.6 to 207.7 mm (TL?).[979] Box plots of data from Wyland Lake bluegills show a similar effect (Figure 65). Age-3 fish in this sample range from 90 to 150 mm FL, but the sampling method probably underestimated the low end of the range.[980] Half the values fall between 105 and 135 mm FL, and all are distributed more or less evenly over the range. Numbers of age-2 fish are skewed, with more in the third quartile and comparatively fewer below the median. The plots are evidence that for Wyland Lake in the 1950s a bluegill's length offered little certainty of its age.

As shown, data are spread most noticeably across the middle age-classes, and age-3 was

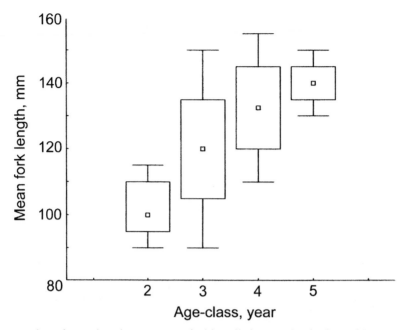

Figure 65. Box plots of mean length vs. ages 2–5 for bluegills from Wyland Lake, Indiana, captured 27 May–15 June 1956. Depicted are medians (squares inside the boxes), 25–75% quartile ranges (the boxes themselves), and minimum and maximum values (vertical lines). The quartile range of a variable is the value of the 75th percentile minus that of the 25th percentile and represents the width of the range about the median in which 50% of the cases occur. Total $n = 513$; n for age-3 $= 406$. Source: Plotted from data in Gerking (1962).

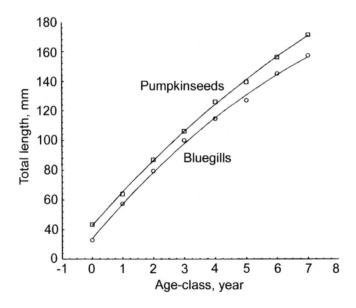

Figure 66. Comparative growth by age-class of bluegills and pumpkinseeds, Lake Opinicon, Ontario, May-November 1971-1973. The slopes of the curves differ significantly: Kendall's $\tau = 1.00$, $z = 3.46$, $n = 8$ (raw $n = 350$ of each species), $p < 0.001$. Data points represent means of ranges and are therefore approximate. Source: Plotted from data in Keast (1978b).

unusually strong (80.7% of the total sample). Among data used to construct the plots were fish of age-3 that fell within the range 88–92 mm FL, but some were also in the groups comprising 148–152 mm FL and every length-group in between. Of the total age-3 bluegills, 12.1% had reached legal angling size (≥ 123 mm FL). Growth slowed near age-5, and natural attrition constricted the range of lengths. Although Wyland Lake bluegills grew slowly they were not stunted, as illustrated in this comparison with a more northern lake (Figure 66).

Growth rate is influenced strongly by temperature and thus indirectly by latitude.[981] Annulus formation starts in early April in Tennessee.[982] In most of the Midwest it occurs between February and June and is most common in May.[983] Based on the appearance of scale annuli, growth starts in May in northern Indiana[984] and extends through September.[985] Growth rates vary widely both by region and bodies of water within regions, and variation within lakes can be as great as between lakes in the same vicinity.[986] This is illustrated by the broad ranges in length of bluegills from 60 Indiana lakes (ranges are in mm FL): age-2 (50–116), age-3 (65–175), age-4 (80–220).[987] Nonetheless, these data represent the expected distribution by being unimodal and symmetric.

Bluegills start to feed when the water reaches 5°C.[988] Some will have fed intermittently all winter. At Lake Onalaska, 233,061 bluegills were caught by angling during one winter season (22 November 1976–22 March 1977) comprising 90.7% of the total catch.[989] That bluegills can be caught by fishing under the ice is well documented.[990] Bluegills at Lake Opinicon obtained in midwinter are thin with empty guts and do not feed consistently until the water warms to 8–10°C in mid-May.[991] Feeding then extends from May–October, and when it begins the condition index (body mass/body length) is 70–80% of its autumn value.[992] Feeding is heavy in May and June, then tapers off. Most of the year's growth in length occurs from the beginning of June through mid-August.[993] Deposits of subcutaneous fat needed to sustain a fish through winter start to peak by the end of July.[994] Daily food intake, which is ~2.5–3.2% of body mass in May and June, declines to ~1.8–2.2% from July through September. Stomach fullness of breeding bluegills increased in spring in Burgess Falls Lake, Tennessee, decreased during the spawning season, and rose again in midsummer.[995] The males generally held less food than females in spring, but more in late summer.

Broad climatic factors (e.g., rainfall, temperature) doubtfully explain interlake differences in growth rates.[996] More likely causes might be unique short-term fluctuations of other factors within lakes,[997] although this hypothesis has been challenged by investigators who favor long-term variation among lakes.[998] Two variables known to fluctuate in the short term are the concentrations of competing species and the nature and abundance of food.[999] In small Michigan lakes, for example, juvenile bluegills and pumpkinseeds compete for common food resources in the littoral zones, but after diet shifting that forces bluegills into the limnos and pumpkinseeds to the benthos their further growth becomes food limited.[1000] Lakes in the western United States often suffer low productivity.[1001] The milder climate surrounding Felt Lake, south of San Francisco, California, extends the potential growing season to twice that of northern Midwestern lakes, but its bluegills grow at approximately the same rate.[1002] Felt Lake's situation is aggravated by seasonal lowering of the water, which precludes development of a littoral zone, and by an impoverished benthic fauna.

Bluegills in southern Michigan lakes grow ~25 mm SL from spring through autumn.[1003] Those near Kalamazoo continued to grow through winter, in one pond adding 20% in length and 50% in mass.[1004] Some of these fish reached 150 mm TL in 17 months The mean length of age-0 bluegills in an Ohio pond nearly doubled from 27.3 to 47.5 mm SL between 20 June and 20 October, or a growth rate of 0.17 mm SL/d.[1005] Growth to preferred length for anglers (≥ 200 mm TL) in 30 Nebraska Sandhill lakes ranged from 4.3 to 14 years.[1006] Bluegills in Michigan lakes that measured 65 mm SL grew 15 mm by late June.[1007] Interlake growth rates vary even when

Table 17. Estimated protein use by individual captive bluegills from Grody Lake, Indiana (year unstated). Dry mass = 27.8% of wet mass, protein = 61.25% of dry mass. Source: Gerking (1954).

Age-class	Body mass, g	Dry mass, g	Protein, g	Protein gain, g	Protein use, %	Protein needed for growth, g
2	5	1.4	0.86			
				3.92	35	11.21
3	28	7.8	4.78			
				5.76	32	18.03
4	62	17.2	10.54			
				7.35	28	26.24
5	105	29.2	17.89			
				5.26	25	21.04
6	136	37.8	23.15			
				5.45	22	24.80
7	168	46.7	28.60			
				2.58	21	12.28
8	183	50.9	31.18			
				1.53	20	7.65
9	192	53.4	32.71			

lakes are nearby. Bluegills at Shoe Lake, Indiana, grew slowly throughout life.[1008] Those of nearby Muskellunge Lake experienced a growth spurt at ages 2–3, and at age-3 were the size of age-5 fish at Shoe Lake. Lake Wawasee bluegills grew slowly at first, but growth accelerated at ages 4–5, and at age-5 they were the size of age-6 fish at Muskellunge Lake.

Females are reported to lag behind males through age-0, but no supporting data have been presented.[1009] After the first year the sexes appear to grow at similar rates, although territorial males ultimately grow larger. I analyzed age-1 through age-5 data from the 1920s through 1941 of 320 bluegills (169 males, 151 females) from four Indiana lakes without finding significant differences in fork length.[1010] However, in age-2 bluegills in Michigan ponds the males averaged 154.1 mm TL and females 142.6 mm, a 7.5% disparity.[1011]

Growth can be defined as an increase in protein, and protein synthesis is growth's most salient feature.[1012] The relationship between length and body mass is represented by a power curve (Figure 67). For growth to occur the protein consumed must exceed that required for energy and maintenance. A bluegill in its active growing phase raises its use of protein with increased food consumption.[1013] The dry mass of captive bluegills after being fed mealworm *Tenebrio molitor* larvae for 50 d was 27.8% of wet mass, 61.25% of which was protein (Table 17).[1014] Therefore, 123.8 g of protein are required to produce a fish of 32.7 g dry mass, or a mean efficiency of 26% (an underestimate because protein for maintenance has not been included).[1015] Estimated protein use and protein needed for growth decline with age (Table 17).

Protein synthesis is seasonal, peaking in spring and fall in bluegills ($\bar{x}$ = 143.1 mm TL) from Burgess Falls Lake, Tennessee, and decreasing in summer and winter.[1016] Cell volumes of muscle and liver tissues diminished in spring and summer, probably in response to gonadal maturation and greater energy required during summer's maximum temperatures. An increase in liver cell volume in October perhaps correlated with decreased energy storage and lower tissue energy demand with falling water temperature.

The relationship between protein nitrogen retained versus that consumed is a nearly perfect correlation (Figure 68). If specimens of 25.9 g grew as projected over one season (150 d) they would weigh 35.1 g, a gain of 9.2 g, 1.56 g of which is protein. This assumes protein to be 17% of fresh mass, an empirically derived number.[1017] During the growing season the daily gain in

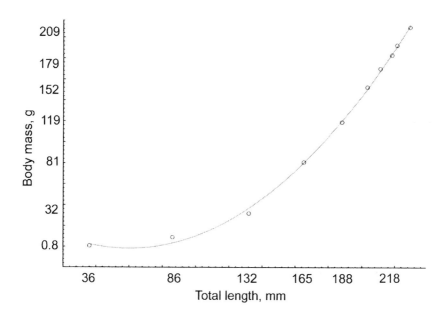

Figure 67. Typical power curve depicting body masses of bluegills regressed against their total lengths: $n = 10$ (means of 530 total specimens grouped by age-classes 1–10), $R^2 = 0.90$, SE = ±24.37, $F_{(1,8)} = 72.80$, $p < 0.0001$; intercept = –80.40, length (ß) is significant at 0.95. The data best fit a polynomial curve in which body mass is predicted by $y = 24.87 - 0.89x + 0.01x^2$. They represent the entire bluegill population of Third Sister Lake, Michigan, collected in summer 1941 after the water was poisoned. Prior to this, angling had been prohibited for 9 years. Source: Plotted from data in Brown and Ball (1942).

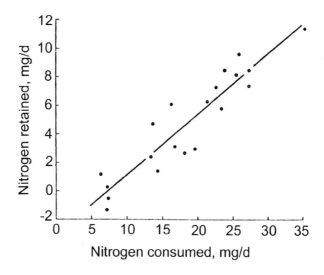

Figure 68. Relationship between nitrogen retained and nitrogen consumed in two 30-d laboratory feeding trials using bluegills. Food consisted of live mealworm larvae. Source: Gerking 1962.

protein would be 1.56/150 = 0.0104 g, or 10.4 mg. Using 0.16 as the nitrogen fraction of animal protein, 0.0104 g × 0.16 = 1.66 mg N/d. As estimated from the curve, to sustain this rate a growing bluegill must ingest 10.4 mg of protein/d, an efficiency of 16%. The mass of food consumed over the growing season (synonymous here with that assimilated) must therefore include 1/0.16 × 1.56 g = 9.75 g of protein.

The growth of bluegills is variable and affected by many factors, but one of the most important is the amount of protein consumed. For example, Indiana bluegills at the start of age-2 ranged from 50 to 150 mm FL, with the larger fish inhabiting lakes in which the population had been reduced abruptly, such as after a winter kill.[1018] Following such an event in Michigan the growth rate of the remaining bluegills reached 35%/year.[1019] With the population reduced, more food was available to the survivors. Food limitation might be a common occurrence in nature. Captive bluegills often eat more than wild ones, in one experiment 8% of body mass daily compared with natural rates of 1.4–3.9%.[1020]

Body size in fishes correlates positively with energy reserves and negatively with metabolic rate.[1021] When energetic factors are paired with survivorship, bigger is often better. Adult male bluegills were collected from Lake Opinicon just after the ice broke, but before foraging commenced.[1022] They ranged from 149 to 206 mm TL (58–175 g wet mass) and were ages 7–10. Total lipid extractions (0.029–3.261 g/fish) correlated positively with both length and mass, demonstrating that larger fish emerged from winter in better energetic condition. However, the metabolic rates of smaller bluegills are less affected by temperature changes.[1023] The bigger-is-better maxim also extends to the biggest of the small: large age-0 bluegills overwintering in Lake Opinicon demonstrated higher survivorship than small ones, and some even appeared to grow.[1024]

As discussed in Chapter 3, foraging requires energy, large prey items are more energetically profitable than small ones, and bluegills appear to forage for optimal energy gain. Adult bluegills in Lake Mendota, Wisconsin, foraged exclusively on macroinvertebrates in the vegetation, consuming 3× more food by mass than zooplankton-feeding adults in nearby Lake Wingra and ultimately growing faster and larger.[1025]

Bluegills in Tennessee still feed in winter, but their intake is greatly reduced. The daily feeding rate of bluegills aged 3–4 in White Oak Lake ranged from 0.8% of body mass in February 1968 to 3.2% in June 1967 and 1968.[1026] At Lake Opinicon, feeding and growth are restricted to ~5 months starting in May.[1027] Between 15 May and 29 September 1984 bluegills of age-2 grew from 63 to 79 mm FL. From 19 June–29 September age-1 fish grew from 44 to 63 mm FL. Age-1 fish in September were the same mean length as those of age-2 in May, indicating negligible winter growth. (As discussed below, later studies indicated growth in overwintering age-0 bluegills.[1028]) Increase in body mass of age-2 fish, including deposition of fat, rose from 7% in mid-May to 14% by late September. Mean whole-body energy increased over the summer from 3.3 to 9.2 kcal (Figure 69). During the growing season, some surplus energy is diverted to increases in length.

Age-1 bluegills at Lake Opinicon are estimated to lose 1.2 kcal over winter, or 0.006 kcal/d, with 0.0043 kcal/d required for nonfeeding metabolism at 6°C.[1029] Bluegills in other northern lakes and ponds feed little while ice cover remains but make use of a variety of aquatic insects and zooplankters.[1030] During February 1968, bluegills of ages 3–4 at White Oak Lake fed under ice at 0.8% of body mass.[1031]

Growth in fishes generally increases with temperature to an optimal rate (if food is not limiting), beyond which it decreases.[1032] Feeding rate, and therefore growth, are largely controlled by temperature, and the eccritic temperature of bluegills is reportedly ~31°C.[1033] Near this value they grow rapidly because food conversion is at maximum efficiency. In one series of experiments, optimal temperature for food conversion and growth was 25°C and continued to be good up to 30°C.[1034] In other aquarium experiments, fish averaging 16.8 g were kept in groups at 25, 28, 31, and 34°C and fed one of two daily rations (either as percentage of body mass or *ad*

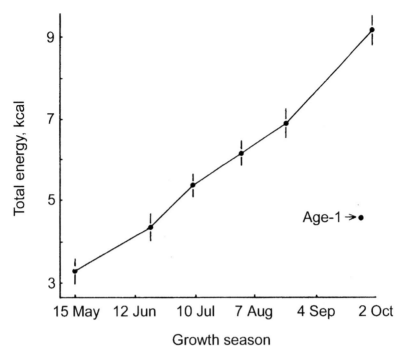

Figure 69. Increase in whole-body energy of age-2 bluegills from Lake Opinicon, Ontario, over summer 1984. Source: Booth and Keast (1986).

libitum). Growth occurred on daily rations of 2% or more.[1035] Daily maintenance rations (the point at which zero growth occurred) were 0.9–1.5% at all tested temperatures. The lowest conversion efficiency was in fish held at 34°C (2%), the highest at 30°C (4%). Bluegills fed *ad libitum* grew 2.2–2.5× faster than those fed daily rations equaling 6% of body mass. Growth was fastest under *ad libitum* feeding at 31°C, but the rate was not significantly faster than at 25°C and 28°C. In some fishes (e.g., the salmonids) growth can be maximized at reduced food intake by moving to cooler water.[1036] The estimated daily maintenance ration of captive bluegills held at 28°C was 36% lower than at 34°C.[1037] However, the physiological cost of rapid acclimation appears to limit the bluegill's response at temperatures too far below the optimal.[1038]

Digestion rate is temperature dependent. The half-life of stomach fullness in captive bluegills held at 18–23°C was 5 h,[1039] but extended to 6 h in force-fed fish at 21°C.[1040] Complete digestion of live foods (e.g., chironomids, dragonfly and mayfly naiads, mealworms) took ~18 h at 18.5–24.6°C ($\bar{x}$ = 21.3°C) in captive bluegills averaging 118.2 and 177.6 mm (TL?) of mean age 1.4 and 3.5 years.[1041] When rations were apportioned by age and size, digestion in larger fish averaged 19.3 mg/h, in smaller ones 6.8 mg/h. Chitin ranged from 0.43% of the live body masses of chironomids to 2.45% of dragonfly naiads and was passed undigested. The estimated daily ration was 2.8% of body mass.

A summer field investigation of bluegills in Lake Opinicon (50–90 mm TL, age-2) estimated the mean daily ration at 1.73–2.40 mg dry mass/g wet mass of fish.[1042] The half-life of stomach fullness decreased linearly over the range of temperatures (10–25°C) according to the regression equation

$$y = 23.4 - 0.901x$$

in which x = water temperature (°C). At a half-life of 4.5 h this agrees closely with an earlier experiment (see above) in which the half-life of stomach fullness of captive bluegills that had not been force-fed was 5 h.

Attempts to correlate environmental factors with growth are sometimes initiated for predictive purposes with the ultimate objective of managing fisheries. The results often fail to meet expectations for three reasons. First, confounding variables are numerous and complex. Resolution tends to be crude, yielding confusing associations of little practical use. Second, correlations, especially positive ones, mislead by implying biological relationships where none exist or the actual effect variable is something else. For example, environmental alkalinity and growth correlate positively in bluegills.[1043] This likely masks a situation in which depressed environmental pH (not necessarily low alkalinity) drives growth retardation,[1044] but not in the obvious way: acidic water is not the cause of physiological acidosis in fishes.[1045] Environmental alkalinity has no effect on internal acid–base balance and such associated factors as reduced branchial ATPase activity and impaired ionic regulation.[1046] Moreover, any pH effects can in turn be masked by more dominating factors, such as those associated with overcrowding,[1047] although at pH values less than 5.5 bluegills spawn sparingly and at less than 5.0 ordinarily not at all.[1048] In measures of water hardness it is the calcium ion concentration, not other covarying electrolytes (e.g., magnesium), that influence the blood ion/acid–base response.[1049] Third, in defining to some extent the associative strengths between and among variables, correlation simultaneously nullifies their estimates as unique parameters.[1050] Collinearity (e.g., shared predictive power) between any two environmental variables, if not accidental, offers little enlightenment unless the interactive effects on growth are known.

Some relationships are well documented. Growth of juvenile bluegills depends on the positive association between food availability and water temperature.[1051] Food ordinarily is more abundant in submerged vegetation than in open water,[1052] and bluegill growth is greater in lakes with large littoral areas.[1053] In lakes in which diet switching occurs (Chapter 4) its timing affects growth. Juveniles that delay moving from vegetation into open water are exposed to fewer risks but grow more slowly.[1054] Juvenile bluegills resolve visual images poorly, which influences prey encounter rate (Chapter 2). Increased encounter rates enhance growth, but the act of switching raises the risk of predation in open water.[1055] In fact, switch size and prey encounter rates in vegetation and open water appear to rank highly among important parameters affecting size structure in some bluegill populations.[1056]

Growth within a bluegill population—that is, the distribution of the lengths and ages of its individuals—is driven mostly by food availability and size-selective predation. Tests in Michigan ponds that were drained and stocked with yolk sac fry showed mortality to be lowest and growth highest when low stocking concentrations were combined with ample food and little competition from other species.[1057] This situation seems to also hold true in natural lakes and ponds.[1058] Experiments using South Carolina bluegills showed that heavy predation on juveniles resulted in more rapid growth, leading to greater age and length at maturity.[1059] Had length differences been exclusively food driven the population would tend to mature at a large size and young age.[1060] Intraspecific competition from fish of the same age-class has an effect: growth in Alabama ponds was faster and relative survival higher at low concentrations of larvae.[1061] Heavy representation by big adults can indicate light fishing pressure. Anglers are size-selective predators who keep the big fish but throw the little ones back (Chapter 8). Were the population of large bluegills predominately males, the cause might be demographic structure, a situation in which big males compete more successfully and delaying reproduction is advantageous (Chapter 6). When females have also delayed breeding until attaining large size, and small males that use alternative mating strategies (Chapter 6) are absent, the most logical possibility left is size-selective predation by piscine predators. Unlike anglers, largemouth bass eat the small bluegills and leave the big ones alone.

Table 18. Characteristics of bluegill populations (mm TL) in some Michigan lakes. Ranges are over multiple years. Compiled from several publications (see Schneider 1999: 100 for references). Source: Schneider (1999).

| Lake or pond | Fish/ha | | Adult mortality, % | | |
	>152 mm	>203 mm	Total	Fishing	Natural
Blueberry	531-1252	306-823	37	Low	
Dead	514-586	40-109	41	Low	
Mill	109-516	1-54	54	0	54
Third Sister	385	168		Low	
Cassidy	309-311	1-1	55-62	Average	
Sugarloaf	86-198	7	68	25-30	40-42
Whitmore	104	10	64-72	Average	
Manistee	12-116	2-11	64	Average	
Fife	10-222	4	55	Average	
Jewett	104-314	2-11	86	23	63
Lodge	86-178	0	83	26	57

What could be called nonselective predation is a factor in southeastern U.S. waters where no angling occurs. Par Pond, South Carolina, contains a size-structured population of largemouth bass averaging 420 mm TL.[1062] These fish are able to swallow bluegills of much larger body depth than the smaller bass typically occurring in lakes and ponds that are fished regularly. Growth rates of bluegills at Par Pond are unusually fast from ages 1–4, possibly because interrupting somatic growth to breed would increase susceptibility to predation. Larger size-classes remain vulnerable because the unusually large and numerous bass can consume large prey. This contrasts with northern lakes where the incidence of predation is comparatively low, and so is the growth rate of bluegills.[1063]

Mortality

Survival drops off rapidly with age. Counts of bluegills from Grody Lake, Indiana, showed this distribution: 965 (age-5), 266 (age-6), 67 (age-7), and 16 (age-8).[1064] In Muskellunge Lake each age-class was ~35% of the preceding one.[1065] Bluegills anywhere rarely live past age-9,[1066] and slowly growing specimens doubtfully outlive those with rapid growth.[1067] The estimated total annual mortality at Grody Lake in the early 1950s was 72.5%, of which 35.0% resulted from summer angling, leaving 37.5% attributable to natural mortality.[1068] Annual mortality of bluegills exceeding 200 mm (TL?) aged 4.3–8.3 years in 19 Nebraska Sandhill lakes averaged 40%, with 10% of this from angling.[1069] At Mid Lake, Wisconsin, prior to its being opened for angling, the natural mortality of adults was 30%.[1070] Adult bluegills at Blueberry Pond, Michigan, under minimal fishing pressure and too large to be eaten by other fishes, died at the rate of 37% annually (Table 18), including 2,400 fish longer than 152 mm TL.[1071] Angling is not permitted at Par Pond, and the annual mortality is 67% for bluegills aged 1–3 and 53% for those aged 4–9.[1072]

Annual mortality for bluegills of age-1 and older has been reported at 65%.[1073] Little of the annual natural mortality (total deaths minus fishing mortality) of adult bluegills results from predation.[1074] The natural mortality of fish longer than 125 mm FL in three Indiana lakes: Muskellunge Lake 47% (1942–1943), Shoe Lake 52–56% (1941–1943), and Lake Wawasee 66% (1939–1940).[1075] Bluegills longer than 125 mm FL in Shoe Lake (16 ha) were estimated at 24,000 in the early 1940s.[1076] Annual natural mortality was 50%, or 30 fish/d, but there were few predators capable of eating them. In 1941 the lake held 16 bowfins (most < 1 kg) and even fewer in 1942. Four spotted gars, most less than 1 kg, were caught in 1941, 12 in 1942, and two in 1943. The largemouth bass population was small too, estimated at less than 40 individuals of which ~10 fish greater than 1 kg were caught annually by anglers. Senile death is apparently the cause of nearly all natural mortality of adult bluegills, a fact often difficult to accept because so few specimens float to the surface.

Management

8 Managing a body of water scientifically and preferentially for bluegills requires knowledge of the habitat's accessible components and control over its most ferocious size-selective predator, the angler. Management strategies traditionally focus on five variables: (1) water quality, (2) lower elements of the food chain, (3) the fishes, (4) the aquatic vegetation, and (5) the angler. What we know is never certain because each lake is dynamic and possessed of unique vulnerabilities. I shall focus on some of what we think we know and how, in sweeping terms, it might be useful.

Predation and Bluegill Quality

The quality of bluegills inhabiting a lake or pond is an assessment based on their relative abundance, population size structure, condition, and growth. These defining elements are linked intimately with parallel attributes of their predators, mainly largemouth bass. Bluegills less than 150 mm TL are typical of small Midwestern ponds containing largemouth bass longer than 300 mm TL, but the trend is reversed when the bass are at high concentrations and smaller (200–290 mm TL).[1077] For example, in 1965 at Deer Ridge Lake, Missouri, only 10% of the bluegills exceeded 150 mm TL, but more than 60% of the bass were 200–225 mm TL.[1078] A minimum length limit of 300 mm TL was imposed for largemouth bass in 1969, and from 1971 to 1973 bluegills larger than 150 mm increased to 54–69% of the population.[1079]

These findings have been affirmed in a more recent investigation of 13 South Dakota ponds where bluegill quality improved with increasing numbers of smaller bass.[1080] High bluegill quality in Nebraska's Sandhill lakes was associated strongly with high relative abundance of largemouth bass of less than 300 mm TL.[1081] Bass populations of extended size structure and low relative abundance were associated with bluegills of lower quality. Largemouths exerted greater influence on bluegill quality than in Minnesota lakes, but the Nebraska lakes also held fewer species of piscine predators.

Sustaining a population of bluegills through all the size ranges—including very large ones—requires constricting the population size structure of the bass that prey on them. Large numbers bass of less than 300 mm TL can consume enough small bluegills to restructure the population until a sizeable proportion consists of fish greater than 150 mm TL.[1082] Angling quickly removes the largest bass, allowing bluegills to outgrow the gapes of those that remain and becoming safe from predation at smaller size.[1083] Therefore, stretching one population's size structure to emphasize the high end of the size range (bluegills) often involves shrinking the other's (largemouth bass) and emphasizing the low end. The result is high predation on age-0 bluegills, much of it by age-0 bass.[1084] Nonetheless, some fishery managers recommend considerably larger minimum legal lengths for largemouths (e.g., 406–457 mm TL) despite mediocre results.[1085]

Factors determining bluegill quality vary by region and body of water. Bluegill quality in southern Michigan lakes depends a great deal on the size of available zooplankton—not necessarily their concentrations—and adult bluegills forage optimally in lakes having reliably abundant large cladocerans, in particular *Daphnia pulicaria*.[1086] Although water fleas were more concentrated in Culver Lake (17/L) than in Lawrence Lake (8/L), individuals were smaller. The predicted between-lake differences in foraging return (0.29 J/s versus 0.13 J/s) correlated with higher growth rates of bluegills in Lawrence Lake (30.2 g/year versus 17.6 g/year).

Water Quality

A comparison of 131 lakes from around the world revealed tenuous effects of chlorophyll concentration, total phosphorus concentration, and Secchi disk transparency on the concentration of macroinvertebrates.[1087] An investigation of 30 Nebraska Sandhill lakes found only weak associations between quality of the bluegill populations and several measurements of environmental quality.[1088] As discussed in Chapter 2, increased turbidity might handicap fishes that rely at least partly on vision.[1089] Its negative influence was implied, but not demonstrated, after evaluation of 32 agriculturally eutrophic lakes in Iowa.[1090] The maximum depth colonized by aquatic angiosperms in the clearest lakes is less than 12 m, or a level of illumination of ~1800 J/cm^2, and becomes rapidly shallower with increasing turbidity.[1091] Because depth distribution (i.e., Secchi depth) and macrophyte biomass (to a lesser extent) are governed largely by solar irradiance, any decline in light transmittance compromises the amount of available foraging and refuge space[1092] and degrades the habitat in other ways (e.g., increased sedimentation, reduced oxygenation).[1093]

Large numbers of benthic foragers, principally the common carp, are associated with high turbidity in the Iowa lakes mentioned above, which mostly lack macrophyte cover.[1094] The CPE (catch per effort) of carp increased with chlorophyll *a*, whereas that of bluegills and other sportfishes declined. Carp destroy bluegill nests and consume the eggs and larvae (Chapter 6), and carp might be among the few fishes with which bluegills fail consistently to compete.[1095] They resuspend sediment with their rooting,[1096] although the extent to which this influences turbidity depends on composition of the substratum.[1097] Nonetheless, rooting activities tend to lower the zooplankton biomass[1098] and diminish macrophyte diversity.[1099] Carp also dislodge plants[1100] and compete with other fishes for benthic insects.[1101] Reduction in the snail communities caused by an abundance of pumpkinseeds or carp can allow epiphytes to blanket the leaves and stems of macrophytes,[1102] eventually killing them.

As the macrophytes die, the nutrients stored in their leaves and stems become available to phytoplankton, which raises the turbidity. The concentration of littoral-zone macroinvertebrates is associated positively with phytoplankton biomass.[1103] However, the decomposition of phytoplankton has a strong negative effect on hypolimnial oxygen.

Aquatic Vegetation

Bluegill populations having a high fraction of specimens exceeding 200 mm TL are often associated with lakes and ponds where the percentage cover of submerged vegetation is meager, the water deep and well-oxygenated, and the relative proportions of piscivorous predators are high.[1104] Bluegills in these environments have reduced recruitment, low competition for food, and experience high predation on their fry and juveniles.[1105] In such environments, heavy macrophyte cover compromises any benefits it might have otherwise, rendering the overall effect detrimental.[1106] In contrast, small weedy lakes are most likely to have a surfeit of bluegills with suppressed growth.[1107] These situations and the results derived from them vary partly by geographic region.

Macrophytes are rooted, their availability for shelter and colonization by macroinvertebrates thus extending from the bottom to the surface. However, aquatic plants alter the surrounding environment starting with a pronounced effect on light penetration. Plants such as Eurasian water milfoil *Myriophyllum spicatum*, which concentrate biomass near the surface, shade everything underneath at all hours of the day.[1108] Rosulate plants (e.g., genus *Vallisneria*), in contrast, attenuate light more strongly when the sun is at low angles. [1109] Eurasian water milfoil sometimes dominates native vegetation, crowding it out and lowering species diversity.[1110] The temperature gradient within a stand of macrophytes can vary 10°C per vertical meter, compared with less than 0.2°C in nearby areas without vegetation.[1111] Heavy stands of macrophytes encourage siltation by interrupting and slowing the movement of water, and by contributing their own tissues to the sediment when they die,[1112] releasing inorganic nutrients in the process. They also cause diel fluctuations in dissolved oxygen, in one case over a projected range of 7–18 mg/L accompanied by pH changes of 7.5–9.5.[1113] Aquatic macrophytes are also leaky, ultimately hastening eutrophication by releasing organic matter.[1114]

When a flourishing stand of Eurasian water milfoil consumes too much of the open substratum, bluegills abandon their nests.[1115] Foraging efficiency is compromised as macrophyte stands become thicker[1116] despite the increase in biomass of associated macroinvertebrates.[1117] As discussed in Chapter 5, foraging efficiency of captive largemouth bass is reduced in heavy simulated macrophyte cover,[1118] allowing more bluegills to survive.[1119]

Thick stands of submerged vegetation have been associated with the decreased growth of bluegills[1120] and their increased abundance.[1121] The relationship between growth and macrophyte thickness is unimodal in laboratory experiments, the highest growth occurring at intermediate stem concentrations. Undersized bluegills in recreational lakes and ponds lower the quality of the fishery. Populations of stunted fish—those in which adults reach only 125–160 mm TL—are traditionally associated with habitats containing heavy growths of submerged macrophytes.[1122] Adult bass, typically a bluegill's main predator, are unable to maneuver through vegetation more concentrated than $300\,g/m^{2,1123}$ and their hunting is restricted to the peripheries of weed beds. As mentioned previously, at fake stem concentrations exceeding $250/m^2$ the success of captive bass hunting bluegills declines nearly to zero.[1124] Small bluegills in pool and pond experiments compete with juvenile bass for resources,[1125] retarding the growth of both species.[1126] Eliminating part of the vegetation makes small bluegills more vulnerable to predation, sometimes resulting in faster growth rates and a higher proportion of large fish among the survivors.[1127]

Most experiments that have measured effects of macrophyte cover on foraging and predation on bluegills were conducted over short periods using a few specimens of a single age-class and implemented on a small scale (Chapter 5). Foraging efficiency implies future growth provided, of course, that the fish survive. These experiments show that foraging while simultaneously avoiding predation requires a compromise in which optimal efficiency occurs in cover of intermediate thickness. Unfortunately, fishery managers often use such information when considering aquatic weed control programs.[1128] Extrapolation from aquarium or pool to pond or lake is a parlous exercise, one in which the probabilities of staying balanced on the tightrope or falling off are not much different. Results from studying captive animals provide insight into hypotheses that need to be tested in the field, not data for making management decisions.

Actually, the unimodal relationship between the growth of either bass or bluegills and macrophyte concentration is nowhere apparent when scaled up. An investigation of 45 Michigan lakes in which nine macrophyte-related variables were used found no support for the notion of optimal growth at intermediate cover, although there was evidence of positive edge effects for largemouths (see below). Nor did mean lake depth, lake area, total alkalinity, or total phosphorus exert a significant effect.

Stands of Eurasian water milfoil can form massive canopies at the surface,[1129] occluding movement of all but the smallest fishes. This impenetrability has an obvious adverse effect on largemouth bass.[1130] Variable stands of native macrophytes, in contrast, ordinarily represent several growth forms of unequal penetrability.[1131] The multiple open areas provided by diverse stem and leaf architecture are thought to enhance foraging success of largemouths,[1132] which in turn should affect the population structure of bluegills and yield more large fish of fewer total numbers.

In the mid-1970s, Eurasian water milfoil invaded Lake Opinicon, which already supported at least 15 species of aquatic macrophytes,[1133] and quickly multiplied. Subsequent investigations indicated that bluegills of age-1 and older preferred feeding and sheltering in stands of two natives, Robbins' pondweed *Potamogeton robbinsii* and wild celery *Vallisneria americana*.[1134] The comparative use of these plants by age-0 bluegills was less pronounced. On occasion, up to 6× more fish could be netted in the littoral zone dominated by these species than in stands of Eurasian water milfoil, in part because there were far greater numbers of macroinvertebrates in the benthos underneath, especially chironomid larvae, which in Lake Opinicon are the bluegill's principal food.[1135] The substratum underneath stands of Eurasian water milfoil accumulated a deeper layer of sediment compared with the native plants, perhaps inhibiting its colonization. Macroinvertebrates on the plants themselves were several times greater on the two natives, the disparity tapering to 2× in August with chironomid larvae still dominant.

Any negative impact of Eurasian water milfoil is inconsistent. Lake Mendota, Wisconsin, supports a diverse macrophyte community, including this exotic and the natives water celery, water stargrass *Heteranthera dubia*, sago pondweed *Potamogeton pectinatus*, leafy pondweed *P. foliosus*, curly-leaf pondweed *P. crispus*, Canadian waterweed, and coontail *Ceratophyllum demersum*.[1136] These plants were distributed by depth throughout the littoral zone with considerable variation in abundance, concentration, and species diversity.[1137] Investigation showed that Lake Mendota's fishes (10 families composed of 29 species) assembled in combinations that depended partly on the patchiness, or spatial heterogeneity, of the macrophyte stands.[1138] Almost 97% of the total catch comprised age-0 fishes, of which bluegills represented 83%. Age-0 bluegills were most numerous in weed beds where Eurasian water milfoil was both abundant and patchy, but species were not highly diverse. Older bluegills shared dominance with yellow perch and occurred most often where vegetation in general was thick and diverse rather than patchy. In general, more of Lake Mendota's bluegills of all ages occurred in abundant, thick, species-diverse vegetation, although bluegills also inhabited areas of the heaviest vegetation and no vegetation. Patchiness might give age-0 fish easier access to open spaces where they can forage for zooplankton. When predators are nearby, age-0 bluegills spend more time foraging among the weeds than in open water where plankton is more prevalent.[1139]

Macrophytes promote sedimentation while simultaneously lowering turbidity, and their inclusion as major components of lake and pond restoration, when accompanied by removal of benthivorous and planktivorous fishes, greatly improves water quality, including water clarity.[1140] Nor are weedy habitats always indicative of stunted bluegills, as shown by investigations in southern Michigan.[1141] Blueberry Pond is 8.0 ha with 83% of its surface covered by macrophytes. Dead Lake is 22.9 ha with 41% surface cover. Vegetation at both locations consists mainly of pondweeds (genus *Potamogeton*) and water lilies (genera *Nuphar* and *Nymphaea*).

Table 19. Mean spring fish biomass and community composition of two Michigan lakes. Source: Schneider (1999).

	Dead Lake		Blueberry Pond	
Species Biomass (kg/ha)		% of total	Biomass (kg/ha)	% of total
Bluegill	70.6	45.6	96.1	54.7
Pumpkinseed	13.6	8.7	21.9	12.5
Largemouth bass	9.4	6.0	20.0	11.4
Yellow perch	7.3	4.7	10.2	5.8
Yellow bullhead	4.9	3.2	8.6	4.9
Lake chubsucker	6.2	4.0	10.8	6.1
Golden shiner	<0.1	<0.1	2.1	1.2
Green sunfish	<0.1	<0.1	1.0	0.6
Bowfin	22.7	14.6	0.0	0.0
Northern pike	10.2	6.5	0.0	0.0
Brown bullhead	8.1	5.2	0.0	0.0
Black crappie	1.9	1.2	0.0	0.0
Warmouth	0.5	0.2	0.0	0.0
Total	155.2	100.0	170.7	100.0

Fishing pressure at the time of this investigation was low. At both sites the proportion of large bluegills (203–228 mm TL) was unusually high: 62% of fish exceeded 152 mm at Blueberry Pond, and 13% were longer than 203 mm at Dead Lake. At Blueberry Pond, bluegills greater than 203 mm TL averaged 504/ha; those exceeding 152 mm TL averaged 815/ha. At Dead Lake these counts were 74 and 551/ha. Maximum survival was exceptionally long (12 years in Blueberry Pond, 11 years in Dead Lake). Total fish biomass was high (Table 19); concentrations of large-mouth bass longer than 254 mm TL averaged 67/ha for Blueberry Pond and 16/ha for Dead Lake. Bluegills at both sites were ~50% of the fish biomass, not unusual for this region.

What factors make these lakes superior to similar ones containing stunted bluegills? Adequate predation, first of all, although the numbers of predators were not high in comparison with many other southern Michigan lakes. Predators consumed an estimated 303,300 bluegills annually in Blueberry Pond, of which 226,000 were eaten by largemouth bass larger than 305 mm TL. Extension of bluegill size structures by bass this size is consistent with some reports,[1142] although not all such waters are fished.[1143] Largemouths seem to be most effective when less than 300 mm TL,[1144] and this situation might be generally true of apex predators in North American lakes. Small northern pike can control an abundance of small fishes effectively.[1145] At Dead Lake and Blueberry Pond, yellow perch longer than 127 mm TL accounted for 33,500 bluegills consumed, yellow bullheads 22,900, grass pickerel 13,600, and other bluegills 7,600. Most bluegills eaten by bass were less than 25 mm TL. Fishing mortality was negligible. The adults, under minimal fishing pressure and too large to be eaten by other fishes, died in large numbers of natural causes (e.g., 37% annually in Blueberry Pond, including 2,400 fish greater than 152 mm TL).

Food was abundant, including ample water fleas and chironomids. Zooplankters are important in these lakes for bluegills of 100–125 mm TL, the size at which they become too big for most largemouth bass. For bluegills of 150–175 mm TL, 50% of the seasonal diet consisted of water fleas (genus *Daphnia*), which fell to 4% in fish exceeding 200 mm TL. The presence of water fleas is associated with enhanced growth in bluegills.[1146] At no time was there evidence of starvation.

Age-0 and age-1 bluegills were uncommon. Limited spawning was the principal mechanism interfering with recruitment. Blueberry Pond contained ~7,000 mature fish capable of producing more than 2 million fingerlings. Assuming half were males and all of them spawned, there could have been 3,500 nests. However, only about 200 nests in a season were seen over 6 years of observation, most of them empty or occasionally occupied by pumpkinseeds. Spawning by females was sometimes incomplete or extended, and females occasionally were captured with eggs that were infertile or being absorbed. Overall, these bluegill lakes are superior to others with extensive weed cover because of low recruitment, minimal fishing pressure, an adequate population of predators, and abundant food of good quality.

Their interstices, numerous surfaces for attachment, and the chemical and physical effects they impose single out stands of submerged vegetation as fundamental lacustrine habitats. Some investigations have also shown a positive association between bluegill quality and emergent, compared with submerged, vegetation.[1147] The consistency of these qualities renders northern and southern lakes and ponds similar despite differences in latitude.

Lake Annie, Florida, is oligotrophic, 35 ha, and 21 m deep. A census was made of its fish population in 1976, and also of nearby Lake Sirena, which is of similar size.[1148] Lake Annie contained 19 species, Lake Sirena 14.[1149] Despite this diversity, bluegills were 38–46% of the estimated fish biomass, the bass 35–37%. Lake Annie's zone of emergent vegetation comprised mainly switch grasses and rushes (genus *Juncus*) extending to a depth of 1.5 m. Beyond were sharply sloping sides populated by sparse stands of bladderwort (genus *Utricularia*) along with pockets of wild celery and spikerush (genus *Eleocharis*). Most bluegills (> 90%) were found between the surface and the top of the vegetation, and larger fish increased in abundance with depth. Nearly all were encountered within 1.5 m of the bottom. Smaller fish occupied the upper 3 m. The littoral zone of Lake Sirena sloped gradually. Emergent vegetation comprised rushes, pickerelweeds, cattails, and water pennyworts (genus *Hydrocotyle*) interspersed with patches of submerged spikerush and filamentous algae, all in water less than 1.2 m deep. Here bluegills were not as common near the bottom, perhaps because the benthic fauna was less productive than Lake Annie's.

A census of two Michigan lakes yielded similar patterns.[1150] In one of them (Lawrence Lake) the littoral slope was covered by water bulrush *Scirpus subterminalis* with bluegills occupying the stratum above, analogous to the stands of bladderwort in Lake Annie, and both lakes had similar phytoplankton production. However, the bladderwort is different from water bulrush in being carnivorous, competing for zooplankton and occasionally eating larval fishes.[1151] Among the several factors in common was species diversity: Lawrence Lake (17 species of fishes, 8 species of centrarchids), Three Lakes (22 total species, 6 species of centrarchids), Lake Annie (19 total species, 7 species of centrarchids). The estimated average biomass of bluegills and largemouth bass combined was 81% (Florida lakes) and 86% (Michigan lakes), although bluegills were more dominant in Michigan (68% versus 46%). Guilds of benthic herbivores and planktivores were similar but composed of different species. Estimates of total biomass/100 m of littoral zone were twice as great for the Michigan lakes, but this was attributed to the greater abundance of bluegills. As in the Florida lakes, most small bluegills were found in water 0.5–1.0 m deep and just above the vegetation.

Removing too much vegetation can substantially affect lacustrine fish communities by reducing available food and eliminating needed places of refuge. Crayfish consume plant material, and their presence in lakes and ponds even at relative low numbers can profoundly affect macrophyte communities.[1152] So can the introduction of herbivorous fishes. Triploid grass carp *Ctenopharyngodon idella* released in 1981 into Lake Conroe, a 8,100-ha Texas reservoir, at a density of 74/ha of vegetative cover, eliminated all vegetation in 2 years.[1153] Prior to their introduction, 3,647 ha, or 45% of the lake's area, had been covered by coontail, a native macrophyte, and the exotics *Hydrilla verticillata*, Eurasian water milfoil, and water hyacinth *Eichhornia crassipes*. Many of the 41 species of fishes were measurably affected. Weedy inshore habitats once dominated by centrarchids became areas of open bottom. As a result, dollar sunfish *Lepomis marginatus*, warmouths, and spotted sunfish *Lepomis punctatus* were nearly eliminated. Redear sunfish persisted, but recruitment dropped nearly to zero. Longear sunfish, which typically shun vegetation,[1154] increased in number, but their average size diminished. The littoral fish community, previously dominated by sunfishes and shads (gizzard shad and threadfin shad, *Dorosoma petenense*), now included large numbers of cyprinids, inland silversides *Menidia beryllina*, and channel catfish. Bluegills declined in biomass per hectare and in mean size, but not in numbers. This was attributed to their generalist feeding habits.

Instead of dredging or raking out excess vegetation or spraying it with herbicides, some fishery managers advocate mowing narrow channels through submerged macrophyte beds, heavy stands of Eurasian water milfoil in particular. Hunting space for bass is increased along the edges of the new channels.[1155] Bass reputedly grow faster because more prey is available,[1156] the bluegills because of reduced competition as more of them are eaten.[1157] The channels ideally extend from surface to substratum, increasing the vertical surface area of the edges to benefit piscivores. Bluegills gain advantage from heavily foliated new growth capable of supporting more epiphytic invertebrates.[1158] The channels themselves open up spaces where planktivores can gather. An ecological model and a field study support this approach.[1159]

The model shows that nearly any manipulation of standing vegetation enhances access to prey fishes by predators.[1160] No optimal level of mowing is apparent for largemouths, although benefits are noticeably less when small (< 10%) or large (> 80%) portions of vegetation are removed. Both species respond positively to ~30% removal (10–50%), bluegills in growth, largemouths in numbers. The model predicts that bluegills will grow 3× faster than bass, but bass should increase in number at twice the rate of bluegills.

Channeling has obvious benefits, but it can disrupt natural succession in lakes and ponds supporting diverse flora. An investigation from 1977 to 1982 of Halverson Lake, Wisconsin, a 4.2-ha pond, found 40–70% of the bottom covered by submerged macrophytes in summer with 30% of the surface blanketed by July.[1161] Macrophytes formed a three-tiered layer during peak growth (mid-May through August). Filamentous algae (e.g., genus *Spirogyra*) spread across the branches of sago pondweed, forming an eventual canopy 60 cm thick. Underneath grew stands of shade-tolerant coontail, slender water-nymph *Najas flexilis*, Canadian waterweed, and water stargrass. The midwater layer contained 80% of the biomass and featured narrow-leaf pondweeds: sago pondweed, slender pondweed, and the introduced curly-leaf pondweed. Openings appeared as certain species senesced, to be invaded by water stargrass, which dominated through ice formation. A channeling program was started, but stargrass became so thick in harvested areas after the second year that the movements of all fishes were restricted. Areas in which stargrass exceeded 200 g/m² (dry mass) were devoid even of fry.

Habitat Structure

Habitat choice directly affects survival, but also drives the types of foods eaten, foraging efficiency, and ultimately growth rate. Sunfishes generally prefer still or slow-moving waters—lakes, ponds, and sluggish streams and rivers—usually near complex structures.[1162] Bluegills might be the least site-specific members of the genus *Lepomis*. Large juveniles and adults occupy any available space regardless of exposure: deep and shallow stands of aquatic weeds, sandy shallows, rocky shelves, submerged snags, gravel bottoms, and open water are all suitable.[1163]

The green sunfish, which coexists with bluegills and pumpkinseeds over much of middle North America,[1164] is perhaps the most structure-specific of the genus *Lepomis*, being rarely far from cover.[1165] Pumpkinseeds gravitate to shallow sandy bottoms and the shallower weed beds.[1166] Where bluegills and green sunfish occur together they partition the space. In both lakes and ponds larger bluegills ordinarily occupy deeper offshore parts of the littoral zone at 1–6 m; green sunfish dominate vegetated, inshore locations less than 1 m deep,[1167] occasionally even displacing bluegills in these habitats.[1168] Additional partitioning of space is evident where all three species coexist. Then pumpkinseeds share the deeper locations offshore with bluegills, but ordinarily occupy positions lower in the water column, often just above the bottom.[1169] If redear[1170] or longear sunfish are present, they too are found near the bottom.[1171] Bluegills are frequently more abundant among water lilies in vegetated lakes.[1172] In some lakes, however, the larger specimens, especially males, are more common in the emergent vegetation.[1173] Green and longear sunfishes prefer the space above open sediments or the confinement of dense stands of muskgrass (genus *Chara*) or bulrushes.[1174]

Bluegills often segregate into habitats by age-classes. Upon leaving the nest, age-0 larvae enter the limnetic zone where they stay for 1–2 months.[1175] Their next move is into thick weed beds. In Lake Opinicon the preference is for thick stands of small pondweed *Potamogeton pusillus* and sago pondweed.[1176] Bluegills join pumpkinseeds in heavy stands of macrophytes through age-0.[1177] Age-1 and age-2 bluegills favor less confined stands of mixed macrophytes, those of ages 3–4 gather in aggregations in the open waters offshore, and the largest (and oldest) fish gravitate to exposed rocky areas inshore.[1178] These comments are general; there are many exceptions based on available food and shelter, the size and nature of the lake or pond, presence of predators, intensity of competition and predation, and so forth.

Stands of aquatic plants are often the preferred habitats of bluegills,[1179] although they and their piscine predators are also common in many shallow nutrient-rich lakes where macrophytes are either absent or nearly so.[1180] After their stay in the limnetic zone, age-0 bluegills, still mostly less than 20 mm TL but sometimes slightly bigger,[1181] eventually take refuge in the littoral vegetation.[1182] Upon first appearing inshore in August, age-0 bluegills at Lake Opinicon remain in open water above the vegetation, ordinarily in groups of ~5, but from late August through the end of September ~50% have shifted to the benthos and presumably into the vegetation.[1183]

When offered choices of habitats, captive bluegills of 10–30 mm SL gravitated to places of quiet water with structure (plastic plants), fine-grained substrata, and dim areas that mimicked shade.[1184] Upon reaching 51–83 mm TL and invulnerable to most piscine predators, bluegills in nature return periodically to open water to forage on zooplankton.[1185] Nutrient-rich lakes with extensive weed beds fronted by open areas are ideal habitats, favoring both juveniles and adults.

Aquatic weeds exert a strong effect on how littoral fishes are distributed in lacustrine environments.[1186] By providing complexity, weed beds increase the abundance and species diversity of fish communities compared with simpler, less structured habitats.[1187] During their early lives, most lacustrine fishes spend time in the littoral zone where macrophytes are concentrated.[1188] Storms and shoreline development destroy weed beds, reducing their relative biomasses and the mean sizes of fishes that depend on them.[1189] Development along the shores of Minnesota's 531 centrarchid-walleye lakes has caused an estimated 20–28% loss of the littoral vegetation,[1190] and the effect on fishes has been direct: the relative biomass of bluegills in these clearwater lakes correlates positively with the yellow water lily (genus *Nuphar*), white water lily *Nymphaea odorata*, and broadleaf cattail *Typha latifolia*; bluegill mean size shows positive correlation with the hardstem bulrush *Scirpus acutus*.

Predation success is thought to diminish with increasing complexity of the habitat. The threat of predators restricts smaller bluegills to complex structures with narrow interstices. Aquatic weeds, rocky reefs, submerged stands of timber, snags (fallen trees and other woody debris), brush, and discarded Christmas trees add heterogeneity to aquatic habitats, providing both food and refuge. Structures do not always increase fish production,[1191] but they increase angling success.[1192] Sunken brush[1193] and conifers[1194] are among the best fish attractants, superior in many cases to manmade modules,[1195] but snags might be the best of all. Snags often shelter more fishes, including bluegills, than other habitats.[1196] Some snags are better than others. In lotic environments snags that slow current velocity and promote the accumulation of sediment are especially attractive,[1197] as are those adjacent to deep pools.[1198]

In an attempt to quantify habitat preference, bluegills (35–95 mm TL) were released into manmade ponds containing structures made of plastic pipes and having interstitial spaces that were small (40 mm), medium (150 mm), and large (350 mm).[1199] The structures composed 0.9% each pond's surface area but attracted 5–10% of the bluegills, probably because there were more fish than spaces available. In the absence of largemouth bass the preference was for small and medium interstices. After the addition of bass, small interstices were chosen over medium and large ones, and this was most apparent in the clearest of the three ponds, where predators were more visible. The experiment was repeated with additional choices of shaded and unshaded areas. Juvenile bluegills (50–100 mm TL) and adults (>150 mm TL) preferred the small (40 mm) spaces regardless of shade or whether largemouth bass were present.[1200]

Water depth also influences habitat selection. The apparatus just described, but with only small (40 mm) and large (350 mm) interstices, was tested in a reservoir at 3.0 m (shallow) and 4.5 m (deep).[1201] Catches of bluegills in shallow water were greater from both small and large interstices, but small ones yielded more fish at both depths. Mean lengths of bluegills from deep water and both interstices were significantly greater than means of bluegills from shallow water. Mean lengths at both depths were greater in fish occupying the large interstices. The smaller spaces yielded smaller bluegills ($\bar{x}$ = 86 mm TL) but also had the most fish longer than 100 mm TL.

Stunting

Stunting is caused mainly by consistent recruitment and size-selective exploitation,[1202] although other factors come into play. One explanation blames homogeneity of the environment for preventing the different age-classes from gaining spatial distance.[1203] An absence of large prey would force both large and small bluegills to compete for smaller organisms, a disadvantage to the larger fish. Moreover, homogeneity of habitats allows prey to be exploited more efficiently, leading to food shortages.[1204] Insufficient food has been considered a mitigating factor.[1205]

Extended size structure of bluegills in Michigan lakes is associated positively with water depth.[1206] In contrast, results of 41 variables evaluated in ~2600 Minnesota lakes showed a negative relationship between maximum depth and growth.[1207] Growth was also associated negatively with recruitment and Secchi depth but positively with population size structure. Moreover, the growth of bluegills was enhanced as the proportion of predators in the total population increased. The negative relationships between growth and recruitment, and population size structure and recruitment, were interpreted as indirect evidence that suppressing recruitment allows the surviving bluegills to grow more quickly. Recruitment was less in smaller lakes. The positive association between Secchi depth and population size structure could imply a benefit from lower turbidity. The greater light transmission of clear water extends the depth at which macrophytes can grow, making more of the habitat available for occupation.[1208]

Biotic variables exerted stronger effects than abiotic ones. Relationships among recruitment, growth, and population size structure were especially strong, suggesting that improvements in the last-mentioned factors necessitates suppressing recruitment, and that growth might be enhanced in populations of certain size structures. Ample evidence supports these results, and they appear to be valid for ponds and small lakes in the northern, Midwestern, and southeastern regions of the United States.[1209]

Physical composition of the habitat, an abiotic variable, counts too. A comparison of 12 southern Wisconsin lakes revealed that sexual dimorphism in males, as measured by size-

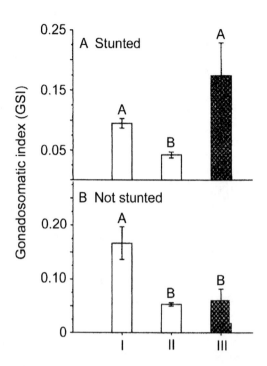

Figure 70. Mean GSIs of male bluegills in ponds with and without large adult males (clear bars) and cohorts collected during resampling of the source populations when the experiment ended (shaded bars). I: No large mature males present. II: Large mature males present. III: Source population. A: Males collected from the stunted population. B: Males collected from the population that was not stunted. Error bars represent ±1 SE. Letters over error bars stand for significant differences between groups (ANOVA, $p \le 0.05$). Source: Aday et al. (2003b).

adjusted mean differences between territorial males and adult females, could be explained by fraction of the lake that was limnos and total lake area.[1210] Dimorphism was greatest in small lakes containing proportionately large pelagic habitats. Growth rate to maturity in territorial males also correlated positively with the amount of pelagic habitat and negatively with number of colonies, making the potential for stunting even greater in lakes and ponds in which the limnos makes up less than half of the habitat.[1211]

Nesting by size-class is under social control,[1212] and stunting is not necessarily a result of environmental factors (Figure 70). When several size-classes are present, nearly all nests are occupied by the largest males. Smaller males typically establish territories only when large males are absent, then they defend nests, mate successfully, and care for the eggs and fry. Small males have lower GSIs when large males are present,[1213] and the absence of large males raises the mean GSIs of small ones.[1214] Big males slow the gonadal development of juvenile males or retard it completely.[1215] Size is apparently important: gonadal development in juveniles is not inhibited by stunted territorial males. Without large males present the remaining males mature while younger and smaller, and their subsequent growth is slowed. Territorial males in Lake Opinicon rarely mature before age-7 and 75 g.[1216] However, F_1 fry from Lake Opinicon stock reared in Illinois ponds without adults produced sperm after 11 months at 3 g.[1217] Mean mass of the Illinois fish was only 12.4 g compared with 106.3 g for the average territorial male at Lake Opinicon.

Growth to maturity of territorial males correlates negatively with the relative abundance of cuckolders,[1218] although cuckoldry and the early maturation of territorial males are distinct biological processes.[1219] This was ascertained clearly in experiments showing that differences in growth rates among pond-raised bluegills altered the proportion maturing as territorial males, but not that of mature cuckolders.[1220] Actually, high growth rate during age-0 stimulates the early maturation of territorial males. Fishery managers, by using GSIs, can distinguish which small mature males are cuckolders and which are early-maturing territorial males.[1221] Assuming that reproductive strategy proves heritable,[1222] managers can decide whether to allow more large males to mature or remove some of the cuckolders.[1223]

Several methods have been used to permanently alter the size structures of bluegill populations and favor growth of large individuals. Supplemental feeding of bluegills in a Kansas lake using commercial fish food swelled the harvest, raising the numbers caught 211% and the total mass 310%.[1224] Neither partial thinning of small fish nor complete annihilation has proved adequate except in the short term.[1225] A long-term experiment in 16 southern Michigan lakes used (1) one-time partial thinning of small bluegills by poisoning with antimycin A at 1–2 ppb, (2) a one-time stocking of fingerling walleyes (37–45/ha) to prey on juvenile bluegills, (3) an extended period of catch–release of age-6 and older of all species in the lakes, and (4) each of the second two treatments with addition of antimycin A.[1226] The results of antimycin treatment were fleeting; stocking walleyes and catch–release angling restrictions provided positive long-term results (i.e., greater size structure, bigger bluegills). Reduced recruitment was not confirmed in any treatment. Catch–release, although popular with fishery managers, is unpopular with anglers. Poisoning and electrofishing of two Alabama lakes to remove largemouth bass increased bluegill recruitment and tripled the angling harvest from 22.3 kg/ha the year prior to treatment to 74.0 kg/ha the year after.[1227]

Angling

The world record bluegill was caught 9 April 1950 at Ketona Lakes in a suburb of Birmingham, Alabama, by T. S. Hudson using a worm and a cane pole. It weighed 4 lb 12 oz, or ~2.15 kg, and was 15 in (~380 mm) long. This was a monster; no other state record has ever approached 4 lb except for a fish caught by Coke McKenzie in the same pond in April 1947 that weighed 4 lb 10 oz. Both apparently were territorial males and probably guarding nests. Fishery biologists who later examined the lake found it populated by numerous largemouth bass. The lake's steep banks restricted nesting areas to some small limestone ledges. Most of the annual bluegill hatch was eaten, but the survivors grew uncommonly big. The lake is now privately owned and closed to angling, although kids reportedly sneak in and later emerge carrying 2-lb bluegills.[1228]

Why do bluegills grow large in some waters and not others (Figure 71)? Individual-based modeling suggests that angling is the dominant factor affecting the size structure of bluegill populations, dwarfing natural history factors (e.g., delayed maturation of small males in the presence of large males).[1229] The model considered exploitation of harvestable males aged 4–8 (> 150 mm) and time to recovery of a population before and after exploitation. The three most significant variables were slope of the growth curve, extent of reproductive activity, and angling pressure. Difference in size before and after angling was greatest when the growth rate was low, percentile of the size structure reaching maturity was low (high reproductive activity), and fish longer than 150 mm were removed. Removing adult males dropped the mean size of harvestable fish by 12–16 mm. Effect on the size distribution was strongest when more adult males than immature males were removed.

Relaxing angling restrictions has been suggested for lakes where bluegills grow slowly or

Figure 71. Darren May of Olney, Illinois, with the state record bluegill caught in a farm pond 10 May 1987. It weighed 3 lb 8 oz. Source: Illinois Department of Natural Resources.

are stunted,[1230] but more stringent regulations are likely to help more. Minnesota waters containing the biggest bluegills also have the lightest angling pressure,[1231] leading to a recommendation that the catch limit be lowered to 10 fish/d.[1232] Mid Lake, Wisconsin, had been closed to angling for years but opened in May 1976. By the end of the month 35% of bluegills 50 mm TL and longer had been caught, the majority in the first 2 d.[1233] No size limits had been imposed, and the catch limit was 50 fish/d. Size structures of all species in the lake quickly shrank. Instead of being dominated by larger and older fishes, they comprised younger individuals of smaller size. The mean length of bluegills declined 35 mm TL through 1979. Creel surveys showed mean lengths diminishing 43 mm TL over 3 years. At Third Sister Lake, Michigan, 24% of the bluegills of legal size were caught in 3 weeks.[1234]

Angler harvest ordinarily is regulated by size limitations and catch (number of fish taken at a given time). Reducing catch limits of bluegills is usually unpopular[1235] and not consistently effective in altering size structure.[1236] Restrictive size limits on large bluegills affect the size structure of the population. Raising the maximum size limit to 175 mm TL and larger has been tried several times;[1237] results show the mean size in the population failing to increase significantly, or actually diminishing. Bracketing the size limit (e.g., 127–175 mm TL) produces the same results. Closing lakes to angling after widespread poisoning of juvenile bluegills in the littoral zones and then introducing piscine predators sometimes improves size structure,[1238] but this is impractical for lakes where people expect to fish. Even poisoning all the fish and restoring bluegills often fails to produce big fish.[1239] Prohibiting the take of largemouth bass is not always effective either.[1240] The principal objective in any management strategy with bluegills should be to reduce recruitment and increase juvenile mortality. The trick, in other words, is to load all possible predation into the front end of the system and worry less about the other end.

Most angling for bluegills is unintentionally sex-specific, focusing on territorial males, which are usually the largest in the population. Heavy angling pressure removes too many desirable fish (territorial males ≥150 mm TL), accelerating the maturity of smaller males and permitting them to breed early but at smaller size.[1241] Because growth slows abruptly after maturation,[1242] the energy ordinarily allocated to somatic growth is transferred instead to the reproductive organs, resulting in a stunted population.

Angling increases the rate of total mortality, although this statement contains less quantitative truth if natural mortality is high too, and in centrarchids it usually is, largemouth bass included.[1243] Disproportionately low numbers of big bluegills (< 20%) indicate slow growth and high adult mortality.[1244] The estimated total annual mortality at Mid Lake was 30% prior to opening the lake to anglers; 2 years later it was 62%.[1245] At Jane Lake, Minnesota, early mortality from fishing pressure showed in the skewed distribution when mean age of mature males guarding nests (5.5 years) was less than the age at 50% maturation (5.9 years).[1246] Nor were mature females exempt. Mean lengths of females from three Minnesota lakes (including Jane Lake) under high angling pressure ranged from 103 to 111 mm TL. Adult females in two other lakes and Lake Opinicon (all under low angling pressure) were 138–167 mm TL. Creel surveys in some southern Wisconsin lakes showed that more than 90% of the catch in late May consisted of large breeding males.[1247]

Implementing size limits on bluegills appears to be ineffective when natural mortality exceeds angling mortality, especially if growth rate within the population does not rise concomitantly.[1248] Length limits are even less useful if fishing pressure is low, and size-selective pressure in heavily fished waters fails to protect larger bluegills while reducing total yield (most sunfish anglers keep their catch). Some fishery managers therefore recommend that investigations of recreational fisheries emphasize growth, exploitation, and natural mortality instead of catch rate and size structure.[1249]

Gizzard Shad

Stocking less desirable fish that compete for the same resources is thought to depress the growth of bluegills.[1250] One such species in Midwestern and southern lakes and ponds is the gizzard shad,[1251] which affects all aspects of the environment, including recruitment of bluegills. The earlier spawning of gizzard shad, combined with their high fecundity, voracious larvae, facile diet switches, and rapid growth places them outside the controlling forces of many fish communities.[1252] Gizzard shad spawn 1–3 weeks before bluegills, and hordes of their larvae (up to 86/m^3)[1253] precede the arrival of bluegill fry. Their huge numbers (females can produce a half-million eggs)[1254] sometimes severely deplete the zooplankton,[1255] leaving little food for larval bluegills.

Gizzard shad have smaller gapes than bluegills.[1256] This, combined with the usually smaller zooplankters found in reservoirs (manmade lakes and ponds), enables them to compete aggressively with other larval fishes and even grow faster on smaller organisms.[1257] Their larvae (18–31 mm TL) forage selectively on small zooplankters (e.g., genera *Bosmina*, *Chydorus*).[1258] Bluegills of the same size have wider gapes and are less selective, but unlike shad they choose larger zooplankters as their gapes increase. Gizzard shad switch from selective feeding to filter feeding at ~25 mm TL and cease to be size selective.[1259] Water fleas (genus *Daphnia*) can prevent phytoplankton blooms after nutrient enrichment (see below), so long as their mortality does not increase,[1260] but this is unlikely in planktivore-dominated waters.

Captive gizzard shad foraged preferentially on plankton smaller than 40 mm.[1261] Gizzard shad also feed heavily on bottom detritus,[1262] and whether feeding in this mode or foraging on plankton, large populations in small bodies of water potentially accelerate eutrophication. Captive gizzard shad feeding on natural detritus excreted nitrogen at 0.4–7.2 mmol/g/h (twice that of bluegills) and phosphorus at 0.01–0.44 mmol/g/h (2.5× that of bluegills).[1263] The biomass of large zooplankton (e.g., cyclopoid copepods, large water fleas) in 39 eutrophic Florida lakes demonstrated weak positive correlation with the trophic state.[1264] These are among the organisms that sustain large bluegills and early age-0 largemouth bass in waters with adequate limnetic areas. Smaller zooplankton (e.g., rotifers, copepod nauplii, ciliated protozoans), in contrast, dominated as eutrophication progressed, rising to 50–90% of the zooplankton biomass. Although fish biomass also increased, emphasis shifted from bass and bluegills to filter-feeding planktivorous fishes such as shad. During experiments using captive gizzard shad, cyclopoid copepods, turbidity, unicellular green algae, pennate diatoms, and particulate phosphorus increased. No comparable increases were seen with bluegills, although fish biomass ultimately determined composition of the plankton communities and water quality.[1265] The presence of gizzard shad ultimately compresses the size structure of bluegills and stunts adults.[1266] This occurs partly because gizzard shad provide alternative prey for largemouth bass.

Gizzard shad are preyed on selectively by esocids[1267] and largemouth bass,[1268] which ought to have a sparing effect on bluegills, but the opposite is true: in Ohio reservoirs the relationship between gizzard shad larvae and larval bluegills is negative.[1269] High early losses of gizzard shad larvae to predation are offset by rapid growth: age-0 fish soon exceed the gape of most predators, including largemouths.[1270] This, combined with the gizzard shad's tremendous fecundity, insulates age-0 fish from substantial losses to predation (only ~20% in one investigation).[1271] With smaller numbers of bluegills migrating to the littoral zone, the growth and reproduction of largemouth bass are depressed. Ultimately, ineffectual top-down control of gizzard shad by predation, combined with the absence of any negative effects from having depleted either the primary or secondary consumers, places southern lakes and ponds apart from the trophic systems that characterize northern lakes.

Gizzard shad eventually affect the recruitment of both bluegills and largemouths (Figure 72).[1272] In their absence the annual recruitment of both species varies. If larval gizzard shad precede bluegills and bass into the limnos then recruitment will be poor to intermediate despite any effect of gizzard shad abundance or zooplankton concentrations. Conversely, if they appear later, recruitment of these other species should be poor to excellent (high numbers of zooplankton) or poor to intermediate (low numbers of zooplankton). Even so, shad and bluegill larvae will overlap, lowering bluegill recruitment. Ultimately, gizzard shad exert a deleterious effect on the recruitment of both bluegills and bass, overwhelming any top-down effect resulting from largemouth predation. Where shad are numerous the sport fishery inevitably declines. This comes about by winning the competition with bluegills at the larval stage. The subsequent diminished recruitment of bluegills then adversely affects the recruitment of largemouths.[1273]

Adult gizzard shad are large (305–406 mm TL)[1274] and deep-bodied, equal in length to many largemouth bass, and nearly invulnerable to predation. Not only can they coexist with piscine predators, they do so while maintaining large populations. In such situations cascade effects on zooplankton and phytoplankton that ordinarily are apparent from manipulation of the piscivore population are suppressed.[1275] In other words, if gizzard shad remain abundant any predation effect by largemouth bass is unlikely to show as noticeable changes in the plankton. We know already that when bluegills persist in large numbers with largemouth bass such cascade effects fail to appear.[1276]

The abundance of age-0 autumn larvae of gizzard shad was lower in experimental ponds with macrophytes than without, although the numbers of larvae were not significantly different among ponds in May and June.[1277] Data from 178 small Missouri lakes containing bluegills were assessed in a parallel study. Of these, 82 also contained gizzard shad. The size structure of bluegill populations was more compressed in lakes with shad than without, and the proportion containing large bluegills correlated positively with macrophyte cover. Lakes without shad held

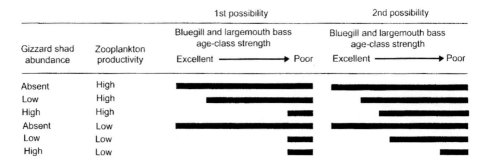

Figure 72. Predicted year-class strength of bluegills and largemouth bass in Ohio reservoirs as dictated by gizzard shad abundance, zooplankton productivity, and relative spawning of gizzard shad and bluegills. In the first possibility, shad appear in the limnetic zone before bluegills; in the second possibility this is reversed. Source: Stein et al. (1995).

more large adult bluegills, but the proportion with large bluegills was unrelated to macrophyte cover.

The Perfect Bluegill Pond

Each little puddle of water is unique; confounding variables are as numerous as stars and just as mysterious, and most of us cling desperately to incomplete information in the unrealized hope that it might actually be useful. Still, if I had the knowledge, money, location, and authority to design, build, and maintain a perfect bluegill pond it would have some of these characteristics. I can picture this pond in my mind's eye and now transfer that image to you along with my reasoning. Fishing, of course, is the classic waste of time, but actually getting ready to fish can keep you pretty busy.

The perfect pond is located in the American South where fishing is comfortable all year. The banks are high to snag breezes and keep out runoff from the pasture. I made sure they were blanketed with thick soft grass and flat on top, convenient places to sit or stand while fishing or even take a nap, weather and angling pressure permitting. The banks are unobstructed, making it easy to throw a fly line. The only object is a large live oak at one end of the pond to provide shade where a couple of anglers might sit with cane poles and bobbers and a can of worms between them on hot summer afternoons. Sure, fly fishing is best, but no bluegill angler can completely discount the value of an active worm. The setting is quiet and bucolic, no highways with snorting diesels or sand hills for dirt bikers, not even a gravel road. You must walk to get there. For companionship I have some cows, each attended by its personal cattle egret, and the oak is loud with birds at dawn and dusk.

The submerged banks slope steeply away with exception of a few narrow stone shelves no deeper than 1 m, stone so no plants can grow on them. The bluegills need level places to spawn, but not too many places. I want the strong and fit to survive; I want only a few good bluegills as apparently exist at Ketona Lakes. The stands of macrophytes drop off quickly because of the steep banks, forming a mere fringe like a monk's haircut and less than 3 m wide. Once again, I want the bluegills to survive—some of them. Eurasian water milfoil, hydrilla, and water hyacinth are nowhere present, nor is any emergent vegetation like cattails and reeds. I have nothing against these last-named plants except their incompatibility with a moving fly line.

Adult bluegills are protected through the breeding season, except on days my friends and I try for the state record. Otherwise we keep the little ones and eat them for supper. Eighty years ago anglers were thought to be the worst enemy of nesting males,[1278] and little has changed. A biologist writing in 1947 advised fishing over active nests, "Since this has been going on for generations and the bluegills appear not to have suffered, it is not to be condemned as bad conservation."[1279] The author continued: "In fact, without some curb there are likely to be too many small fish." We know now that angling over nests is indeed destructive to the size structure of populations, and removing large males only encourages the proliferation of smaller fish.

Protracted reproduction (Chapter 6) appears to be an evolutionary mechanism for enhanced survival in unstable environments.[1280] The roller coaster life history of bluegills is evidence that effective management should be based on the full spectrum of their biology and behavior, not just annual recruitment, size- or age-related growth, nest counts, and other traditional tools of fishery management. Fry that hatch from late-summer spawns often make important contributions to their age-classes.[1281] Consequently, to reduce the incidence of stunting all breeding adults, but territorial males especially,[1282] are off-limits to anglers so long as they occupy nests, if necessary from early spring through autumn.[1283] One model shows that varying angling regulations, including catch limits, has little effect, and only closing the season to nesting fish stretches the size structure so that many large bluegills remain available.[1284] An extended size structure in a bluegill population can take years to recover after prolonged exploitation.[1285] Stunting has undesirable effects on other species. For example, an abundance of small bluegills suppresses the growth of northern pike.[1286]

Age-related mortality is high for bluegills that have outgrown the gape of all but the biggest predators, but so is their natural mortality even in waters with low angling pressure. Estimates of both yield and size structure in 18 Nebraska Sandhill lakes rose with hypothetical implementation of a 200-mm TL limit.[1287] Exploitation of bluegills in excess of 200 mm was already low (~10% of the annual mortality), and results were compared with the existing situation (no size limit). The model showed a decline in yield of 39%; the number removed dropped 62%. Bluegills in these lakes would need to reach 200 mm in 4.2 years to sustain no losses.

Large numbers of cuckolding males are not inevitable. They might actually be typical of crowded waters, although this is simply conjecture. Par Pond, a nuclear reactor cooling reservoir in South Carolina, has never been open for angling.[1288] During the early 1990s bluegills ranged from ages 1–9 and 37–278 mm TL. Rapid growth occurred to age-4 (~240 mm TL) after which little increase in size was apparent; males and females were not significantly different in length-at-age from ages 1–5. In comparison, growth in regularly fished waters in the southeastern U.S. demonstrated decreasing rates of growth with age, not the two phases evident in Par Pond. Bluegills at Par Pond generally grew faster and larger than the others and at ages 2–4 were significantly larger. Reproduction occurred at larger size and greater age. Those less than 175 mm TL were seldom mature, not starting to spawn until 175–215 mm TL, and by 235 mm TL they were all mature. Distribution of reproductive males was unimodal ($\bar{x}$ = 257 mm TL), indicating the absence of cuckolders; for females, the mean size was 243 mm TL. The concentration of juveniles averaged 0.52/m², considerably less than the littoral zone of Lawrence Lake (1.6/m²)[1289] and most other northern waters.

Largemouth bass at Par Pond averaged 420 mm TL (0.84 kg),[1290] exceeding by a wide margin the specimens of 300–380 mm TL that normally occur in southeastern lakes and ponds.[1291] Par Pond bass were 10–30% larger and 3–4× more abundant than in other lakes. At 35 kg/ha their collective mass, or standing crop, was also greater compared with the mean of 11.2 kg/ha for 22 public lakes in Georgia.

Angling regulations at my perfect pond? I mentioned the breeding adults. You can keep any small bluegill and any largemouth bass bigger than 300 mm TL (round that off to 12 in). Waters where angling is not allowed can simultaneously support size-structured populations of bluegills and bass, but this is doubtfully possible in lakes and ponds that are fished. Still, we have to try.

Thinning the macrophytes would not be necessary. The steep banks keep them from marching into the center of the pond. Effects of herbicides on aquatic macrophytes are usually temporary.[1292] Their extended application to reduce bluegill recruitment and enhance predation by largemouth bass is probably a bad idea. Long-term effects on humans and the environment of such compounds as fluoridone are unknown.[1293] Plants die after poisoning instead of being consumed, and where herbicides are applied regularly the masses of dead and dying vegetation degrade into low-density silt that blankets the benthos and billows to the surface at the slightest disturbance. Steadily increasing turbidity induces negative effects with no discernible upside.

Fishery managers seem generally disinclined to use biological controls, but these are the best permanent solutions. Triploid grass carp consume aquatic vegetation relentlessly, apparently without impact on bluegills or largemouth bass (presumably their nests) unless the vegetation has been consumed entirely.[1294] Success in their use has ranged from unimpressive[1295] through confusing[1296] and inconsistent[1297] to excessive.[1298] The objective should be the control of vegetation, not its eradication, and initial low stocking is preferable. The grass carp typically offered by producers (200–280 mm TL) are vulnerable to predation by largemouth bass of 460–510 mm TL.[1299] Stocking larger fish might improve performance and yield consistent results. A large literature exists on the grass carp, and its efficacy can undoubtedly be refined and rendered more predictable. Crayfish are far less easy to manage, especially if largemouth bass populations are low,[1300] and they should probably not be released for any reason, even to control macrophytes. Their use as bait ought to be prohibited to prevent accidental introduction.

I considered stocking shad in my pond, but only in a fleeting moment of irrationality. Managers usually stock shad as food for largemouth bass, but their effect on bluegill populations is unpredictable,[1301] and like other fecund planktivorous fishes they can quickly degrade water quality and hasten eutrophication.[1302] Threadfin shad might be preferable to gizzard shad, although their northern range is more restricted.[1303] Threadfin shad are smaller (maximum adult size ~127 mm TL)[1304] and less likely to exceed gape sizes of typical piscine predators. Largemouth bass, for example, feed preferentially on age-1 gizzard shad (up to ~226 g).[1305] Threadfin shad reproduce from spring into summer in Alabama,[1306] but not until August in Ohio, or after most of the bluegills have spawned for the final time.[1307] Unlike the situation with gizzard shad larvae, the delayed reproduction of threadfin shad might mute direct competition with larval bluegills. Nonetheless, threadfin shad in Ohio reservoirs exerted a negative effect overall by still competing with bluegill larvae for zooplankton,[1308] reducing their survivorship, and, in a domino effect, lowering the survivorship of age-0 largemouth bass. Anyway, I want the bass to keep the number of small bluegills under control and remain undeterred from this purpose.

Water in the pond is clear, making it easy to watch the bluegills spawning in spring. Reducing the phytoplankton biomass improves water clarity, but this is seldom successful without simultaneously reducing the biomass of planktivorous fishes. Gizzard shad and turbidity are closely linked. Ultimately, water clarity depends on whether the relationship between the biomasses of the fishes and the phytoplankton is linear or sigmoid.[1309] If linear then reducing piscine planktivores will improve clarity, if sigmoid it will not. The relationship was sigmoid in experiments with captive gizzard shad. Turbidity in lakes and ponds likely will not improve until enough shad have been removed to allow zooplankton to increase and nutrient concentrations to decline.[1310] Before this can happen the biomass of gizzard shad would need to be lowered to less than 10 g/m^3, or below 200 kg/ha. Whether this can be achieved and subsequently maintained is questionable.

In designing this pond I took a top-down approach. Angling lakes have traditionally been managed using a bottom-up approach.[1311] Where turbidity and related water quality factors are of no concern, eutrophication is often induced by addition of fertilizers to enhance productivity.[1312] Phosphorus is usually the limiting nutrient.[1313] The purpose of fertilization is to increase phytoplankton production, which in turn increases the zooplankton biomass. The positive association between these factors is undeniable,[1314] and the biomass of phytoplankton again increases as zooplankters are cropped by burgeoning numbers of planktivorous fishes.[1315] Sometimes the result is a jump in the zooplankton population without an accompanying change in chlorophyll *a*.[1316] In the case of bluegills, adults shift foraging activities from the littoral zone to the limnos, causing large zooplankters to decline (Chapter 3).

Fish predation affects zooplankton populations (Chapter 3), but so does phytoplankton abundance. Stimulating this bottom-up effect to grow more zooplankters for bluegill food is the purpose of spiking with nutrients.[1317] Nitrogen as NH_4NO_3 and phosphorus as KH_2PO_4 added to enclosures in Dynamite Lake, Illinois, to produce nitrogen concentrations of 21.43 mmol/L and phosphorus concentrations of 0.32 mmol/L yielded 10× more water fleas (genera *Ceriodaphnia* and *Diaphanosoma*) than untreated controls. This N:P ratio of 30 mirrored the natural ratio in the lake. Nutrient enrichment also increased populations of the rotifers *Monostyla bulla* and *Lecane luna*.

Fertilizers are also suggested for killing submerged macrophytes by denying them light.[1318] According to this procedure, thick blooms of phytoplankton turn the pond green with phytoplankton, occluding downward illumination. The advice urges applying fertilizers directly over weed beds starting early in spring, then continuing applications every 2–4 weeks until the plants become blanketed with filamentous algae, die, and start to decay. As their stems break, "Large masses of floating, decaying weeds and 'scum' are present in the pond until the spring and early summer."[1319] Grass carp or long rakes would obviously be useful then. Granular fertilizer is broadcast along the water's edge or from a boat. The source just cited recommended 18 kg/ha of 6–8–4 (nitrogen-phosphorus-potassium) in addition to 4.5 kg of sodium nitrate.[1320] Another source suggested 45 kg/ha of 20–20–5 (nitrogen-phosphorus-potassium).[1321]

Powerful top-down effects have been reported in complex marine ecosystems along with advice to manage the fishes instead of the nutrients.[1322] Recent limnological evidence also points to an important top-down effect on lacustrine food webs starting with piscivorous fishes, which control the biomass of planktivorous fishes.[1323] These, in turn, ultimately affect phytoplankton populations through shifts in the numbers and sizes of zooplankters, and the results are most pronounced in eutrophic lakes.[1324] Nutrient concentrations change community structure at every level.[1325] Rising phosphorus concentrations in 71 shallow Danish lakes caused a significant drop in the species diversity of zooplankton and submerged macrophytes. Low phosphorus concentrations were associated with increased abundance of piscivorous fishes and a high ratio of piscivorous/planktivorous fishes. Large-bodied zooplankters dominated, and their biomass ratio to that of phytoplankters was high. Phytoplankton biomass was low, and submerged macrophytes were abundant. Keeping planktivorous fishes in check—including bluegills—improves a lake's environmental quality. I have no intention of fertilizing, and if the macrophytes should ever get out of control I plan to add a few grass carp.

I installed a short dock where I tie up the rowboat, and beside the dock is a small beach where you can wade into the water and take a swim on a hot day. Watch out for alligators. I keep this area free of weeds. Aquatic vegetation is often considered a nuisance, although it improves water clarity by stabilizing sediments, intercepting runoff from the land, and absorbing nutrients that might otherwise promote algal growth.[1326] Fishes that rely on nearshore vegetation for spawning or growth can be affected adversely when efforts are undertaken to remove too much of it for boating, swimming, and construction of docks and beaches.[1327] But it will never happen at this pond.

Endnotes

Preface

1. Hoffman (1999).
2. Gilbert (1998); Catalog of Fishes, California Academy of Sciences, http://www.calacademy.org/re
   search/ichthyology/catalog/fishcatsearch.html
3. Bailey et al. (2004), Eddy and Surber (1947), Etnier and Starnes (1993), Gerking (1955), Harlan and
   Speaker (1969), Hubbs et al. (2004), Minckley (1973), Page and Burr (1991), Pflieger (1975), Robison
   and Buchanan (1988?), Ross (2001), Smith-Vaniz (1968), Wydoski and Whitney (1979).
4. Ross (2001), Scott and Crossman (1998).
5. Nelson et al. (2004).
6. Ogburn, C. (1966:70).
7. Beckman (1945).

Chapter 1

8. Young (2005).
9. Zhu et al. (2002).
10. Gibb et al. (1994).
11. Drucker and Lauder (1999).
12. Drucker and Lauder (1999).
13. Drucker and Lauder (1999).
14. Gibb et al. (1994).
15. Gibb et al. (1994).
16. Gibb et al. (1994).
17. Drucker and Lauder (1999).
18. Gibb et al. (1994).
19. Drucker and Lauder (1999).
20. Drucker and Lauder (1999).
21. Gibb et al. (1994).
22. Drucker and Lauder (1999).
23. Lauder (2000).
24. Dickinson (1996).
25. Drucker and Lauder (1999).
26. Gibb et al. (1994).

27. Drucker and Lauder (1999).
28. Gibb et al. (1994).
29. Lauder (2000).
30. Lauder (2000).
31. Lauder (2000).
32. Lauder (2000:116, Fig. 14).
33. Lauder et al. (2002).
34. Lauder et al. (2002).
35. Lauder et al. (2002).
36. Lauder et al. (2002).
37. Zhu et al. (2002).
38. Drucker and Lauder (2001).
39. Lauder et al. (2002).
40. Standen and Lauder (2005).
41. Jayne et al. (1996).
42. Lauder et al. (2002).
43. Drucker and Lauder (2001).
44. Drucker and Lauder (2001), Jayne et al. (1996).
45. Drucker and Lauder (2001), Jayne et al. (1996).
46. Drucker and Lauder (2001).
47. Drucker and Lauder (2001).
48. Drucker and Lauder (2001).
49. Standen and Lauder (2005).
50. Drucker and Lauder (2001).
51. Drucker and Lauder (2001:433).
52. Lauder et al. (2002).
53. Higham et al. (2005a), Webb (1984).
54. Higham et al. (2005b).
55. Jayne et al. (1996).
56. Breder (1926).

Chapter 2

57. Kalmijn (1989).
58. Engelmann et al. (2000), Kalmijn (1989).
59. Kalmijn (1989).
60. Engelmann et al. (2000), Kalmijn (1989).
61. Bassett et al. (2006).
62. Montgomery et al. (1997).
63. Engelmann et al. (2000).
64. Kalmijn (1989), Popper et al. (2003).
65. Kalmijn (1989).
66. Popper et al. (2003).
67. Popper et al. (2003).
68. Kalmijn (1989).
69. Kalmijn (1989).
70. Kalmijn (1989).
71. Popper and Platt (1993).
72. Denton and Gray (1989), Enger et al. (1989), Kalmijn (1989).
73. Kalmijn (1988).
74. Kalmijn (1989).
75. Kalmijn (1989).
76. Müller et al. (1997).

77. Hanke and Bleckmann (2004).
78. Hanke and Bleckmann (2004), Hanke et al. (2000).
79. Pohlmann et al. (2001).
80. Hanke and Bleckmann (2004).
81. Hanke and Bleckmann (2004).
82. Kalmijn (1989).
83. Tou (1991).
84. See references in Bleckmann (1994:49-65).
85. New et al. (2001).
86. Margenau et al. (1998).
87. Kalmijn (1988, 1989).
88. Kalmijn (1989).
89. Enger et al. (1989).
90. Kalmijn (1988).
91. Helfman (1981).
92. Janssen et al. (1995).
93. Janssen and Corcoran (1993).
94. Popper et al. (2003).
95. Brackenbury (2001, 2004)
96. Popper et al. (2003).
97. Popper and Platt (1993).
98. Popper et al. (2003), Schellart and Wubbels (1998).
99. See references in Scholik and Yan (2002).
100. Yan et al. (2000), but see Popper et al. (2003:13-15).
101. Popper et al. (2003).
102. Popper and Fay (1973).
103. Popper et al. (2003:18)
104. Breck and Gitter (1983), Li et al. (1985), Tamura and Wisby (1963), Walton et al. (1994, 1997).
105. Breck and Gitter (1983), Hairston et al. (1982).
106. Breck and Gitter (1983).
107. Breck and Gitter (1983).
108. Luo and Brandt (1994).
109. Tamura and Wisby (1963).
110. Williamson and Keast (1988).
111. Hairston et al. (1982).
112. Breck and Gitter (1983), Hairston et al. (1982).
113. Hairston et al. (1982).
114. Breck and Gitter (1983).
115. Breck and Gitter (1983).
116. Breck and Gitter (1983).
117. Confer and Blades (1975a).
118. Breck and Gitter (1983).
119. Gardner (1981b).
120. Williamson and Keast (1988).
121. Luecke and O'Brien (1981), O'Brien et al. (1985).
122. Sivak (1973).
123. Mittelbach (1981b), Sarker (1977), Shoup et al. (2004).
124. Williamson and Keast (1988).
125. Williamson and Keast (1988).
126. Sivak (1973).
127. Luecke and O'Brien (1981).
128. Miner and Stein (1996).
129. Miner and Stein (1993).
130. Vinyard and O'Brien (1976).

131. Claramunt and Wahl (2000).
132. Luecke and O'Brien (1981).
133. Luecke and O'Brien (1981).
134. Muntz (1975).
135. Douglas and Hawryshyn (1990)
136. Lythgoe (1979).
137. Lythgoe (1979).
138. Muntz (1975).
139. Kawamura and Shimowada (1993).
140. Lythgoe (1966).
141. Levine and MacNichol (1982).
142. Douglas and Hawryshyn (1990).
143. Hawryshyn et al. (1988).
144. Levine and MacNichol (1982).
145. Douglas and Hawryshyn (1990).
146. Chou and Hawryshyn (1987).
147. Hawryshyn et al. (1988).
148. For example, Vinyard and O'Brien (1976).
149. Hawryshyn et al. (1988).
150. Hawryshyn et al. (1988).
151. Breck and Gitter (1983).
152. Hawryshyn et al. (1988).
153. Hawryshyn et al. (1988).
154. Walton et al. (1997).

Chapter 3

155. Egertson and Downing (2004).
156. Keast (1978b), Keast and Webb (1966).
157. Desselle et al. (1978).
158. Figiel and Semlitsch (1990), Werschkul and Christensen (1977).
159. Applegate (1966).
160. Gerking (1962).
161. Forbes and Richardson (1920).
162. Engel (1987).
163. Seaburg and Moyle (1964).
164. Keast (1985b).
165. Hildebrand and Towers (1927).
166. Kitchell and Windell (1970).
167. Gerking (1962).
168. Engel (1987), Keast (1978a).
169. Yonekura et al. (2002).
170. Crossman (1976).
171. Scott and Crossman (1998).
172. Helfman (1981).
173. Peterson et al. (1993).
174. Musselman et al. (1995).
175. Desselle et al. (1978).
176. Desselle et al. (1978).
177. Tomasso and Grosell (2005).
178. Murdy et al. (1997).
179. Bailey et al. (1954).
180. Swift et al. (1977).
181. Renfro (1960).

182. Keast and Webb (1966).
183. Dewey et al. (1997), Sadzikowski and Wallace (1976).
184. Gerking (1962), Keast (1978a, 1978b).
185. Keast (1978a).
186. Breck (1993).
187. Mittelbach (1984).
188. Keast (1978a).
189. Lauder (1980).
190. Lauder (1980).
191. Lauder (1980).
192. Carroll et al. (2004).
193. Lauder (1980).
194. Carroll et al. (2004).
195. Higham et al. (2005a).
196. Coble et al. (1985).
197. Kieffer and Colgan (1992).
198. Brown and Colgan (1986).
199. Brown and Colgan (1986).
200. Dugatkin and Wilson (1992, 1994), but see the rebuttal of Lamprecht and Hofer (1994).
201. Wildhaber and Crowder (1995).
202. Vince et al. (1976).
203. Stoner (1982).
204. Werner and Hall (1974).
205. Bartell (1982), O'Brien et al. (1976), Werner and Hall (1974).
206. Bartell (1982), O'Brien et al. (1976), Werner and Hall (1974).
207. Mittelbach (1981b), Werner (1974).
208. Mittelbach (1981b).
209. Rettig and Mittelbach (2002).
210. Shiozawa and Barnes (1977).
211. Mittelbach (1981b).
212. Harrel and Dibble (2001), Mittelbach (1981b).
213. Harrel and Dibble (2001).
214. Walton et al. (1992).
215. Catania and Remple (2005).
216. Mittelbach (1981b).
217. Gardner (1981b), Werner and Hall (1974).
218. Eggers (1977), Miller et al. (1988).
219. Werner and Hall (1974).
220. Wetterer and Bishop (1985), Wright and O'Brien (1982).
221. Wright and O'Brien (1982).
222. O'Brien et al. (1979).
223. O'Brien et al. (1979).
224. Confer and Blades (1975a, 1975b), Giguère and Northcote (1987).
225. Wright and O'Brien (1982).
226. Giguère and Northcote (1987).
227. McFarland and Munz (1975).
228. Duffy et al. (2005).
229. Pyke (1984).
230. Li et al. (1985).
231. Butler and Bence (1984).
232. Gardner (1981b), Werner and Hall (1974), Werner et al. (1983a).
233. Mittelbach (1981b).
234. See Ehlinger (1990).
235. Breck (1993).

236. Mittelbach (1983).
237. Mittelbach (1981b).
238. Harrel and Dibble (2001), Mittelbach (1981b), Walton et al. (1992).
239. Gerking (1962), Harrel and Dibble (2001), Keast (1978b), Mittelbach (1981b), Walton et al. (1997), Werner et al. (1983a).
240. Mittelbach (1981b).
241. Harrel and Dibble (2001).
242. Seaburg and Moyle (1964).
243. Keast (1978b).
244. Keast (1978b).
245. Keast (1978b).
246. Drucker and Lauder (1999).
247. Keast and Welsh (1968).
248. Mittelbach (1981b).
249. Harrel and Dibble (2001).
250. Mittelbach (1984).
251. Garvey et al. (2002).
252. Breck (1993).
253. Garvey et al. (2002).
254. Breck (1993:477).
255. DeVries et al. (1989).
256. Wildhaber et al. (1994).
257. Wildhaber and Crowder (1990, 1991).
258. Wildhaber et al. (1994).
259. Werner et al. (1981).
260. Wildhaber and Crowder (1991).
261. Wildhaber et al. (1994).
262. Gunning and Shoop (1963).
263. Fish and Savitz (1983).
264. Paukert et al. (2004).
265. Hasler et al. (1958).
266. Goodyear and Bennett (1979).
267. Wildhaber and Crowder (1990).
268. Wildhaber and Crowder (1990).
269. Wildhaber and Crowder (1990).
270. Wildhaber (2001).
271. Wildhaber (2001).
272. O'Brien et al. (1976), Walton et al. (1992), Wetterer and Bishop (1985).
273. Butler and Bence (1984).
274. Butler and Bence (1984).
275. Wright and O'Brien (1984).
276. O'Brien et al. (1985).
277. Butler and Bence (1984).
278. Li et al. (1985).
279. Wetterer (1989).
280. Werner and Hall (1974).
281. Mittelbach (1981b), Werner et al. (1983a).
282. Li et al. (1985).
283. Walton et al. (1997).
284. Walton et al. (1997).
285. Li et al. (1985).
286. Douglas et al. (1988).
287. Wetterer and Bishop (1985).
288. Wetterer and Bishop (1985).

289. Walton et al. (1992).
290. Wetterer and Bishop (1985).
291. Hawryshyn et al. (1988).
292. Gardner (1981b).
293. Mittelbach (1981b).
294. Walton et al. (1997).
295. Walton et al. (1992).
296. Hambright et al. (1991).
297. Li et al. (1985).
298. Walton et al. (1992).
299. O'Brien et al. (1985).
300. O'Brien et al. (1976).
301. Walton et al. (1992).
302. Walton et al. (1992).
303. Khadka and Ramakrishna (1986).
304. O'Brien et al. (1985).
305. Wetterer (1989).
306. Eggers (1982), Wetterer and Bishop (1985).
307. Hairston et al. (1982).
308. Butler and Bence (1984).
309. Wetterer (1989).
310. Eggers (1982), Werner and Hall (1974), Wetterer and Bishop (1985).
311. Butler and Bence (1984).
312. Wetterer (1989).
313. Eggers (1982).
314. Luo and Brandt (1994).
315. Gardner (1981b).
316. Luo and Brandt (1994).
317. Eggers (1977).
318. Gardner (1981b).
319. Gardner (1981b).
320. Gardner (1981a, 1981b).
321. Gardner (1981b).
322. Butler and Bence (1984).
323. Butler and Bence (1984).
324. Wetterer and Bishop (1985).
325. Janssen (1982), O'Brien et al. (1985), Wright and O'Brien (1982).
326. Brewer and Coughlin (1995).
327. Tsuda et al. (1998), Tucker and Woolpy (1984), Zaret (1980).
328. Confer and Blades (1975b).
329. O'Brien et al. (1979), Zaret (1972).
330. Bando (1993).
331. Douglas and Hawryshyn (1990).
332. O'Brien et al. (1985).
333. O'Brien et al. (1985).
334. Eggers (1977).
335. Wright and O'Brien (1984).
336. Confer and Blades (1975a).
337. Wright and O'Brien (1984).
338. Vinyard (1980).
339. Nowlin and Drenner (2000).
340. Eggers (1977).
341. Li and Li (1979).
342. Swaffar and O'Brien (1996).

343. Kolar and Wahl (1998).
344. Kacelnik and Marsh (2002).
345. Pompilio et al. (2006).
346. Kacelnik and Marsh. (2002).
347. Kacelnik and Marsh (2002).
348. Pompilio et al. (2006).
349. Luo and Brandt (1994).
350. DeVries et al. (1989).
351. Marschall et al. (1989).
352. Vinyard (1980).
353. Keast (1978a).
354. Keast and Welsh (1968).
355. Keast and Welsh (1968).
356. Sarker (1977).
357. Sarker (1977).
358. Dewey et al. (1997).
359. Petraitis (1979).
360. Seaburg and Moyle (1964).
361. Helfman (1981).
362. Werner et al. (1977).
363. Mittelbach (1981b).
364. Killgore et al. (1989).
365. Beckett et al. (1992), El-Shamy (1978), Gerking (1957), Richardson et al. (1998), Rosine (1955), Schramm and Jirka (1989), Schramm et al. (1987).
366. Dionne and Folt (1991).
367. Rosine (1955).
368. Beckett et al. (1992).
369. Cyr and Downing (1988).
370. Mittelbach (1981a).
371. Keast (1977a), Mittelbach (1981a), Seaburg and Moyle (1964).
372. Mittelbach (1981a).
373. Mittelbach (1981a).
374. Mittelbach (1981b).
375. Mittelbach (1984).
376. Keast (1978b).
377. Mittelbach (1984).
378. Seaburg and Moyle (1964).
379. Mittelbach (1984).
380. Schramm and Jirka (1989).
381. Schramm and Jirka (1989).
382. Anderson et al. (1978), Benke et al. (1984, 1985), Nilsen and Larimore (1973), Thorp et al. (1985).
383. Marzolf (1978).
384. K. Marley and M. Delong, unpublished data cited in Lehtinen et al. (1997).
385. Benke et al. (1984).
386. Benke et al. (1985).
387. Benke et al. (1985).
388. Ehlinger and Wilson (1988), Janssen (1982).
389. Ehlinger (1989).
390. Ehlinger (1989).
391. Ehlinger (1990).
392. Janssen (1982).
393. Ehlinger and Wilson (1988).
394. Layzer and Clady (1987).
395. Ehlinger (1990), Ehlinger and Wilson (1988).

396. Ehlinger and Wilson (1988).
397. Ehlinger and Wilson (1988), Yonekura et al. (2002).
398. Wilson et al. (1996).
399. Yonekura et al. (2002).
400. Smith et al. (1999).
401. Werner and McPeek (1994).
402. Mittelbach and Osenberg (1993), Smith et al. (1999), Vanni (1987).
403. Werner et al. (1977).
404. Mittelbach (1981b).
405. Werner et al. (1977).
406. Haney and Hall (1975), Osenberg et al. (1988).
407. Mittelbach (1981b), Mittelbach and Osenberg (1993).
408. Dawidowicz et al. (1990), Zaret and Suffern (1976).
409. Partridge and DeVries (1999), Siefert (1972).
410. Gilbert (1988).
411. Carpenter et al. (1985).
412. Mittelbach and Osenberg (1993), Vanni (1987), Walton et al. (1992).
413. Vanni (1987).
414. Vanni (1987).
415. Vanni (1987).
416. Vanni (1987).
417. Mittelbach and Osenberg (1993).
418. Taylor and Hendricks (1987); also see Mather et al. (1995).
419. Drenner et al. (1990).
420. Mather et al. (1995).
421. Brown and Ball (1942).

Chapter 4

422. Keast (1978a).
423. Harrel and Dibble (2001).
424. Harrel and Dibble (2001).
425. Mittelbach (1984), Werner and Hall (1988).
426. Mittelbach (1984), Osenberg et al. (1988, 1992).
427. Mittelbach and Osenberg (1993).
428. Mittelbach and Osenberg (1993).
429. Werner and Hall (1988).
430. Werner and Hall (1988).
431. Osenberg et al. (1992).
432. Werner and Hall (1988).
433. Clady (1974), Murphy (1949).
434. Keast (1978a).
435. Kramer and Smith (1962).
436. Werner and Hall (1988).
437. Werner and Hall (1988).
438. Werner and Hall (1988).
439. Brenden and Murphy (2004).
440. Olson et al. (1995).
441. Werner and Hall (1988).
442. Werner and Hall (1988).
443. Werner and Hall (1979).
444. Mittelbach (1981b).
445. Werner and Hall (1988).
446. Kolehmainen (1974).

447. Dewey et al. (1997).
448. Cloe and Garman (1996).
449. Claramunt and Wahl (2000).
450. Rettig (1998).
451. Layzer and Clady (1987).
452. Conrow et al. (1990).
453. Werner and Hall (1988).
454. Werner and Hall (1988).
455. Werner and Hall (1988).
456. Keast and Fox (1992).
457. Mittelbach (1984), Osenberg et al. (1988), Sadzikowski and Wallace (1976).
458. Keast (1978b), Mittelbach (1984).
459. Osenberg et al. (1988).
460. Mittelbach and Osenberg (1993).
461. Mittelbach (1988).
462. Osenberg et al. (1992).
463. Werner and Hall (1979).
464. Werner and Hall (1976, 1979).
465. Werner and Hall (1976).
466. Werner and Hall (1979).
467. Werner and Hall (1979).
468. Keast (1978a).
469. Keast (1978b).
470. Keast (1978a).
471. Keast (1977b, 1978b).
472. Keast (1978a).
473. Schoener (1970).
474. Mittelbach (1984).
475. Mittelbach (1984).
476. Mittelbach (1984).
477. Mittelbach (1984).
478. Mittelbach (1984).
479. Werner and Hall (1976).
480. Werner and Hall (1977).
481. Werner et al. (1983a).
482. Hall and Werner (1977).
483. Keast (1978a).
484. Partridge and DeVries (1999).
485. Toetz (1966).
486. Breck (1993).
487. Werner (1974).
488. Breck (1993).
489. Bremigan and Stein (1994).
490. Rettig and Mittelbach (2002).
491. Rettig and Mittelbach (2002).
492. Paszkowski (1986).
493. Keast (1985a).
494. See the discussion in Keast (1985a).
495. Keast (1985a).
496. Keast (1968).
497. Keast (1977b).
498. Keast 1978a)
499. Keast (1985a).
500. Keast (1977a).

501. Keast (1985a).
502. Margenau et al. (1998).
503. Keast (1978a).
504. Werner et al. (1977).
505. Keast (1985a). Also see Amundrud et al. (1974).
506. Swisher et al. (1998).
507. Osenberg et al. (1992).
508. Osenberg et al. (1992).
509. Osenberg et al. (1992).
510. Wainwright et al. (1991).
511. Osenberg et al. (1992).
512. VanderKooy et al. (2000).
513. VanderKooy et al. (2000).
514. Horn (1966).
515. VanderKooy et al. (2000).
516. Pace et al. (1998).
517. Raikow (2004).
518. Pace et al. (1998).
519. Petranka and Fakhoury (1991).
520. McPeek (1989).
521. Petranka and Fakhoury (1991).
522. Blois-Heulin et al. (1990).
523. Resetarits (2001).
524. Werschkul and Christensen (1977).
525. Semlitsch (1987).
526. Figiel and Semlitsch (1990).
527. Smith et al. (1999), Werner and McPeek (1994).
528. Smith et al. (1999).

Chapter 5

529. Hambright et al. (1991), Lawrence (1958).
530. Ricker (1945).
531. Ricker (1945).
532. Mundahl et al. (1998).
533. Schneider and Lockwood (2002).
534. Keast (1978a).
535. Otis et al. (1998).
536. Belk and Hales (1993), Trebitz et al. (1997).
537. Belk and Hales (1993).
538. Seaburg and Moyle (1964).
539. Margenau et al. (1998).
540. Ricker (1945).
541. Burke (2006). The whopper that wasn't. New York *Times* website, 28. March. [http://
     www.nytimes.com/2006/03/28/opinion/28burke.html?_r=1&oref-slogin]
542. Hambright et al. (1991).
543. Keast (1978a).
544. Keast (1978a).
545. Dewey et al. (1997).
546. Santucci and Wahl (2003).
547. Webb (1986).
548. Hambright et al. (1991).
549. Webb (1986).
550. Moody et al. (1983), Webb (1986).

551. Webb (1986).
552. Heidinger (1975).
553. Webb (1986).
554. Einfalt and Wahl (1997).
555. Hoyle and Keast (1987, 1988).
556. Savino and Stein (1989b).
557. Nyberg (1971).
558. Savitz and Janssen (1982).
559. Hoyle and Keast (1987).
560. Paukert et al. (2004).
561. Meesters (1940).
562. Desselle et al. (1978).
563. Margenau et al. (1998).
564. Tomcko et al. (1984), Wahl and Stein (1988).
565. Wahl and Stein (1988).
566. Tomcko and Pierce (2005).
567. Savitz and Janssen (1982).
568. Keast (1978a).
569. Einfalt and Wahl (1997).
570. Einfalt and Wahl (1997).
571. Margenau et al. (1998).
572. Coble (1973).
573. Mauck and Coble (1971).
574. Moody et al. (1983).
575. Wahl and Stein (1988).
576. Savitz and Janssen (1982).
577. Wahl and Stein (1988).
578. Savino and Stein (1989b).
579. Einfalt and Wahl (1997), Howick and O'Brien (1983), Moody et al. (1983), Savino and Stein (1989a).
580. Savino and Stein (1989b).
581. Chipps et al. (2004).
582. Lawrence (1958).
583. Hoyle and Keast (1988), Lawrence (1958).
584. Hoyle and Keast (1987).
585. Hoyle and Keast (1987).
586. Savitz and Janssen (1982).
587. Pierce et al. (2001).
588. Gotceitas (1990), Hall and Werner (1977), Mittelbach (1981a, 1981b), Werner et al. (1983b).
589. Werner et al. (1983b).
590. Gotceitas (1990).
591. Gotceitas and Colgan (1987).
592. Gotceitas and Colgan (1990).
593. Werner and Hall (1988).
594. Werner and Hall (1988).
595. Egertson and Downing (2004).
596. Annett (1998).
597. Annett (1998).
598. Ostrand et al. (2004).
599. Anderson (1984), Annett (1998), Savino and Stein (1982, 1989a).
600. Savino and Stein (1989a).
601. Savino and Stein (1989a).
602. Anderson (1984), Savino and Stein (1982, 1989a), Werner et al. (1983b).
603. Savino and Stein (1982).
604. Sheldon and Boylen (1977).

605. Savino and Stein (1989a).
606. Savino and Stein (1989a).
607. Savino and Stein (1989b).
608. Wahl and Stein (1988).
609. Engel (1987).
610. Gotceitas and Colgan (1987).
611. Savino and Stein (1982).
612. Hayse and Wissing (1996).
613. Engel (1987).
614. Valley and Bremigan (2002).
615. Valley and Bremigan (2002).
616. Butler (1988).

Chapter 6

617. Roff (1984).
618. Gross (1982, 1991), Keast (1977b).
619. Belk (1995), Belk and Hales (1993).
620. Belk and Hales (1993).
621. Swingle and Smith (1942).
622. Krumholz (1946).
623. Belk (1998).
624. Belk (1995, 1998).
625. Belk (1995).
626. Roff (1984).
627. Belk and Hales (1993).
628. Gross (1982).
629. Belk (1998).
630. Keast (1978a).
631. James (1946).
632. Bulow et al. (1981).
633. Rohde et al. (1994).
634. Belk (1995).
635. Robison and Buchanan (1988?).
636. Rohde et al. (1994).
637. Miller (1963).
638. Swift et al. (1977).
639. Pflieger (1975).
640. Phillips et al. (1982).
641. Miller and Robison (2004).
642. Simon (1951).
643. Storck et al. (1978).
644. Churchill and Over (1933).
645. Harlan and Speaker (1969).
646. La Rivers (1994).
647. McGinnis (1984).
648. Simpson and Wallace (1982).
649. Minckley (1973).
650. Avila (1976).
651. Partridge and DeVries (1999).
652. Swingle and Smith (1942).
653. Clark and Keenleyside (1967).
654. Breder and Rosen (1966), Clark and Keenleyside (1967).
655. Clark and Keenleyside (1967).

656. Clarke at al. (1984).
657. Ballantyne and Colgan (1978a), Clarke et al. (1984).
658. Clarke et al. (1984), Hinch and Collins (1993).
659. Clark and Keenleyside (1967).
660. Miller (1963).
661. Clark and Keenleyside (1967), Miller (1963).
662. Dorn and Mittelbach (2004), Gross and MacMillan (1981), Richardson (1913).
663. Gross (1982), Gross and Charnov (1980).
664. Coggeshall (1924).
665. Gross and MacMillan (1981).
666. Gross and MacMillan (1981).
667. Colgan et al. (1979).
668. Ingram and Odum (1941), Miller (1963).
669. Avila (1976), Miller (1963).
670. Clark and Keenleyside (1967).
671. Clark and Keenleyside (1967), Richardson (1913).
672. Breder (1936).
673. Clark and Keenleyside (1967).
674. Breder (1936).
675. Coggeshall (1924), Gross and MacMillan (1981), Richardson (1913).
676. Clark and Keenleyside (1967).
677. Birdsong and Yerger (1967), Breder and Rosen (1966), King (1947), Schneider (1999).
678. Colle et al. (1987).
679. Breder (1936), Breder and Rosen (1966).
680. Coggeshall (1924).
681. Avila (1976).
682. Neff et al. (2004).
683. Avila (1976).
684. Côté and Gross (1993), Gross and MacMillan (1981).
685. Ehlinger (1999).
686. Dominey (1981a).
687. Ehlinger (1999), Neff et al. (2004).
688. Hildebrand and Towers (1927).
689. Ehlinger (1997, 1999), Gross (1982).
690. Ehlinger (1999).
691. Neff et al. (2004).
692. Gross (1991), Neff (2001).
693. Gross (1982).
694. Miller (1963).
695. Except where indicated, the nest-sweeping description is based on that of Miller (1963).
696. Avila (1976).
697. Miller (1963).
698. Miller (1963).
699. Breder (1936), Richardson (1913).
700. Breder (1936), Neff and Sherman (2005), Richardson (1913).
701. Avila (1976), Coggeshall (1924), Richardson (1913).
702. Breder (1936).
703. Dominey (1981a).
704. Gross and Charnov (1980), Neff et al. (2003).
705. Gross (1982).
706. Coleman and Fischer (1991), Gross (1982).
707. Coggeshall (1924).
708. Santucci and Wahl (2003).
709. Jennings et al. (1997).

710. Clark and Keenleyside (1967).
711. Clark and Keenleyside (1967).
712. Clark and Keenleyside (1967).
713. Dominey (1980, 1981a).
714. Clark and Keenleyside (1967).
715. Neff et al. (2003).
716. Fu et al. (2001).
717. Neff et al. (2003).
718. Avila (1976), Dominey (1980, 1981a), Miller (1963).
719. Avila (1976).
720. W. C. Dominey, personal communication in Helfman (1981).
721. Breder (1936), Noble (1934).
722. Breder (1936).
723. Avila (1976), Gross and Charnov (1980).
724. Jordan and Evermann (1963. reprint).
725. Noble (1934) proposed that sunfishes use coloration in sexual selection; Breder (1936) discounted it.
726. Hildebrand and Towers (1927).
727. Eddy and Surber (1947).
728. Eddy and Surber (1947), Neff (2003a).
729. Coggeshall (1924).
730. Coggeshall (1924).
731. Gross and MacMillan (1981).
732. Avila (1976), Miller (1963), Ballantyne and Colgan (1978a), Clarke et al. (1984), Colgan et al. (1979).
733. Ballantyne and Colgan (1978a, 1978b).
734. Ballantyne and Colgan (1978a).
735. Hubbs and Hubbs (1932:428).
736. Stacey and Chiszar (1975).
737. Ballantyne and Colgan (1978a: 128).
738. Ballantyne and Colgan (1978b).
739. Jennings et al. (1997).
740. Kindler et al. (1989).
741. Kindler et al. (1991).
742. Dominey (1981a).
743. Dominey (1980).
744. Dominey (1981a).
745. Dominey (1981a).
746. Breder (1936).
747. Swingle (1959).
748. Miller (1963).
749. Coleman and Fischer (1991).
750. Coleman and Fischer (1991).
751. Breder (1936), Miller (1963).
752. Werner et al. (1977).
753. Clark and Keenleyside (1967).
754. Dominey (1981a).
755. Clark and Keenleyside (1967).
756. Clark and Keenleyside (1967).
757. Breder (1936).
758. Breder (1936).
759. Thorpe (1963:61).
760. Wilson (1975:274). Miller (1963:111) reported habituation in nesting male pumpkinseeds, describing the desultory threats among neighbors as "ambivalent thrusts."
761. Avila (1976), Miller (1963).
762. Colgan et al. (1979).

763. Colgan et al. (1979:33).
764. Bain and Helfrich (1983).
765. Bain and Helfrich (1983).
766. Gross and MacMillan (1981).
767. Bain and Helfrich (1983), Gross and MacMillan (1981).
768. Dorn and Mittelbach (2004).
769. Bain and Helfrich (1983).
770. Gross and MacMillan (1981).
771. Dominey (1981b).
772. Coggeshall (1924).
773. Pearse (1921).
774. Elliott et al. (1997).
775. Gross and MacMillan (1981).
776. Gross and MacMillan (1981).
777. Dominey (1981a).
778. Clark and Keenleyside (1967).
779. Gross and MacMillan (1981).
780. Breder (1936:20).
781. Gross and MacMillan (1981).
782. Gross and MacMillan (1981).
783. Gross and MacMillan (1981).
784. Gross and MacMillan (1981).
785. Dominey (1981b, 1983), Gross and MacMillan (1981).
786. Dominey (1981a).
787. Gross and MacMillan (1981).
788. Gross and MacMillan (1981).
789. Pierce et al. (1987).
790. Gross and MacMillan (1981).
791. Franklin (1914).
792. Keast (1978b).
793. Côté and Gross (1993).
794. Birdsong and Yerger (1967), Breder (1936), Dawley (1987), Hubbs and Hubbs (1932), Scott and Crossman (1998), Trautman (1981).
795. Birdsong and Yerger (1967).
796. Trautman (1981).
797. Gilbert (1998).
798. Clark and Keenleyside (1967), Hubbs and Hubbs (1932).
799. Clark and Keenleyside (1967).
800. Clark and Keenleyside (1967), unpublished data cited.
801. Dawley (1987).
802. Dawley et al. (1985).
803. Dawley (1987).
804. Gross (1996).
805. Fu et al. (2001).
806. Gross (1991).
807. Dominey (1981a).
808. Taborsky (1998).
809. Dominey (1981a).
810. Gross (1991, 1996).
811. Gross (1996).
812. Neff (2004), Taborsky (1998).
813. Neff (2001).
814. Gross (1982).
815. Drake et al. (1997).

816. Drake et al. (1997).
817. Gross (1982), Gross and Charnov (1980).
818. Drake et al. (1997, Fig. 1:534).
819. Fu et al. (2001), Gross (1982), Neff et al. (2004).
820. Gross (1982).
821. Gross (1982).
822. Gross (1982).
823. Gross (1982).
824. Drake et al. (1997).
825. Dominey (1980), Gross (1982), Gross and Charnov (1980).
826. Gross (1982).
827. Dominey (1980), Gross (1982).
828. Neff et al. (2004).
829. Dominey (1980, 1981a).
830. Dominey (1981a).
831. Dominey (1980, 1981a).
832. Dominey (1981a). See, for example, Avila (1976:199-200).
833. Dominey (1980), Gross (1982). Although see Dominey (1981a).
834. Gross (1982), Neff (2001).
835. Dominey (1980, 1981a), Gross (1982), Neff et al. (2003), Neff and Gross (2001).
836. Dominey (1981a).
837. Gross (1982).
838. Fu et al. (2001), Gross (1982), Gross and Charnov (1980).
839. Gross and Charnov (1980).
840. Gross (1982).
841. Gross and Charnov (1980).
842. Dominey (1981a), Gross and Charnov (1980), Neff (2004), Taborsky (1997).
843. Gross (1982).
844. Gross (1982), Gross and Charnov (1980), Neff (2004).
845. Neff and Gross (2001).
846. Gross (1991).
847. Gross (1982).
848. Gross (1991).
849. Gross (1991).
850. Dominey (1981a), Gross (1991).
851. Gross (1982, 1991), Gross and Charnov (1980).
852. Gross (1991).
853. Drake et al. (1997).
854. Drake et al. (1997).
855. Aday et al. (2003b), Jennings et al. (1997).
856. Gross and Charnov (1980).
857. Gross (1982).
858. Parker (1970).
859. Billard (1986).
860. Billard (1986).
861. Neff et al. (2003).
862. Leach and Montgomerie (2000)
863. Leach and Montgomerie (2000).
864. Neff et al. (2003).
865. Schulte-Hostedde and Burness (2005).
866. Neff et al. (2003).
867. Neff et al. (2003).
868. Fu et al. (2001), Gross (1982, 1991), Gross and Charnov (1980), Neff et al. (2003).
869. Fu et al. (2001).

870. Fu et al. (2001).
871. Neff et al. (2003).
872. Neff et al. (2003).
873. Neff et al. (2003).
874. Fu et al. (2001).
875. Gross (1982).
876. Taborsky (1994).
877. Neff et al. (2003).
878. Fu et al. (2001).
879. Gross (1982).
880. Fu et al. (2001).
881. Neff et al. (2003).
882. Taborsky (1994).
883. Ehlinger (1997).
884. Gross (1982), Gross and Charnov (1980).
885. Ehlinger (1997).
886. Neff et al. (2003).
887. Drake et al. (1997).
888. Taborsky (1994:75-76).
889. Gross (1982).
890. Fu et al. (2001), Neff et al. (2003).
891. Neff et al. (2003).
892. Neff et al. (2003).
893. Neff et al. (2003).
894. Philipp and Gross (1994).
895. Neff (2003b).
896. Neff (2003b).
897. Coleman and Fischer (1991), Dominey (1981a).
898. Avila (1976).
899. W. C. Dominey, personal communication in Helfman (1981).
900. Coleman and Fischer (1991).
901. Gross (1982), Neff (2003b).
902. Coleman and Fischer (1991).
903. Neff (2003b).
904. Neff and Gross (2001).
905. Neff and Gross (2001).
906. Neff and Gross (2001).
907. Neff and Sherman (2003, 2005).
908. Neff (2003b).
909. Neff and Gross (2001).
910. Coleman et al. (1985).
911. Coleman et al. (1985).
912. Coleman et al. (1985).
913. Dawley (1987).
914. Taborsky (1994, 1998).
915. Neff (2004).
916. Dominey (1981a).
917. Neff (2001).
918. Gross (1982), Gross and Charnov (1980).
919. Gross (1982:11-12).
920. Belk and Hales (1993).

Chapter 7

921. Connor (1979), Hardy (1978), Kim and Park (1987), Nakamura et al. (1971), Toetz (1966).
922. Conner (1979), Holland-Bartels et al. (1990).
923. Rettig (1998).
924. Brown and Colgan (1981).
925. Kim and Park (1987).
926. Kim and Park (1987), Nakamura et al. (1971).
927. Miller et al. (1988).
928. Kim and Park (1987), Nakamura et al. (1971).
929. Nakamura et al. (1971).
930. Banner and Van Arman (1973).
931. Banner and van Arman (1973).
932. Swingle (1959).
933. Amundrud et al. (1974).
934. Kim and Park (1987).
935. Nakamura et al. (1971).
936. Krumholz (1946).
937. Bain and Helfrich (1983), Richardson (1913).
938. Kim and Park (1987).
939. Bain and Helfrich (1983).
940. Bain and Helfrich (1983), Stevenson et al. (1969).
941. Cargnelli and Gross (1996).
942. Cargnelli and Gross (1996), Garvey et al. (2002).
943. Osenberg et al. (1988).
944. Nakamura et al. (1971).
945. Nakamura et al. (1971).
946. Toetz (1966).
947. Keast (1980), Partridge and DeVries (1999).
948. Partridge and DeVries (1999), Siefert (1972).
949. Nakamura et al. (1971).
950. Bremigan and Stein (1994).
951. Partridge and DeVries (1999).
952. Miller et al. (1988).
953. Miller et al. (1988).
954. Toetz (1966).
955. Neff (2004).
956. Partridge and DeVries (1999).
957. Dominey (1980), Gross and Charnov (1980), Hoxmeier et al. (2001), Mayhew (1956), Regier (1962), Schramm (1989).
958. Taubert and Coble (1977).
959. Gerking (1954).
960. Brown et al. (1977).
961. Gross and Charnov (1980), Tomcko and Pierce (2001).
962. Breck (1993).
963. Breck (1993).
964. Breck (1993), Keast (1980).
965. Breck (1993).
966. Breck (1993).
967. Krumholz (1946).
968. Breck (1993).
969. Miller et al. (1988).
970. Keast (1980).
971. Cargnelli and Gross (1996), Garvey et al. (2002).

972. Santucci and Wahl (2003).
973. Cady (1945).
974. Cargnelli and Gross (1996).
975. Miller et al. (1988), Putman et al. (1995).
976. Osenberg et al. (1988).
977. Breck (1993), Miller et al. (1988).
978. Gerking (1954, 1962), Osenberg et al. (1988).
979. Tomcko and Pierce (2001).
980. Gerking (1954).
981. Beitinger and Fitzpatrick (1979).
982. Kolehmainen (1974).
983. Ricker (1942).
984. Ricker (1942).
985. Gerking (1962).
986. Osenberg et al. (1988).
987. Ricker (1942).
988. Ricker (1942).
989. Rach and Meyer (1982).
990. Eddy and Surber (1947), Jordan and Evermann (1916), Schrenkeisen (1938).
991. Keast (1978a).
992. Keast (1977b).
993. Keast (1977b).
994. Keast (1978a).
995. Bulow et al. (1981).
996. Osenberg et al. (1988).
997. Osenberg et al. (1988).
998. Cheruveilil et al. (2005).
999. Osenberg et al. (1988).
1000. El-Shamy (1978), Mittelbach (1981b, 1984, 1988), Osenberg et al. (1988), Werner and Hall (1988).
1001. Wohlschlag and Juliano (1959).
1002. Wohlschlag and Juliano (1959).
1003. Mittelbach and Osenberg (1993).
1004. Krumholz (1946).
1005. Hayse and Wissing (1996).
1006. Paukert et al. (2002b).
1007. Werner and Hall (1988).
1008. Ricker (1945).
1009. Nakamura et al. (1971).
1010. Ricker (1942:205, Table 4); t-test of independent sample means, $t = -1.10.$ to $-0.20, p \geq 0.29, n = 66$; Levene's test of homogeneity, $F_{(1)} = 0.03$–$0.97, p \geq 0.18$.
1011. Krumholz (1946).
1012. Gerking (1954).
1013. Gerking (1962).
1014. Gerking (1954).
1015. Gerking (1954).
1016. Bulow et al. (1981).
1017. Gerking (1962).
1018. Gerking (1962).
1019. Beckman (1950).
1020. Beitinger and Fitzpatrick (1979).
1021. Brett and Groves (1979).
1022. Cargnelli and Gross (1997).
1023. O'Hara (1968).
1024. Garvey et al. (2002).

1025. El-Shamy (1978).
1026. Kolehmainen (1974).
1027. Booth and Keast (1986).
1028. Garvey et al. (2002).
1029. Booth and Keast (1986).
1030. Moffett and Hunt (1943).
1031. Kolehmainen (1974).
1032. Beitinger and Fitzpatrick (1979).
1033. Beitinger (1977), Coutant (1977), Wildhaber and Crowder (1990); also references in Beitinger and Fitzpatrick (1979) and Beitinger and Magnuson (1976, 1979).
1034. Keast (1978a).
1035. Beitinger and Magnuson (1979).
1036. Brett et al. (1969).
1037. Beitinger and Magnuson (1979).
1038. Wildhaber and Crowder (1990).
1039. Seaburg and Moyle (1964).
1040. Windell (1966).
1041. Windell (1966).
1042. Booth (1990).
1043. Claramunt and Wahl (2000), Tomcko and Pierce (2001).
1044. Wood (1989).
1045. Wood (1989).
1046. Wood (1989).
1047. Wiener and Hanneman (1982).
1048. Swingle (1959).
1049. Wood (1989).
1050. Nibbelink and Carpenter (1998).
1051. Richardson et al. (1998).
1052. Richardson et al. (1998).
1053. Tomcko and Pierce (2001).
1054. Nibbelink and Carpenter (1998).
1055. Nibbelink and Carpenter (1998).
1056. Nibbelink and Carpenter (1998).
1057. Krumholz (1946).
1058. Claramunt and Wahl (2000).
1059. Belk (1995).
1060. Belk (1995).
1061. Partridge and DeVries (1999).
1062. Belk and Hales (1993).
1063. Werner and Hall (1988).
1064. Gerking (1954).
1065. Ricker (1945).
1066. Ricker (1945).
1067. Ricker (1942).
1068. Gerking (1954).
1069. Paukert et al. (2002b).
1070. Goedde and Coble (1981).
1071. Schneider (1999).
1072. Belk and Hales (1993).
1073. Breck (1993).
1074. Ricker (1945).
1075. Ricker (1945).
1076. Ricker (1942).

Chapter 8

1077. Anderson (1976, 1978), Novinger and Legler (1978).
1078. Anderson (1976).
1079. Anderson (1976).
1080. Guy and Willis (1990).
1081. Paukert et al. (2002a).
1082. Guy and Willis (1990).
1083. Belk and Hales (1993)
1084. Santucci and Wahl (2003).
1085. Otis et al. (1988).
1086. Mittelbach and Osenberg (1993).
1087. Rasmussen and Kalff (1987).
1088. Paukert et al. (2002a).
1089. Bruton (1985), Gardner (1981a) Weithman and Anderson (1977).
1090. Egertson and Downing (2004).
1091. Chambers and Kalff (1985).
1092. Egertson et al. (2004).
1093. Lillie and Budd (1992).
1094. Egertson and Downing (2004).
1095. Cooper et al. (1971).
1096. Breukelaar et al. (1994), Lougheed et al. (1998).
1097. Crivelli (1983).
1098. Lougheed et al. (1998).
1099. Lougheed et al. (1998).
1100. Crivelli (1983).
1101. Tátrai et al. (1994).
1102. Brönmark and Weisner (1992).
1103. Rasmussen and Kalff (1987).
1104. Schneider (1999).
1105. Schneider (1999).
1106. Keast (1984), Pothoven et al. (1999).
1107. Schneider (1999).
1108. Titus and Adams (1979).
1109. Carpenter and Lodge (1986).
1110. Boylen et al. (1999).
1111. Dale and Gillespie (1977).
1112. Carpenter and Lodge (1986).
1113. Ondok et al. (1984).
1114. Søndergaard (1981).
1115. Keast (1984).
1116. Crowder and Cooper (1982), Harrel and Dibble (2001).
1117. Beckett et al. (1992).
1118. Salvino and Stein (1982).
1119. Gotceitas and Colgan (1989), Savino and Stein (1982).
1120. Olson et al. (1998), Pothoven et al. (1999), Trebitz et al. (1997), Trebitz and Nibbelink (1996).
1121. Hinch and Collins (1993).
1122. Colle et al. (1987), Schneider (1999).
1123. Engel (1987).
1124. Savino and Stein (1982).
1125. Aday et al. (2005), Olson et al. (1995).
1126. Swingle (1959).
1127. Pothoven et al. (1999).
1128. Cheruveilil et al. (2005).

1129. Lillie and Budd (1992).
1130. Colle and Shireman (1980), Engel (1995).
1131. Valley and Bremigan (2002).
1132. Colle and Shireman (1980), Killgore et al. (1989), Olson et al. (1998).
1133. Keast (1978a).
1134. Keast (1984).
1135. Keast (1984).
1136. Weaver et al. (1997).
1137. Weaver et al. (1997).
1138. Weaver et al. (1997).
1139. Werner and Hall (1988).
1140. Grimm and Backx (1990).
1141. Schneider (1999).
1142. McHugh (1990).
1143. Belk and Hales (1993).
1144. Guy and Willis (1990).
1145. Grimm and Backx (1990).
1146. Osenberg et al. (1988), Paukert et al. (2002a).
1147. Paukert et al. (2002a).
1148. Werner et al. (1978).
1149. Werner et al. (1978).
1150. Werner et al. (1977, 1978).
1151. Forbes (1884).
1152. Chambers et al. (1990).
1153. Bettoli et al. (1993).
1154. Laughlin and Werner (1980).
1155. Eicher (1946), Engel (1987).
1156. Eicher (1946).
1157. Schneider (1999).
1158. Lillie and Budd (1992).
1159. Olson et al. (1998), Trebitz et al. (1997).
1160. Trebitz et al. (1997).
1161. Engel (1987).
1162. Lehtinen et al. (1997).
1163. Guillory (1979), Keast et al. (1978).
1164. Hubbs et al. (2004).
1165. Werner and Hall (1976).
1166. Keast (1978a), Keast et al. (1978).
1167. Werner and Hall (1976), Werner et al. (1977).
1168. Werner and Hall (1976).
1169. Walters et al. (1991), Werner and Hall (1976), Werner et al. (1977).
1170. Werner et al. (1978).
1171. Werner et al. (1977).
1172. Werner et al. (1977).
1173. Paukert et al. (2002a).
1174. Werner et al. (1977).
1175. Keast (1978a).
1176. Keast (1978a).
1177. Keast (1978a).
1178. Keast (1978a).
1179. Annett (1998), Hinch and Collins (1993), Lobb and Orth (1991), Werner et al. (1978).
1180. Egertson and Downing (2004).
1181. Brown and Colgan (1985).
1182. Mittelbach (1981b), Turner and Mittelbach (1990), Werner et al. (1983a).

1183. Brown and Colgan (1985).
1184. Casterlin and Reynolds (1978).
1185. Keast et al. (1978), Mittelbach (1984), Mittelbach and Osenberg (1993), Werner (1969), Werner and Hall (1988).
1186. Radomski and Goeman (2001), Weaver et al. (1997).
1187. Killgore et al. (1989), Brazner and Magnuson (1994), Bryan and Scarnecchia (1992), Weaver et al. (1997).
1188. Radomski and Goeman (2001).
1189. Radomski and Goeman (2001).
1190. Radomski and Goeman (2001).
1191. Pardue and Nielsen (1979).
1192. Paxon and Stevenson (1979), Wege and Anderson (1979).
1193. Barwick et al. (2004), Rodeheffer (1939).
1194. Johnson and Lynch (1992), Newbrey et al. (2005).
1195. Rold et al. (1996), Wege and Anderson (1979).
1196. Angermeier and Karr (1984), Lehtinen et al. (1997).
1197. Lehtinen et al. (1997).
1198. Lobb and Orth (1991).
1199. D. L. Johnson et al. (1988).
1200. Lynch and Johnson (1989).
1201. Walters et al. (1991).
1202. Coble (1988).
1203. Keast (1978a).
1204. Keast (1978a).
1205. El-Shamy (1978), Gerking (1962), Ricker (1942).
1206. Schneider (1999).
1207. Tomcko and Pierce (2005).
1208. Pearse (1921).
1209. Guy and Willis (1990).
1210. Ehlinger (1997).
1211. Ehlinger (1997).
1212. Aday et al. (2003b), Jennings et al. (1997).
1213. Aday et al. (2003b), Jennings et al. (1997).
1214. Aday et al. (2003b).
1215. Aday et al. (2003b).
1216. Gross (1982).
1217. Drake et al. (1997).
1218. Ehlinger (1997).
1219. Ehlinger et al. (1997).
1220. Ehlinger et al. (1997).
1221. Drake et al. (1997).
1222. Schneider and Lockwood (2002).
1223. Ehlinger et al. (1997).
1224. Berger (1982).
1225. Schneider and Lockwood (2002).
1226. Schneider and Lockwood (2002).
1227. McHugh (1990).
1228. Bignami, L. 2005. The second best bluegill. http://www.finefishing.com/aaspecies/panfish/bgillrec.htm
1229. Beard and Essington (2000).
1230. Coble (1988), Ricker (1942).
1231. Drake et al. (1997).
1232. Jacobson (2005).
1233. Goedde and Coble (1981).

1234. Brown and Ball (1942).
1235. Tomcko and Pierce (2005).
1236. Jacobson (2005).
1237. References in Tomcko and Pierce (2005).
1238. Schneider and Lockwood (2002).
1239. Cooper et al. (1971).
1240. Otis et al. (1998), Tomcko and Pierce (2005).
1241. Drake et al. (1997), Jennings et al. (1997), Schneider and Lockwood (2002).
1242. Drake et al. (1997).
1243. Anderson (1978).
1244. Gerking (1962).
1245. Goedde and Coble (1981); Coble (1988) says 61%.
1246. Drake et al. (1997), Ehlinger (1997).
1247. Ehlinger (1997).
1248. Crawford and Allen (2006).
1249. Crawford and Allen (2006).
1250. Ricker (1942).
1251. Porath and Hurley (2005).
1252. Garvey and Stein (1998), Stein et al. (1995).
1253. DeVries and Stein (1992).
1254. Bodola (1966).
1255. DeVries and Stein (1992).
1256. Bremigan and Stein (1994).
1257. Stein et al. (1995).
1258. Bremigan and Stein (1994).
1259. Cramer and Marzolf (1970), Guest et al. (1990).
1260. Sarnelle (1992).
1261. Drenner et al. (1986).
1262. Mundahl (1991).
1263. Mather et al. (1995).
1264. Bays and Crisman (1983).
1265. Lazzaro et al. (1992).
1266. Aday et al. (2003a), Swingle (1946).
1267. Wahl and Stein (1988).
1268. B. M. Johnson et al. (1988).
1269. DeVries and Stein (1992).
1270. Garvey and Stein (1998), Swingle (1946).
1271. B. M. Johnson et al. (1988).
1272. Stein et al. (1995).
1273. Stein et al. (1995).
1274. Robison and Buchanan (1988?).
1275. Hambright et al. (1991).
1276. Hambright et al. (1986).
1277. Michaletz and Bonneau (2005).
1278. Coggeshall (1924).
1279. King (1947:38).
1280. Garvey et al. (2002).
1281. Garvey et al. (2002).
1282. Beard et al. (1997).
1283. Garvey et al. (2002).
1284. Beard et al. (1997).
1285. Beard and Essington (2000).
1286. Margenau et al. (1998).
1287. Paukert et al. (2002b)

1288. Belk and Hales (1993).

1289. Mittelbach (1988).

1290. Gibbons et al. (1978). I must accept the total length measurement and body mass on faith. This reference gives the data in standard length without a conversion factor. Body mass is not mentioned.

1291. Belk and Hales (1993).

1292. Pothoven et al. (1999).

1293. Pothoven et al. (1999).

1294. Baur et al. (1979).

1295. Kirk (1992).

1296. Bailey (1978).

1297. Kirk (1992).

1298. Bettoli et al. (1993).

1299. Kirk (1992).

1300. Maezono et al. (2005).

1301. DeVries and Stein (1990).

1302. Jeppesen et al. (2000). Also see Grimm and Backx (1990).

1303. Boschung and Mayden (2004).

1304. Robison and Buchanan (1988?).

1305. B. M. Johnson et al., (1988).

1306. Boschung and Mayden (2004).

1307. DeVries et al. (1991).

1308. DeVries et al. (1991).

1309. Lazzaro et al. (1992).

1310. Lazzaro et al. (1992).

1311. Olive et al. (2005), Swingle and Smith (1942).

1312. Hogan (1946), Olive et al. (2005), Swingle and Smith (1942).

1313. Sarnelle (1992).

1314. McCauley and Kalff (1981).

1315. Carpenter et al. (1985).

1316. Sarnelle (1992).

1317. Vanni (1987).

1318. Swingle and Smith (1942).

1319. Swingle and Smith (1942:21).

1320. Swingle and Smith (1942).

1321. Geihsler and Holder (1983).

1322. Halpern et al. (2006).

1323. Carpenter et al. (1985), Jeppesen et al. (2000).

1324. Sarnelle (1992).

1325. Jeppesen et al. (2000).

1326. Engel (1987).

1327. Bryan and Scarnecchia (1992).

References

Aday, D. D., R. J. H. Hoxmeier, and D. H. Wahl. 2003a. Direct and indirect effects of gizzard shad on bluegill growth and population size structure. Transactions of the American Fisheries Society 132:47–56.

Aday, D. D., D. H. Wahl, and D. P. Philipp. 2003b. Assessing population-specific and environmental influences on bluegill life histories: a common garden approach. Ecology 84:3370–3375.

Aday, D. D., D. E. Shoup, J. A. Neviackas, J. L. Kline, and D. H. Wahl. 2005. Prey community responses to bluegill and gizzard shad foraging: implications for growth of juvenile largemouth bass. Transactions of the American Fisheries Society 134:1091–1102.

Amundrud, J. R., D. J. Faber, and A. Keast. 1974. Seasonal succession of free-swimming perciform larvae in Lake Opinicon, Ontario. Canadian Journal of Fisheries and Aquatic Sciences 31:1661–1665.

Anderson, N. H., J. H. Sedell, L. M. Roberts, and F. J. Triska. 1978. The role of aquatic invertebrates in processing of wood debris in coniferous forest streams. American Midland Naturalist 100:64–82.

Anderson, R. O. 1976. Management of small warm water impoundments. Fisheries 1(6):5–7, 26–28.

Anderson, R. O. 1978. New approaches to recreational fishery management. Pages 73–78 in G. D. Novinger and J. G. Dillard, editors. New approaches to the management of small impoundments. American Fisheries Society, North Central Division, Special Publication 5, Bethesda, Maryland.

Anderson, O. 1984. Optimal foraging by largemouth bass in structured environments. Ecology 65:851–861.

Angermeier, P. L., and J. R. Karr. 1984. Relationships between woody debris and fish habitat in a small warmwater stream. Transactions of the American Fisheries Society 113:716–726.

Annett, C. A. 1998. Hunting behavior of Florida largemouth bass, *Micropterus salmoides floridanus*, in a channelized river. Environmental Biology of Fishes 53:75–87.

Applegate, R. L. 1966. The use of a bryozoan, *Fredericella sultana*, as food by sunfish in Bull Shoals Reservoir. Limnology and Oceanography 11:129–130.

Avila, V. L. 1976. A field study of nesting behavior of male bluegill sunfish (*Lepomis macrochirus* Rafinesque). American Midland Naturalist 96:195–206.

Bailey, R. M., H. E. Winn, and C. L. Smith. 1954. Fishes from the Escambia River, Alabama and Florida, with ecologic and taxonomic notes. Proceedings of the Academy of Natural Sciences of Philadelphia 106:109–164.

Bailey, R. M., W. C. Latta, and G. R. Smith. 2004. An atlas of Michigan fishes with keys and illustrations for their identification. University of Michigan, Museum of Zoology, Miscellaneous Publications, Ann Arbor.

Bailey, W. M. 1978. A comparison of fish populations before and after extensive grass carp stocking. Transactions of the American Fisheries Society 107:181–206.

Bain, M. B., and L. A. Helfrich. 1983. Role of male parental care in survival of larval bluegills. Transactions of the American Fisheries Society 112:47–52.

Ballantyne, P. K., and P. W. Colgan. 1978a. Sound production during agonistic and reproductive behaviour in the pumpkinseed (*Lepomis gibbosus*), the bluegill (*L. macrochirus*), and their hybrid sunfish. 1. Context. Biology of Behaviour 3:113–135.

Ballantyne, P. K., and P. W. Colgan. 1978b. Sound production during agonistic and reproductive behaviour in the pumpkinseed (*Lepomis gibbosus*), the bluegill (*L. macrochirus*), and their hybrid sunfish. 2. Recipients. Biology of Behaviour 3:207–220.

Bando, T. 1993. Discrimination of random dot texture patterns in bluegill sunfish, *Lepomis macrochirus*. Journal of Comparative Physiology 172:663–669.

Banner, A., and J. A. van Arman. 1973. Thermal effects on eggs, larvae and juveniles of bluegill sunfish. Environmental Protection Agency, Ecological Research Series R3–73-041, Washington, D.C.

Bartell, S. M. 1982. Influence of prey abundance on size-selective predation by bluegills. Transactions of the American Fisheries Society 111:453–461.

Barwick, R. D., T. J. Kwak, R. L. Noble, and D. H. Barwick. 2004. Fish populations associated with habitat-modified piers and natural woody debris in Piedmont Carolina reservoirs. North American Journal of Fisheries Management 24:1120–1133.

Bassett, D. K., A. G. Carton, and J. C. Montgomery. 2006. Flowing water decreases hydrodynamic signal detection in a fish with an epidermal lateral-line system. Marine and Freshwater Research 57:611–617.

Baur, R. J., D. H. Buck, and C. R. Rose. 1979. Production of age-0 largemouth bass, smallmouth bass, and bluegills in ponds stocked with grass carp. Transactions of the American Fisheries Society 108:496–498.

Bays, J. S., and T. L. Crisman. 1983. Zooplankton and trophic state relationships in Florida lakes. Canadian Journal of Fisheries and Aquatic Sciences 40:1813–1819.

Beard, T. D., Jr., M. T. Drake, J. E. Breck, and N. A. Nate. 1997. Effects of simulated angling regulations on stunting in bluegill populations. North American Journal of Fisheries Management 17:525–532.

Beard, T. D., Jr., and T. E. Essington. 2000. Effects of angling and life history processes on bluegill size structure: insights from an individual-based model. Transactions of the American Fisheries Society 129:561–568.

Beckett, D. C., T. P. Aartila, and A. C. Miller. 1992. Contrasts in density of benthic invertebrates between macrophyte beds and open littoral patches in Eau Galle Lake, Wisconsin. American Midland Naturalist 127:77–90.

Beckman, W. C. 1945. The length-weight relationship, factors for conversions between standard and total lengths, and coefficients of condition for seven Michigan fishes. Transactions of the American Fisheries Society 75:237–256.

Beckman, W. C. 1950. Changes in growth rates of fishes following reduction in population densities by winter kill. Transactions of the American Fisheries Society 78:82–90.

Beitinger, F. L. 1977. Thermopreference behavior of bluegill (*Lepomis macrochirus*) subjected to restrictions in available temperature range. Copeia 1977:536–541.

Beitinger, T. L., and L. C. Fitzpatrick. 1979. Physiological and ecological correlates of preferred temperature in fish. American Zoologist 19:319–329.

Beitinger, T. L., and J. J. Magnuson. 1976. Low thermal responsiveness in the bluegill, *Lepomis macrochirus*. Journal of the Fisheries Research Board of Canada 33:293–295.

Beitinger, T. L., and J. J. Magnuson. 1979. Growth rates and temperature selection of bluegill, *Lepomis macrochirus*. Transactions of the American Fisheries Society 108:378–382.

Belk, M. C. 1995. Variation in growth and age at maturity in bluegill sunfish: genetic or environmental effects? Journal of Fish Biology 47:237–247.

Belk, M. C. 1998. Predator-induced delayed maturity in bluegill sunfish (*Lepomis macrochirus*): variation among populations. Oecologia 113:203–209.

Belk, M. C., and L. S. Hales, Jr. 1993. Predation-induced differences in growth and reproduction of bluegills (*Lepomis macrochirus*). Copeia 1993:1034–1044.

Benke, A. C., T. C. van Arsdall, Jr., D. M. Gillespie, and F. K. Parrish. 1984. Invertebrate productivity in a subtropical blackwater river: the importance of habitat and life history. Ecological Monographs

54:25–63.

Benke, A. C., R. L. Henry, III, D. M. Gillespie, and R. J. Hunter. 1985. Importance of snag habitat for animal production in southeastern streams. Fisheries 10(5):8–13.

Berger, T. A. 1982. Supplemental feeding of a wild bluegill population. North American Journal of Fisheries Management 2:158–163.

Bettoli, P. W., M. J. Maceina, R. L. Noble, and R. K. Betsill. 1993. Response of a reservoir fish community to aquatic vegetation removal. North American Journal of Fisheries Management 13:110–124.

Billard, R. 1986. Spermatogenesis and spermatology of some teleost fish species. Reproduction, Nutrition, Development 26:877–920.

Birdsong, R. S., and R. W. Yerger. 1967. A natural population of hybrid sunfishes: *Lepomis macrochirus* × *Chaenobryttus gulosus*. Copeia 1967:62–71.

Bleckmann, H. 1994. Reception of hydrodynamic stimuli in aquatic and semiaquatic animals. Gustav Fischer Verlag, Stuttgart.

Blois-Heulin, C., P. H. Crowley, M. Arrington, and D. M. Johnson. 1990. Direct and indirect effects of predators on the dominant invertebrates of two freshwater littoral communities. Oecologia 84:295–306.

Bodola, A. 1966. Life history of the gizzard shad *Dorosoma cepedianum* (LeSueur) in western Lake Erie. Fishery Bulletin (NOAA) 65:391–425.

Booth, D. J. 1990. Effect of water temperature on stomach evacuation rates, and estimation of daily food intake of bluegill sunfish (*Lepomis macrochirus* Rafinesque). Canadian Journal of Zoology 68:591–595.

Booth, D. J., and J. A. Keast. 1986. Growth energy partitioning by juvenile bluegill sunfish, *Lepomis macrochirus* Rafinesque. Journal of Fish Biology 28:37–45.

Boschung, H. T., Jr., and R. L. Mayden. 2004. Fishes of Alabama. Smithsonian Books, Washington, D.C.

Boylen, C. W., L. W. Eichler, and J. D. Madsen. 1999. Loss of native aquatic plant species in a community dominated by Eurasian watermilfoil. Hydrobiologia 415:207–211.

Brackenbury, J. 2001. The vortex wake of the free-swimming larva and pupa of *Culex pipiens* (Diptera). Journal of Experimental Biology 204:1855–1867.

Brackenbury, J. 2003. Escape manoeuvres in damsel-fly larvae: kinematics and dynamics. Journal of Experimental Biology 206:389–397.

Brackenbury, J. 2004. Kinematics and hydrodynamics of swimming in the mayfly larva. Journal of Experimental Biology 207:913–922.

Brazner, J. C., and J. J. Magnuson. 1994. Patterns of fish species richness and abundance in coastal marshes and other nearshore habitats in Green Bay, Lake Michigan. Verhandlungen der Internationale Vereinigung für Theoretische und Angewandte Limnologie 25:2098–2104.

Breck, J. E. 1993. Hurry up and wait: growth of young bluegills in ponds and in simulations with an individual-based model. Transactions of the American Fisheries Society 122:467–480.

Breck, J. E., and M. J. Gitter. 1983. Effect of fish size on the reactive distance of bluegill (*Lepomis macrochirus*). Canadian Journal of Fisheries and Aquatic Sciences 40:162–167.

Breder, C. M., Jr. 1926. The locomotion of fishes. Zoologica (New York) 4:159–296.

Breder, C. M., Jr. 1936. The reproductive habits of the North American sunfishes (family Centrarchidae). Zoologica (New York) 21:1–48.

Breder, C. M., Jr., and D. E. Rosen. 1966. Modes of reproduction in fishes. Natural History Press, New York.

Bremigan, M. T., and R. A. Stein. 1994. Gape-dependent larval foraging and zooplankton size: implications for fish recruitment across systems. Canadian Journal of Fisheries and Aquatic Sciences 51:913–922.

Brenden, T. O., and B. R. Murphy. 2004. Experimental assessment of age-0 largemouth bass and juvenile bluegill competition in a small impoundment in Virginia. North American Journal of Fisheries Management 24:1058–1070.

Brett, J. R., J. E. Shelbourn, and C. T. Shoop. 1969. Growth rate and body composition of fingering sockeye salmon, *Oncorhynchus nerka*, in relation to temperature and ration size. Journal of the Fisheries Research Board of Canada 26:2363–2394.

Brett, J. R., and T. D. D. Groves. 1979. Physiological energetics. Pages 279–352 *in* W. S. Hoar, D. J. Randall, and J. R. Brett, editors. Fish physiology, volume 8. Academic Press, New York.

Breukelaar, A. W., E. H. R. R. Lammens, J. G. P. Klein Breteler, and I. Tátrai. 1994. Effects of benthivorous bream (*Abramis brama*) and carp (*Cyprinus carpio*) on sediment resuspension and concentrations of nutrients and chlorophyll *a*. Freshwater Biology 32:113–121.

Brewer, M. C., and J. N. Coughlin. 1995. Virtual plankton: a novel approach to the investigation of aquatic predator-prey interactions. Marine and Freshwater Behavior and Physiology 26:91–100.

Brönmark, C., and S. E. B. Weisner. 1992. Indirect effects of fish community structure on submerged vegetation in shallow, eutrophic lakes: an alternative mechanism. Hydrobiologia 243/244:293–301.

Brown, C. J. D., and R. C. Ball. 1942. A fish population study of Third Sister Lake. Transactions of the American Fisheries Society 72:177–186.

Brown, D., E. E. Miller, and C. E. von Geldern, Jr. 1977. Detection of delayed annulus formation among bluegill, *Lepomis macrochirus*, populations at Lake Nacimiento, California. California Fish and Game 63:29–42.

Brown, J. A., and P. W. Colgan. 1981. The use of lateral-body bar markings in identification of young-of-year sunfish (*Lepomis*) in Lake Opinicon, Ontario. Canadian Journal of Zoology 59:1852–1855.

Brown, J. A., and P. W. Colgan. 1985. The ontogeny of social behavior in four species of centrarchid fish. Behaviour 92:254–276.

Brown, J. A., and P. W. Colgan. 1986. Individual and species recognition in centrarchid fishes: evidence and hypotheses. Behavioral Ecology and Sociobiology 19:373–379.

Bruton, M. N. 1985. The effects of suspensoids on fish. Hydrobiologia 125:221–241.

Bryan, M. D., and D. L. Scarnecchia. 1992. Species richness, composition, and abundance of fish larvae and juveniles inhabiting natural and developed shorelines of a glacial Iowa lake. Environmental Biology of Fishes 35:329–341.

Bulow, F. J., M. E. Zeman, J. R. Winningham, and W. F. Hudson. 1981. Seasonal variations in RNA-DNA ratios and in indicators of feeding, reproduction, energy storage, and condition in a population of bluegill, *Lepomis macrochirus* Rafinesque. Journal of Fish Biology 18:237–244.

Butler, M. J., IV. 1988. In situ observations of bluegill (*Lepomis macrochirus* Raf.) foraging behavior: the effects of habitat complexity, group size, and predators. Copeia 1988:939–944.

Butler, S. M., and J. R. Bence. 1984. A diet model for planktivores that follow density-independent rules for prey selection. Ecology 65:1885–1894.

Cady, E. R. 1945. Fish distributions, Norris Reservoir, Tennessee, 1943. I. Depth distribution of fish in Norris Reservoir. Journal of the Tennessee Academy of Science 20:103–114.

Cargnelli, L. M., and M. R. Gross. 1996. The temporal dimension in fish recruitment: birth date, body size, and size-dependent survival in a sunfish (bluegill: *Lepomis macrochirus*). Canadian Journal of Fisheries and Aquatic Sciences 53:360–367.

Cargnelli, L. M., and M. R. Gross. 1997. Fish energetics: larger individuals emerge from winter in better condition. Transactions of the American Fisheries Society 126:153–156.

Carpenter, S. R., and D. M. Lodge. 1986. Effects of submersed macrophytes on ecosystem processes. Aquatic Botany 26:341–370.

Carpenter, S. R., J. F. Kitchell, and J. R. Hodgson. 1985. Cascading trophic interactions and lake productivity. Bioscience 35:634–639.

Carroll, A. M., P. C. Wainwright, S. H. Huskey, D. C. Collar, and R. G. Turingan. 2004. Morphology predicts suction feeding performance in centrarchid fishes. Journal of Experimental Biology 207:3873–3881.

Casterlin, M. E., and W. W. Reynolds. 1978. Habitat selection by juvenile bluegill sunfish, *Lepomis macrochirus*. Hydrobiologia 59:75–79.

Catania, K. C., and F. E. Remple. 2005. Asymptotic prey profitability drives star-nosed moles to the foraging speed limit. Nature (London) 433:519–522.

Chambers, P. A., and J. Kalff. 1985. Depth distribution and biomass of submersed macrophyte communities in relation to Secchi depth. Canadian Journal of Fisheries and Aquatic Sciences 42:701–709.

Chambers, P. A., J. M. Hanson, J. M. Burke, and E. E. Prepas. 1990. The impact of the crayfish *Orconectes virilis* on aquatic macrophytes. Freshwater Biology 24:81–91.

Cheruveilil, K. S., N. A. Nate, P. A. Soranno, and M. T. Bremigan. 2005. Lack of a unimodal relationship between fish growth and macrophyte cover in 45 north temperate lakes. Archiv für Hydrobiologie 164:193–215.

Chipps, S. R., J. A. Dunbar, and D. H. Wahl. 2004. Phenotypic variation and vulnerability to predation in juvenile bluegill sunfish (*Lepomis macrochirus*). Oecologia 138:32–38.

Chou, B. R., and C. W. Hawryshyn. 1987. Spectral transmittance of the ocular media of the bluegill (*Lepomis macrochirus*). Canadian Journal of Zoology 65:1214–1217.

Churchill, E. P., and W. H. Over. 1933. Fishes of South Dakota. South Dakota Department of Game and Fish, Pierre.

Clady, M. D. 1974. Food habits of yellow perch, smallmouth bass and largemouth bass in two unproductive lakes in northern Michigan. American Midland Naturalist 91:453–459.

Claramunt, R. M., and D. H. Wahl. 2000. The effects of abiotic and biotic factors in determining larval fish growth rates: a comparison across species and reservoirs. Transactions of the American Fisheries Society 129:835–851.

Clark, F. W., and M. A. Keenleyside. 1967. Reproductive isolation between the sunfish, *Lepomis gibbosus* and *L. macrochirus*. Journal of the Fisheries Research Board of Canada 24:495–514.

Clarke, S. E., P. W. Colgan, and N. P. Lester. 1984. Courtship sequences and ethological isolation in two species of sunfish (*Lepomis* spp.) and their hybrids. Behaviour 91:93–113.

Cloe, W. W., III, and G. C. Garman. 1996. The energetic importance of terrestrial arthropod inputs to three warm-water streams. Freshwater Biology 36:105–114.

Coble, D. W. 1973. Influence of appearance of prey and satiation of predator on food selection by northern pike (*Esox lucius*). Journal of the Fisheries Research Board of Canada 30:317–320.

Coble, D. W. 1988. Effects of angling on bluegill populations: management implications. North American Journal of Fisheries Management 8:277–283.

Coble, D. W., G. B. Farabee, and R. O. Anderson. 1985. Comparative learning ability of selected fishes. Canadian Journal of Fisheries and Aquatic Sciences 42:791–796.

Coggeshall, L. T. 1924. A study of the productivity and breeding habits of the bluegill, *Lepomis pallidus* (Mitch). Proceedings of the Indiana Academy of Science 33:315–320.

Coleman, R. M., and R. U. Fischer. 1991. Brood size, male fanning effort and the energetics of a nonshareable parental investment in bluegill sunfish, *Lepomis macrochirus* (Teleostei: Centrarchidae). Ethology 87:177–188.

Coleman, R. M., M. R. Cross, and R. C. Sargent. 1985. Parental investment decision rules: a test in bluegill sunfish. Behavioral Ecology and Sociobiology 18:59–66.

Colgan, P. W., W. A. Nowell, M. R. Gross, and J. W. A. Grant. 1979. Aggressive habituation and rim circling in the social organization of bluegill sunfish (*Lepomis macrochirus*). Environmental Biology of Fishes 4:29–36.

Colle, D. E., and J. V. Shireman. 1980. Coefficients of condition for largemouth bass, bluegill, and redear sunfish in *Hydrilla*-infested lakes. Transactions of the American Fisheries Society 109:521–528.

Colle, D. E., J. V. Shireman, W. T. Haller, J. C. Joyce, and D. E. Canfield, Jr. 1987. Influence of hydrilla on harvestable sport-fish populations, angler use, and angler expenditures at Orange Lake, Florida. North American Journal of Fisheries Management 7:410–417.

Confer, J. L., and P. I. Blades. 1975a. Omnivorous zooplankton and planktivorous fish. Limnology and Oceanography 20:571–579.

Confer, J. L., and P. I. Blades. 1975b. Reaction distance to zooplankton by *Lepomis gibbosus*. Verhandlungen der Internationale Vereinigung für Theoretische und Angewandte Limnologie 19:2493–2497.

Connor, J. V. 1979. Identification of larval sunfishes (Centrarchidae: Elassomatidae) from southern Louisiana. Pages 17–52 *in* R. D. Hoyt, editor. Proceedings of the third symposium on larval fishes. Western Kentucky University, Bowling Green.

Conrow, R., A. V. Zale, and R. W. Gregory. 1990. Distributions and abundances of early life stages of fishes in a Florida lake dominated by aquatic macrophytes. Transactions of the American Fisheries Society 119:521–528.

Cooper, E. L., C. C. Wagner, and G. E. Krantz. 1971. Bluegills dominate production in a mixed population of fishes. Ecology 52:280–290.

Côté, I. M., and M. R. Gross. 1993. Reduced disease in offspring: a benefit of coloniality in sunfish. Behavioral Ecology and Sociobiology 33:269–274.

Coutant, C. C. 1977. Compilation of temperature preference data. Journal of the Fisheries Research Board of Canada 34:739–745.

Cramer, J. D., and G. R. Marzolf. 1970. Selective predation on zooplankton by gizzard shad. Transactions of the American Fisheries Society 99:320–332.

Crawford, S., and M. S. Allen. 2006. Fishing and natural mortality of bluegills and redear sunfish at Lake Panasoffkee, Florida. North American Journal of Fisheries Management 26:42–51.

Crivelli, A. J. 1983. The destruction of aquatic vegetation by carp. Hydrobiologia. 106:37–41.

Crossman, E. J. 1976. Quetico fishes. Royal Ontario Museum, Toronto.

Crowder, L. B., and W. E. Cooper. 1982. Habitat structural complexity and the interaction between bluegills and their prey. Ecology 63:1802–1813.

Cyr, H., and J. A. Downing. 1988. Empirical relationships of phytomacrofaunal abundance to plant biomass and macrophyte bed characteristics. Canadian Journal of Fisheries and Aquatic Sciences 45:976–984.

Dale, H. M., and T. J. Gillespie. 1977. The influence of submersed aquatic plants on temperature gradients in shallow water bodies. Canadian Journal of Botany 55:2216–2225.

Dawidowicz, P., J. Pijanowska, and K. Ciechomski. 1990. Vertical migration of *Chaoborus* larvae is induced by the presence of fish. Limnology and Oceanography 35:1631–1637.

Dawley, R. M. 1987. Hybridization and polyploidy in a community of three sunfish species (Pisces: Centrarchidae). Copeia 1987:326–335.

Dawley, R. M., J. H. Graham, and R. J. Schultz. 1985. Triploid progeny of pumpkinseed × green sunfish hybrids. Journal of Heredity 76:251–257.

Denton, E. J., and J. A. B. Gray. 1989. Some observations on the forces acting on neuromasts in fish lateral line canals. Pages 230–246 *in* S. Coombs, P. Görner, and H. Münz, editors. The mechanosensory lateral line: neurobiology and evolution. Springer-Verlag, New York.

Desselle, W. J., M. A. Poirrier, J. S. Rogers, and R. C. Cashner. 1978. A discriminant functions analysis of sunfish (*Lepomis*) food habits and feeding niche segregation in the Lake Pontchartrain, Louisiana estuary. Transactions of the American Fisheries Society 107:713–719.

DeVries, D. R., and R. A. Stein. 1990. Manipulating shad to enhance sport fisheries in North America: an assessment. North American Journal of Fisheries Management 10:209–223.

DeVries, D. R., and R. A. Stein. 1992. Complex interactions between fish and zooplankton: quantifying the role of an open-water planktivore. Canadian Journal of Fisheries and Aquatic Sciences 49:1216–1227.

DeVries, D. R., R. A. Stein, and P. L. Chesson. 1989. Sunfish foraging among patches: the patch-departure decision. Animal Behaviour 37:455–464.

DeVries, D. R., R. A. Stein, J. G. Miner, and G. G. Mittelbach. 1991. Stocking threadfin shad: consequences for young-of-year fishes. Transactions of the American Fisheries Society 120:368–381.

Dewey, M. R., W. B. Richardson, and S. J. Zigler. 1997. Patterns of foraging and distribution of bluegill sunfish in a Mississippi River backwater: influence of macrophytes and predation. Ecology of Freshwater Fishes 6:8–15.

Dickinson, M. H. 1996. Unsteady mechanisms of force generation in aquatic and aerial locomotion. American Zoologist 36:537–554.

Dionne, M., and C. L. Folt. 1991. An experimental analysis of macrophyte growth forms as fish foraging habitat. Canadian Journal of Fisheries and Aquatic Sciences 48:123–131.

Dominey, W. J. 1980. Female mimicry in male bluegill sunfish—a genetic polymorphism? Nature 284:546–548.

Dominey, W. J. 1981a. Maintenance of female mimicry as a reproductive strategy in bluegill sunfish (*Lepomis macrochirus*). Environmental Biology of Fishes 6:59–64.

Dominey, W. J. 1981b. Anti-predator function of bluegill sunfish nesting colonies. Nature (London) 290:586–588.

Dominey, W. J. 1983. Mobbing in colonially nesting fishes, especially the bluegill, *Lepomis macrochirus*. Copeia 1983:1086–1088.

Dorn, N. J., and G. G. Mittelbach. 2004. Effects of a native crayfish (*Orconectes virilis*) on the reproductive success and nesting behavior of sunfish (*Lepomis* spp.). Canadian Journal of Fisheries and Aquatic Sciences 61:2135–2143.

Douglas, R. H., and C. W. Hawryshyn. 1990. Behavioural studies of fish vision: an analysis of visual capabilities. Pages 373–400 *in* R. H. Douglas and M. B. A. Djamgoz, editors. The visual system of fish.

Chapman and Hall, London.

Douglas, R. H., J. Eva, and N. Guttridge. 1988. Size constancy in goldfish (*Carassius auratus*). Behavior and Brain Research 30:37–42.

Drake, M. T., J. E. Claussen, D. P. Philipp, and D. L. Pereira. 1997. A comparison of bluegill reproductive strategies and growth among lakes with different fishing intensities. North American Journal of Fisheries Management 17:496–507.

Drenner, R. W., J. D. Smith, J. R. Mummert, and H. F. Lancaster. 1990. Responses of a eutrophic pond community to separate and combined effects of N:P supply and planktivorous fish: a mesocosm experiment. Hydrobiologia 208:161–167.

Drenner, R. W., S. T. Threlkeld, and M. D. McCracken. 1986. Experimental analysis of the direct and indirect effects of an omnivorous filter-feeding clupeid on plankton community structure. Canadian Journal of Fisheries and Aquatic Sciences 43:1935–1945.

Drucker, E. G., and G. V. Lauder. 1999. Locomotor forces on a swimming fish: three-dimensional vortex wake dynamics quantified using digital particle image velocimetry. Journal of Experimental Biology 202:2393–2412.

Drucker, E. G., and G. V. Lauder. 2001. Locomotor function of the dorsal fin in teleost fishes: experimental analysis of wake forces in sunfish. Journal of Experimental Biology 204:2943–2958.

Drucker, E. G., and G. V. Lauder. 2002. Wake dynamics and locomotor function in fishes: interpreting evolutionary patterns in pectoral fin design. Integrative and Comparative Biology 42:997–1008.

Duffy, M. A., S. R. Hall, A. J. Tessier, and M. Huebner. 2005. Selective predators and their parasitized prey: are epidemics in zooplankton under top-down control? Limnology and Oceanography 50:412–420.

Dugatkin, L. A., and D. S. Wilson. 1992. The prerequisites for strategic behaviour in bluegill sunfish, *Lepomis macrochirus*. Animal Behaviour 44:223–230.

Dugatkin, L. A., and D. S. Wilson. 1994. Choice experiments and cognition: a reply to Lamprecht and Hofer. Animal Behaviour 47:1459–1461.

Eddy, S., and T. Surber. 1947. Northern fishes with special reference to the upper Mississippi Valley, 2nd edition. University of Minnesota Press, Minneapolis.

Egertson, C. J., and J. A. Downing. 2004. Relationship of fish catch and composition to water quality in a suite of agriculturally eutrophic lakes. Canadian Journal of Fisheries and Aquatic Sciences 61:1784–1796.

Egertson, C. J., J. A. Kopaska, and J. A. Downing. 2004. A century of change in macrophyte abundance and composition in response to agricultural eutrophication. Hydrobiologia 524:145–156.

Eggers, D. M. 1977. The nature of prey selection by planktivorous fish. Ecology 58:46–59.

Eggers, D. M. 1982. Planktivore preference by prey size. Ecology 63:381–390.

Ehlinger, T. J. 1989. Learning and individual variation in bluegill foraging: habitat-specific techniques. Animal Behaviour 38:643–658.

Ehlinger, T. J. 1990. Habitat choice and phenotype-limited feeding efficiency in bluegill: individual differences and trophic polymorphism. Ecology 71:886–896.

Ehlinger, T. J. 1997. Male reproductive competition and sex-specific growth patterns in bluegill. North American Journal of Fisheries Management 17:508–515.

Ehlinger, T. J. 1999. Ecology, phenotype, and character evolution in sunfish: a population comparative approach. Pages 121–138 *in* S. A. Foster and J. E. Endler, editors. Geographic variation in behavior: perspectives on evolutionary mechanisms. Oxford University Press, New York.

Ehlinger, T. J., and D. S. Wilson. 1988. Complex foraging polymorphism in bluegill sunfish. Proceedings of the National Academy of Sciences 85:1878–1882.

Ehlinger, T. J., M. R. Gross, and D. P. Philipp. 1997. Morphological and growth rate differences between bluegill males of alternative reproductive life histories. North American Journal of Fisheries Management 17:533–542.

Eicher, G. J., Jr. 1946. Localized weed control in management of game fish. Transactions of the American Fisheries Society 76:177–182.

Einfalt, L. M., and D. H. Wahl. 1997. Prey selection by juvenile walleye as influenced by prey morphology and behavior. Canadian Journal of Fisheries and Aquatic Sciences 54:2618–2626.

Elliott, J. K., J. M. Elliott, and W. C. Leggett. 1997. Predation by *Hydra* on larval fish: field and laboratory experiments with bluegill (*Lepomis macrochirus*). Limnology and Oceanography 42:1416–1423.

El-Shamy, F. M. 1978. Dynamics of feeding and growth of bluegill (*Lepomis macrochirus*) in Lake Wingra and Lake Mendota, Wisconsin. Hydrobiologia 60:113–124.

Engel, S. 1987. Impact of submerged macrophytes on largemouth bass and bluegills. Lake and Reservoir Management 3:227–234.

Engel, S. 1995. Eurasian watermilfoil as a fishery management tool. Fisheries 20(3):20–27.

Engelmann, J., W. Hanke, J. Mogdans, and H. Bleckmann. 2000. Hydrodynamic stimuli and the fish lateral line. Nature (London) 408:51–52.

Enger, P. S., A. J. Kalmijn, and O. Sand. 1989. Behavioral investigations on the functions of the lateral line and inner ear in predation. Pages 575–587 *in* S. Coombs, P. Görner, and H. Münz, editors. The mechanosensory lateral line: neurobiology and evolution. Springer-Verlag, New York.

Etnier, D. A., and W. C. Starnes. 1993. The fishes of Tennessee. University of Tennessee Press, Knoxville.

Figiel, C. R., Jr., and R. D. Semlitsch. 1990. Population variation in survival and metamorphosis of larval salamanders (*Ambystoma maculatum*) in the presence and absence of fish predation. Copeia 1990:818–826.

Fish, P. A., and J. Savitz. 1983. Variations in home ranges of largemouth bass, yellow perch, bluegills, and pumpkinseeds in an Illinois lake. Transactions of the American Fisheries Society 112:147–153.

Forbes, S. A. 1884. Destruction of fish-food by bladderwort (*Utricularia*). Bulletin of the U.S. Fish Commission 4:443.

Forbes, S. A., and R. E. Richardson. 1920. The fishes of Illinois, 2nd edition. Natural History Survey Division, Springfield, Illinois.

Franklin, D. 1914. Note on a nesting sunfish. Copeia (11):1.

Fu, P., B. D. Neff, and M. R. Gross. 2001. Tactic-specific success in sperm competition. Proceedings of the Royal Society of London 268B:1105–1112.

Gardner, M. B. 1981a. Effects of turbidity on feeding rates and selectivity of bluegills. Transactions of the American Fisheries Society 110:446–450.

Gardner, M. B. 1981b. Mechanisms of size selectivity by planktivorous fish: a test of hypotheses. Ecology 62:571–578.

Garvey, J. E., and R. A. Stein. 1998. Linking bluegill and gizzard shad prey assemblages to growth of age-0 largemouth bass in reservoirs. Transactions of the American Fisheries Society 127:70–83.

Garvey, J. E., T. P. Herra, and W. C. Leggett. 2002. Protracted reproduction in sunfish: the temporal dimension in fish recruitment revisited. Ecological Applications 12:194–205.

Geihsler, M. R., and D. R. Holder. 1983. Status of fish populations in Georgia ponds 1–4 years after stocking. North American Journal of Fisheries Management 3:189–196.

Gerking, S. D. 1954. The food turnover of a bluegill population. Ecology 35:490–498.

Gerking, S. D. 1955. Key to the fishes of Indiana. Investigations of Indiana Lakes and Streams 4(2):49–86.

Gerking, S. D. 1957. A method of sampling the littoral macrofauna and its application. Ecology 38:219–225.

Gerking, S. D. 1962. Production and food utilization in a population of bluegill sunfish. Ecological Monographs 32:31–78.

Gibb, A. C., B. C. Jayne, and G. V. Lauder. 1994. Kinematics of pectoral fin locomotion in the bluegill sunfish, *Lepomis macrochirus*. Journal of Experimental Biology 189:133–161.

Gibbons, J. W., D. H. Bennett, G. W. Esch, and T. C. Hazen. 1978. Effects of thermal effluent on body condition of largemouth bass. Nature (London) 274:470–471.

Giguère, L. A., and T. G. Northcote. 1987. Ingested prey increase risks of visual predation in transparent *Chaoborus* larvae. Oecologia 73:48–52.

Gilbert, C. R. 1998. Type catalog of recent and fossil North American freshwater fishes: families Cyprinidae, Catostomidae, Ictaluridae, Centrarchidae and Elassomatidae. Florida Museum of Natural History, Special Publication No. 1, Tallahassee.

Gilbert, J. J. 1988. Suppression of rotifer populations by *Daphnia*: a review of the evidence, the mechanisms, and the effects on zooplankton community structure. Limnology and Oceanography 33:1286–1303.

Goedde, L. E., and D. W. Coble. 1981. Effects of angling on a previously fished and an unfished warmwater fish community in two Wisconsin lakes. Transactions of the American Fisheries Society 110:594–603.

Goodyear, C. P., and D. H. Bennett. 1979. Sun compass orientation of immature bluegill. Transactions of the American Fisheries Society 108:555–559.

Gotceitas, V. 1990. Variation in plant stem density and its effects on foraging success of juvenile bluegill sunfish. Environmental Biology of Fishes 27:63–70.

Gotceitas, V., and P. Colgan. 1987. Selection between densities of artificial vegetation by young bluegills avoiding predation. Transactions of the American Fisheries Society 116:40–49.

Gotceitas, V., and P. Colgan. 1989. Predator foraging success and habitat complexity: quantitative test of the threshold hypothesis. Oecologia 80:158–166.

Gotceitas, V., and P. Colgan. 1990. The effects of prey availability and predation risk on habitat selection by juvenile bluegill sunfish. Copeia 1990:409–417.

Grimm, M. P., and J. J. G. M. Backx. 1990. The restoration of shallow eutrophic lakes, and the role of northern pike, aquatic vegetation and nutrient concentration. Hydrobiologia 200/201:557–566.

Gross, M. R. 1982. Sneakers, satellites and parentals: polymorphic mating strategies in North American sunfishes. Zeitschrift für Tierpsychologie 60:1–26.

Gross, M. R. 1991. Evolution of alternative reproductive strategies: frequency-dependent sexual selection in male bluegill sunfish. Philosophical Transactions of the Royal Society of London 332B:59–66.

Gross, M. R. 1996. Alternative reproductive strategies and tactics: diversity within sexes. Trends in Ecology and Evolution 11:92–98.

Gross, M. R., and E. L. Charnov. 1980. Alternative male life histories in bluegill sunfish. Proceedings of the National Academy of Sciences 77:6937–6940.

Gross, M. R., and A. M. MacMillan. 1981. Predation and the evolution of colonial nesting in bluegill sunfish (Lepomis macrochirus). Behavioral Ecology and Sociobiology 8:163–174.

Guest, W. C., R. W. Drenner, S. T. Threlkeld, F. D. Martin, and J. D. Smith. 1990. Effects of gizzard shad and threadfin shad on zooplankton and young-of-the-year white crappie production. Transactions of the American Fisheries Society 119:529–536.

Guillory, V. 1979. Species assemblages of fish in Lake Conway. Florida Scientist 42:158–162.

Gunning, G. E., and C. R. Shoop. 1963. Occupancy of home range by longear sunfish, Lepomis m. megalotis (Rafinesque), and bluegill, Lepomis m. macrochirus Rafinesque. Animal Behaviour 11:325–330.

Guy, C. S., and D. W. Willis. 1990. Structural relationships of largemouth bass and bluegill populations in South Dakota ponds. North American Journal of Fisheries Management 10:338–343.

Hairston, N. G., Jr., K. T. Li, and S. S. Easter, Jr. 1982. Fish vision and the detection of planktonic prey. Science 218:1240–1242.

Hall, D. T., and E. E. Werner. 1977. Seasonal distribution and abundance of fishes in the littoral zone of a Michigan lake. Transactions of the American Fisheries Society 106:545–555.

Halpern, B. S., K. Cottenie, and B. R. Broitman. 2006. Strong top-down control in southern California kelp forest ecosystems. Science 312:1230–1232.

Hambright, K. D., R. J. Trebatoski, R. W. Drenner, and D. Kettle. 1986. Experimental study of the impacts of bluegill (Lepomis macrochirus) and largemouth bass (Micropterus salmoides) on pond community structure. Canadian Journal of Fisheries and Aquatic Sciences 43:1171–1176.

Hambright, K. D., R. W. Drenner, S. R. McComas, and N. G. Hairston, Jr. 1991. Gape-limited piscivores, planktivore size refuges, and the trophic cascade hypothesis. Archiv für Hydrobiologie 121:389–404.

Haney, J. F., and D. J. Hall. 1975. Diel vertical migration and filter-feeding activities of Daphnia. Archiv für Hydrobiologie 75:413–441.

Hanke, W., and H. Bleckmann. 2004. The hydrodynamic trails of Lepomis gibbosus (Centrarchidae), Colomesus psittacus (Tetraodontidae) and Tysochromis ansorgii (Cichlidae) investigated with scanning particle image velocimetry. Journal of Experimental Biology 207:1585–1596.

Hanke, W., C. Brücker, and H. Bleckmann. 2000. The ageing of the low-frequency water disturbances caused by swimming goldfish and its possible relevance to prey detection. Journal of Experimental Biology 203:1193–1200.

Hardy, J. D., Jr. 1978. Development of fishes of the Mid-Atlantic Bight: an atlas of egg, larval and juvenile stages. Volume III, Aphredoderidae through Rachycentridae. U.S. Fish and Wildlife Service, Biological Service Program FWS/OBS-78/12, Washington, D.C.

Harlan, J. R., and E. B. Speaker. 1969. Iowa fish and fishing, 4th edition. Iowa Conservation Commission, Des Moines.

Harrel, S. L., and E. D. Dibble. 2001. Foraging efficiency of juvenile bluegill, Lepomis macrochirus, among different vegetated habitats Environmental Biology of Fishes 62:441–453.

Harris, J. E. 1938. The role of the fins in the equilibrium of the swimming fish. II. The role of the pelvic fins. Journal of Experimental Biology 15:32–47.

Hasler, A. D., R. M. Horrall, W. J. Wisby, and W. Braemer. 1958. Sun-orientation and homing in fishes. Limnology and Oceanography 3:353–361.

Hawryshyn, C. W., M. G. Arnold, W. N. McFarland, and E. R. Loew. 1988. Aspects of color vision in bluegill sunfish (*Lepomis macrochirus*): ecological and evolutionary relevance. Journal of Comparative Physiology 164:107–116.

Hayse, J. W., and T. E. Wissing. 1996. Effects of stem density of artificial vegetation on abundance and growth of age-0 bluegills and predation by largemouth bass. Transactions of the American Fisheries Society 125:422–433.

Heidinger, R. C. 1975. Life history and biology of the largemouth bass. Pages 11–20 *in* R. H. Stroud and H. Clepper, editors. Black bass biology and management. Sport Fishing Institute, Washington, D.C.

Helfman, G. S. 1981. Twilight activities and temporal structure in a freshwater fish community. Canadian Journal of Fisheries and Aquatic Sciences 38:1405–1420.

Higham, T. E., S. W. Day, and P. C. Wainwright. 2005a. Sucking while swimming: evaluating the effects of ram speed on suction generation in bluegill sunfish *Lepomis macrochirus* using digital particle image velocimetry. Journal of Experimental Biology 208:2653–2660.

Higham, T. E., B. Malas, B. C. Jayne, and G. V. Lauder. 2005b. Constraints on starting and stopping: behavior compensates for reduced pectoral fin area during braking of the bluegill sunfish *Lepomis macrochirus*. Journal of Experimental Biology 208:4735–4746.

Hildebrand, S. F., and I. L. Towers. 1927. Annotated list of fishes collected in the vicinity of Greenwood, Miss., with descriptions of three new species. U.S. Bureau of Fisheries Bulletin 43(Part 2):105–136.

Hinch, S. G., and N. C. Collins. 1993. Relationships of littoral fish abundance to water chemistry and macrophyte variables in central Ontario lakes. Canadian Journal of Fisheries and Aquatic Sciences 50:1870–1878.

Hoffman, G. L. 1999. Parasites of North American freshwater fishes, 2nd edition. Comstock Publishing Associates, Ithaca, New York.

Hogan, J. 1946. The control of aquatic plants with fertilizers in rearing ponds at the Lonoke Hatchery, Arkansas. Transactions of the American Fisheries Society 76:183–189.

Holland-Bartels, L. E., S. K. Littlejohn, and M. L. Huston. 1990. A guide to larval fishes of the upper Mississippi River. University of Minnesota, Minnesota Extension Service, St. Paul.

Horn, H. S. 1966. Measurement of "overlap" in comparative ecological studies. American Naturalist 100:419–424.

Howick, G. L., and W. J. O'Brien. 1983. Piscivorous feeding behavior of largemouth bass: an experimental analysis. Transactions of the American Fisheries Society 112:508–516.

Hoxmeier, R. J. H., D. D. Aday, and D. H. Wahl. 2001. Factors influencing precision of age estimation from scales and otoliths of bluegills in Illinois reservoirs. North American Journal of Fisheries Management 21:374–380.

Hoyle, J. A., and A. Keast. 1987. The effect of prey morphology and size on handling time in a piscivore, the largemouth bass (*Micropterus salmoides*). Canadian Journal of Zoology 65:1972–1977.

Hoyle, J. A., and A. Keast. 1988. Prey handling time in two piscivores, *Esox americanus vermiculatus* and *Micropterus salmoides*, with contrasting mouth morphologies Canadian Journal of Zoology 66:540–542.

Hubbs, C. L., and L. C. Hubbs. 1932. Experimental verification of natural hybridization between distinct genera of sunfishes. Papers of the Michigan Academy of Science, Arts, and Letters 15:427–437.

Hubbs, C. L., K. F. Lagler, and G. R. Smith. 2004. Fishes of the Great Lakes region, Revised edition. University of Michigan Press, Ann Arbor.

Ingram, W. M., and E. P. Odum. 1941. Nests and behavior of *Lepomis gibbosus* (Linnaeus) in Lincoln Pond, Rensselaerville, New York. American Midland Naturalist 26:182–193.

Jacobson, P. C. 2005. Experimental analysis of a reduced daily bluegill limit in Minnesota. North American Journal of Fisheries Management 25:203–210.

James, M. F. 1946. Histology of gonadal changes in the bluegill, *Lepomis macrochirus* Rafinesque, and the largemouth bass, *Huro salmoides* (Lacépède). Journal of Morphology 79:63–86.

Janssen, J. 1982. Comparison of searching behavior for zooplankton in an obligate planktivore, blueback herring (*Alosa aestivalis*) and a facultative planktivore, bluegill (*Lepomis macrochirus*). Canadian Journal of Fisheries and Aquatic Sciences 39:1649–1654.

Janssen, J., and J. Corcoran. 1993. Lateral line stimuli can override vision to determine sunfish strike trajectory. Journal of Experimental Biology 176:299–305.

Janssen, J., W. R. Jones, A. Whang, and P. E. Oshel. 1995. Use of the lateral line in particulate feeding in the dark by juvenile alewife (*Alosa pseudoharengus*). Canadian Journal of Fisheries and Aquatic Sciences 52:358–363.

Jayne, B. C., A. Lozada, and G. V. Lauder. 1996. Function of the dorsal fin in bluegill sunfish: motor patterns during four locomotor behaviors. Journal of Morphology 228:307–326.

Jennings, M. J., J. E. Claussen, and D. P. Philipp. 1997. Effect of population size structure on reproductive investment in male bluegill. North American Journal of Fisheries Management 17:516–524.

Jeppesen, E., J. P. Jensen, M. Søndergaard, T. Lauridsen, and F. Landkildehus. 2000. Trophic structure, species richness and biodiversity in Danish lakes: changes along a phosphorus gradient. Freshwater Biology 45:201–218.

Johnson, B. M., R. A. Stein, and R. F. Carline. 1988. Use of a quadrat rotenone technique and bioenergetics modeling to evaluate prey availability to stocked piscivores. Transactions of the American Fisheries Society 117:127–141.

Johnson, D. L., and W. E. Lynch, Jr. 1992. Panfish use of and angler success at evergreen tree, brush, and stake-bed structures. North American Journal of Fisheries Management 12:222–229.

Johnson, D. L., R. A. Beaumier, and W. E. Lynch, Jr. 1988. Selection of habitat structure interstice size by bluegills and largemouth bass in ponds. Transactions of the American Fisheries Society 117:171–179.

Jordan, D. S., and B. W. Evermann. 1916. American food and game fishes. A popular account of all the species found in America north of the Equator, with keys for ready identification, life histories and methods of capture. Doubleday, Page, Garden City, New York.

Jordan, D. S., and B. W. Evermann. 1963. The Fishes of North and middle America, volume 2. Smithsonian Institution/T.F.H. Publications, Washington, D.C. (Reprint edition.)

Kacelnik, A., and B. Marsh. 2002. Cost can increase preference in starlings. Animal Behaviour 63:245–250.

Kalmijn, A. J. 1988. Hydrodynamic and acoustic field detection. Pages 83–130 *in* J. Atema, R. R. Fay, A. N. Popper, and W. N. Tavolga, editors. Sensory biology of aquatic animals. Springer-Verlag, New York.

Kalmijn, A. J. 1989. Functional evolution of lateral line and inner ear sensory systems. Pages 187–216 *in* S. Coombs, P. Görner, and H. Münz, editors. The mechanosensory lateral line: neurobiology and evolution. Springer-Verlag, New York.

Kawamura, G., and T. Shimowada. 1993. Optic critical duration and contrast thresholds in the freshwater fish, *Lepomis macrochirus*, as determined behaviourally Fisheries Research 17:251–258.

Keast, A. 1968. Breeding biology of the black crappie, *Pomoxis nigromaculatus*. Journal of the Fisheries Research Board of Canada 25:285–297.

Keast, A. 1977a. Feeding and food overlaps between the year classes relative to the resource base, in the yellow perch, *Perca flavescens*. Environmental Biology of Fishes 2:53–70.

Keast, A. 1977b. Mechanisms expanding niche width and minimizing intraspecific competition in two centrarchid fishes. Pages 333–395 *in* M. K. Hecht, W. C. Steere, and B. Wallace, editors. Evolutionary biology, volume 10. Plenum, New York.

Keast, A. 1978a. Trophic and spatial interrelationships in the fish species of an Ontario temperate lake. Environmental Biology of Fishes 3:7–31.

Keast, A. 1978b. Feeding interrelations between age-groups of pumpkinseed (*Lepomis gibbosus*) and comparisons with bluegill (*L. macrochirus*). Journal of the Fisheries Research Board of Canada 35:12–27.

Keast, A. 1980. Food and feeding relationships of young fish in the first weeks after beginning of exogenous feeding in Lake Opinicon, Ontario. Environmental Biology of Fishes 5:305–314.

Keast, A. 1984. The introduced aquatic macrophyte, *Myriophyllum spicatum*, as habitat for fish and their invertebrate prey. Canadian Journal of Zoology 62:1289–1303.

Keast, A. 1985a. The piscivore feeding guild of fishes in small freshwater ecosystems. Environmental Biology of Fishes 12:119–129.

Keast, A. 1985b. Planktivory in a littoral-dwelling lake fish association: prey selection and seasonality.

Canadian Journal of Fisheries and Aquatic Sciences 42:1114–1126.

Keast, A., and M. G. Fox. 1992. Space use and feeding patterns of an offshore fish assemblage in a shallow mesotrophic lake. Environmental Biology of Fishes 34:159–170.

Keast, A., and D. Webb. 1966. Mouth and body form relative to feeding ecology in the fish fauna of a small lake, Lake Opinicon, Ontario. Journal of the Fisheries Research Board of Canada 23:1845–1874.

Keast, A., and L. Welsh. 1968. Daily feeding periodicities, food uptake rates, and dietary changes with hour of day in some lake fishes. Journal of the Fisheries Research Board of Canada 25:1133–1144.

Keast, A., J. Harker, and D. Turnbull. 1978. Nearshore fish habitat utilization and species associations in Lake Opinicon (Ontario, Canada). Environmental Biology of Fishes 3:173–184.

Khadka, R. B., and R. T. Ramakrishna. 1986. Prey size selection by common carp (*Cyprinus carpio* var. *communis*) larvae in relation to age and prey density Aquaculture 54:89–96.

Kieffer, J. D., and P. W. Colgan. 1992. Differences in learning by foraging juvenile pumpkinseed and bluegill sunfish in a structured habitat. Environmental Biology of Fishes 33:359–366.

Killgore, K. J., R. P. Morgan, I. I., and N. B. Rybicki. 1989. Distribution and abundance of fishes associated with submersed aquatic plants in the Potomac River. North American Journal of Fisheries Management 9:101–111.

Kim, Y.-U., and Y.-S. Park. 1987. Development of eggs, larvae and juveniles of bluegill, *Lepomis macrochirus* Rafinesque. Bulletin of the Korean Fisheries Society 20:24–32.

Kindler, P. M., D. P. Philipp, M. R. Gross, and J. M. Bahr. 1989. Serum 11-ketotestosterone and testosterone concentrations associated with reproduction in male bluegill (*Lepomis macrochirus*: Centrarchidae). General and Comparative Endocrinology 75:446–453.

Kindler, P. M., J. M. Bahr, M. R. Gross, and D. P. Philipp. 1991. Hormonal regulation of parental care behavior in nesting male bluegills: do the effects of bromocriptine suggest a role for prolactin? Physiological Zoology 64:310–322.

King, W. 1947. Important food and game fishes of North Carolina. Department of Conservation and Development, Division of Game and Inland Fisheries, Raleigh, North Carolina.

Kirk, J. P. 1992. Efficacy of triploid grass carp in controlling nuisance aquatic vegetation in South Carolina farm ponds. North American Journal of Fisheries Management 12:581–584.

Kitchell, J. F., and J. T. Windell. 1970. Nutritional value of algae to bluegill sunfish, *Lepomis macrochirus*. Copeia 1970:186–190.

Kolar, C. S., and D. H. Wahl. 1998. Daphnid morphology deters fish predators. Oecologia 116:556–564.

Kolehmainen, S. E. 1974. Daily feeding rates of bluegill (*Lepomis macrochirus*) determined by a refined radioisotope method. Journal of the Fisheries Research Board of Canada 31:67–74.

Kramer, R. H., and L. L. Smith, Jr. 1962. Formation of year classes in largemouth bass. Transactions of the American Fisheries Society 91:29–41.

Krumholz, L. A. 1946. Rates of survival and growth of bluegill yolk fry stocked at different intensities in hatchery ponds. Transactions of the American Fisheries Society 76:190–203.

La Rivers, I. 1994. Fishes and fisheries of Nevada. University of Nevada Press, Reno.

Lamprecht, J., and H. Hofer. 1994. Cooperation among sunfish: do they have the cognitive abilities? Animal Behaviour 47:1457–1458.

Lauder, G. V. 1980. The suction feeding mechanism in sunfishes (*Lepomis*): an experimental analysis. Journal of Experimental Biology 88:49–72.

Lauder, G. V. 2000. Function of the caudal fin during locomotion in fishes: kinematics, flow visualization, and evolutionary patterns. American Zoologist 40:101–122.

Lauder, G. V., J. C. Nauen, and E. G. Drucker. 2002. Experimental hydrodynamics and evolution: function of median fins in ray-finned fishes. Integrative and Comparative Biology 42:1009–1017.

Laughlin, D. R., and E. E. Werner. 1980. Resource partitioning in two coexisting sunfish: pumpkinseed (*Lepomis gibbosus*) and northern longear sunfish (*Lepomis megalotis peltastes*). Canadian Journal of Fisheries and Aquatic Sciences 37:1411–1420.

Lawrence, J. M. 1958. Estimated sizes of various forage fishes largemouth bass can swallow. Southeastern Association of Game and Fish Commissioners 11:220–225.

Layzer, J. B., and M. D. Clady. 1987. Phenotypic variation of young-of-year bluegills (*Lepomis macrochirus*) among microhabitats. Copeia 1987:702–707.

Lazzaro, X., R. W. Drenner, R. A. Stein, and J. D. Smith. 1992. Planktivores and plankton dynamics: effects of fish biomass and planktivore type. Canadian Journal of Fisheries and Aquatic Sciences 49:1466–1473.

Leach, B., and R. Montgomerie. 2000. Sperm characteristics associated with different male reproductive tactics in bluegills (*Lepomis macrochirus*). Behavioral Ecology and Sociobiology 49:31–37.

Lee, T. Y., and S. Y. Kim. 1987. Experimental studies on the mechanism of reproductive cycles in the bluegill, *Lepomis macrochirus*. Bulletin of the Korean Fisheries Society 20:489–500.

Lehtinen, R. M., N. D. Mundahl, and J. C. Madejczyk. 1997. Autumn use of woody snags by fishes in backwater and channel border habitats of a large river. Environmental Biology of Fishes 49:7–19.

Levine, J. S., and E. F. MacNichol. 1982. Color vision in fishes. Scientific American 246(2):140–149.

Li, J. L., and H. W. Li. 1979. Species-specific factors affecting predator-prey interactions of the copepod *Acanthocyclops vernalis* with its natural prey. Limnology and Oceanography 24:613–626.

Li, K. T., J. K. Wetterer, and N. G. Hairston, Jr. 1985. Fish size, visual resolution, and prey selectivity. Ecology 66:1729–1735.

Lillie, R. A., and J. Budd. 1992. Habitat architecture of *Myriophyllum spicatum* L. as an index to habitat quality for fish and macroinvertebrates. Journal of Freshwater Ecology 7:113–125.

Lobb, M. D., III, and D. J. Orth. 1991. Habitat use by an assemblage of fish in a large warmwater stream. Transactions of the American Fisheries Society 120:65–78.

Lougheed, V. L., B. Crosbie, and P. Chow-Fraser. 1998. Predictions on the effect of common carp (*Cyprinus carpio*) exclusion on water quality, zooplankton, and submergent macrophytes in a Great Lakes wetland. Canadian Journal of Fisheries and Aquatic Sciences 55:1189–1197.

Luecke, C., and W. J. O'Brien. 1981. Prey location volume of a planktivorous fish: a new measure of prey vulnerability. Canadian Journal of Fisheries and Aquatic Sciences 38:1264–1270.

Luo, J., and S. B. Brandt. 1994. Virtual reality of planktivores: are fish really size selective? Pelagic fish and plankton interactions in marine ecosystems. International Council for the Exploration of the Sea C.M. 1994/R:1, Copenhagen.

Lynch, W. E., Jr., and D. L. Johnson. 1989. Influences of interstice size, shade, and predators on the use of artificial structures by bluegills. North American Journal of Fisheries Management 9:219–225.

Lythgoe, J. N. 1966. Visual pigments and underwater vision. Pages 375–391 *in* R. Bainbridge, G. C. Evans, and O. Rackham, editors. Light as an ecological factor. Wiley, New York.

Lythgoe, J. N. 1979. The ecology of vision. Clarendon Press, Oxford.

Maezono, Y., R. Kobayashi, M. Kusahara, and T. Miyashita. 2005. Direct and indirect effects of bass and bluegill on exotic and native organisms in farm ponds. Ecological Applications 15:638–650.

Margenau, T. L., P. W. Rasmussen, and J. M. Kampa. 1998. Factors affecting growth of northern pike in small northern Wisconsin lakes. North American Journal of Fisheries Management 18:625–639.

Marschall, E. A., P. L. Chesson, and R. A. Stein. 1989. Foraging in a patchy environment: prey-encounter rate and residence time distributions. Animal Behaviour 37:444–454.

Marzolf, G. R. 1978. The potential effects of clearing and snagging on stream ecosystems. U.S. Department of the Interior, Fish and Wildlife Service FWS/OBS-78/14, Washington, D.C.

Mather, M. E., M. J. Vanni, T. E. Wissing, S. A. Davis, and M. H. Shaus. 1995. Regeneration of nitrogen and phosphorus by bluegill and gizzard shad: effect of feeding history. Canadian Journal of Fisheries and Aquatic Sciences 52:2327–2338.

Mauck, W. L., and D. W. Coble. 1971. Vulnerability of some fishes to northern pike (*Esox lucius*) predation. Journal of the Fisheries Research Board of Canada 28:957–969.

Mayhew, J. 1956. The bluegill, *Lepomis macrochirus* (Rafinesque) in West Okoboji, Iowa. Proceedings of the Iowa Academy of Science 63:705–713.

McCauley, E., and J. Kalff. 1981. Empirical relationships between phytoplankton and zooplankton biomass in lakes. Canadian Journal of Fisheries and Aquatic Sciences 38:458–463.

McFarland, W. N., and F. W. Munz. 1975. Part III: The evolution of photopic visual pigments in fishes. Vision Research 15:1071–1080.

McGinnis, S. M. 1984. Freshwater fishes of California. University of California Press, Berkeley.

McHugh, J. J. 1990. Responses of bluegills and crappies to reduced abundance of largemouth bass in two Alabama impoundments. North American Journal of Fisheries Management 10:344–351.

McPeek, M. A. 1989. Differential dispersal tendencies among *Enallagma* damselflies (Odonata) inhabiting different habitats. Oikos 56:187–195.

Meesters, A. 1940. Über die Organisation des gesichtsfeldes der fishe. Zeitschrift für Tierpsychologie 4:84–149.

Michaletz, P. H., and J. L. Bonneau. 2005. Age-0 gizzard shad abundance is reduced in the presence of macrophytes: implications for interactions with bluegills. Transactions of the American Fisheries Society 134:149–159.

Miller, H. C. 1963. The behavior of the pumpkinseed sunfish, *Lepomis gibbosus* (Linnaeus) with notes on the behavior of other species of *Lepomis* and the pigmy sunfish, *Elassoma evergladei*. Behaviour 22:88–151.

Miller, R. J., and H. W. Robison. 2004. Fishes of Oklahoma. University of Oklahoma Press, Norman.

Miller, T. J., L. B. Crowder, J. A. Rice, and E. A. Marshall. 1988. Larval size and recruitment mechanisms in fishes: toward a conceptual framework. Canadian Journal of Fisheries and Aquatic Sciences 45:1657–1670.

Minckley, W. L. 1973. Fishes of Arizona. Arizona Fish and Game Department, Phoenix.

Miner, J. G., and R. A. Stein. 1993. Interactive influence of turbidity and light on larval bluegill (*Lepomis macrochirus*) foraging. Canadian Journal of Fisheries and Aquatic Sciences 50:781–788.

Miner, J. G., and R. A. Stein. 1996. Detection of predators and habitat choice by small bluegills: effects of turbidity and alternative prey. Transactions of the American Fisheries Society 125:97–103.

Mittelbach, G. G. 1981a. Patterns of invertebrate size and abundance in aquatic habitats. Canadian Journal of Fisheries and Aquatic Sciences 38:896–904.

Mittelbach, G. G. 1981b. Foraging efficiency and body size: a study of optimal diet and habitat use by bluegills. Ecology 62:1370–1386.

Mittelbach, G. G. 1983. Optimal foraging and growth in bluegills. Oecologia 59:157–162.

Mittelbach, G. G. 1984. Predation and resource partitioning in two sunfishes (Centrarchidae). Ecology 65:499–513.

Mittelbach, G. G. 1988. Competition among refuging sunfishes and effects of fish density on littoral zone invertebrates. Ecology 69:614–623.

Mittelbach, G. G., and C. W. Osenberg. 1993. Stage-structured interactions in bluegill: consequences of adult resource variation. Ecology 74:2381–2394.

Moffett, J. W., and B. P. Hunt. 1943. Winter feeding habits of bluegills, *Lepomis macrochirus* Rafinesque, and yellow perch, *Perca flavescens* (Mitchill), in Cedar Lake, Washtenaw County, Michigan. Transactions of the American Fisheries Society 73:231–242.

Montgomery, J. C., C. F. Baker, and A. G. Carton. 1997. The lateral line can mediate rheotaxis in fish. Nature (London) 389:960–963.

Moody, R. C., J. M. Helland, and R. A. Stein. 1983. Escape tactics used by bluegills and fathead minnows to avoid predation by tiger muskellunge. Environmental Biology of Fishes 8:61–65.

Müller, U. K., B. L. E. van den Heuvel, E. J. Stamhuis, and J. J. Videler. 1997. Fish foot prints: morphology and energetics of the wake behind a continuously swimming mullet (*Chelon labrosus* Risso). Journal of Experimental Biology 200:2893–2906.

Mundahl, N. D. 1991. Sediment processing by gizzard shad, *Dorosoma cepedianum* (Lesueur), in Acton Lake, Ohio, U.S.A. Journal of Fish Biology 38:565–572.

Mundahl, N. D., C. Melnytschuk, C., D. K. Spielman, J. P. Harkins, K. Funk, and A. M. Bilicki. 1998. Effectiveness of bowfin as a predator on bluegill in a vegetated lake. North American Journal of Fisheries Management 18:286–294.

Muntz, W. R. A. 1975. Visual pigments and the environment. Pages 565–578 *in* M. A. Ali, editor. Vision in fishes. Plenum, New York.

Murdy, E. O., R. S. Birdsong, and J. A. Musick. 1997. Fishes of Chesapeake Bay. Smithsonian Institution Press, Washington, D.C.

Murphy, G. I. 1949. The food of young largemouth black bass (*Micropterus salmoides*) in Clear Lake, California. California Fish and Game 35:159–163.

Musselman, N. J., M. S. Peterson, and W. J. Diehl. 1995. The influence of salinity and prey salt content on growth and intestinal Na^+/K^+-ATPase activity of juvenile bluegill, *Lepomis macrochirus*. Environmental Biology of Fishes 42:303–311.

Nakamura, N., S. Kasahara, and T. Yada. 1971. Studies on the usefulness of the bluegill sunfish, *Lepomis macrochirus* Rafinesque, as an experimental standard animal. II. On the developmental stages and growth from the egg through one year. Journal of the Faculty of Fisheries and Animal Husbandry, Hiroshima University 10:139–151.

Neff, B. D. 2001. Genetic paternity analysis and breeding success in bluegill sunfish (*Lepomis macrochirus*). Journal of Heredity 92:111–119.

Neff, B. D. 2003a. Decisions about parental care in response to perceived paternity. Nature (London) 422:716–719.

Neff, B. D. 2003b. Paternity and condition affect cannibalistic behavior in nest-tending bluegill sunfish. Behavioral Ecology and Sociobiology 54:377–384.

Neff, B. D. 2004. Increased performance of offspring sired by parasitic males in bluegill sunfish. Behavioral Ecology 15:327–331.

Neff, B. D., and M. R. Gross. 2001. Dynamic adjustment of parental care in response to perceived paternity. Proceedings of the Royal Society of London 268B:1559–1565.

Neff, B. D., and P. W. Sherman. 2003. Nestling recognition via direct cues by parental male bluegill sunfish (*Lepomis macrochirus*). Animal Cognition 6:87–92.

Neff, B. D., and P. W. Sherman. 2005. In vitro fertilization reveals offspring recognition via self-referencing in a fish with paternal care and cuckoldry. Ethology 111:425–438.

Neff, B. D., P. Fu, and M. R. Gross. 2003. Sperm investment and alternative mating tactics in bluegill sunfish (*Lepomis macrochirus*). Behavioral Ecology 14:634–641.

Neff, B. D., L. M. Cargnelli, and I. M. Côté. 2004. Solitary nesting as an alternative breeding tactic in colonial nesting bluegill sunfish (*Lepomis macrochirus*). Behavioral Ecology and Sociobiology 56:381–387.

Nelson, J. S., E. J. Crossman, H. Espinosa-Pérez, L. T. Findley, C. R. Gilbert, R. N. Lea, and J. D. Williams, editors. 2004. Common and scientific names of fishes from the United States, Canada, and Mexico, 6th edition. American Fisheries Society, Special Publication 29, Bethesda, Maryland.

New, J. G., L. A. Fewkes, and A. N. Khan. 2001. Strike feeding behavior in the muskellunge, *Esox masquinongy*: contributions of the lateral line and visual sensory systems. Journal of Experimental Biology 204:1207–1221.

Newbrey, M. G., M. A. Bozek, M. J. Jennings, and J. E. Cook. 2005. Branching complexity and morphological characteristics of coarse woody structure as lacustrine fish habitat. Canadian Journal of Fisheries and Aquatic Sciences 62:2110–2123.

Nibbelink, N. P., and S. R. Carpenter. 1998. Interlake variation in growth and size structure of bluegill (*Lepomis macrochirus*): inverse analysis of an individual-based model. Canadian Journal of Fisheries and Aquatic Sciences 55:387–396.

Nilson, H. C., and R. W. Larimore. 1973. Establishment of invertebrate communities on log substrates in the Kaskaskia River, Illinois. Ecology 54:366–374.

Noble, G. K. 1934. Sex recognition in the sunfish, *Eupomotis gibbosus* (Linné). Copeia (4):151–155.

Novinger, G. D., and R. E. Legler. 1978. Bluegill population structure and dynamics. Pages 37–49 *in* G. D. Novinger and J. G. Dillard, editors. New approaches to the management of small impoundments. American Fisheries Society, North Central Division, Special Publication 5, Bethesda, Maryland.

Nowlin, W. H., and R. W. Drenner. 2000. Context-dependent effects of bluegill in experimental mesocosm communities. Oecologia 122:421–426.

Nyberg, D. W. 1971. Prey capture in the largemouth bass. American Midland Naturalist 86:128–144.

O'Brien, W. J., B. Evans, and C. Luecke. 1985. Apparent size choice of zooplankton by planktivorous sunfish: exceptions to the rule. Environmental Biology of Fishes 13:225–233.

O'Brien, W. J., D. Kettle, and H. Riessen. 1979. Helmets and invisible armor: structures reducing predation from tactile and visual planktivores. Ecology 60:287–294.

O'Brien, W. J., N. A. Slade, and G. L. Vinyard. 1976. Apparent size as the determinant of prey selection by bluegill sunfish (*Lepomis macrochirus*). Ecology 57:1304–1310.

O'Hara, J. 1968. The influence of weight and temperature on the metabolic rate of sunfish. Ecology 49:159–161.

Ogburn, C., Jr. 1966. The winter beach. William Morrow, New York.

Olive, J. A., L. E. Miranda, and W. D. Hubbard. 2005. Centrarchid assemblages in Mississippi state-operated fishing lakes. North American Journal of Fisheries Management 25:7–15.

Olson, M. H., G. G. Mittelbach, and C. W. Osenberg. 1995. Competition between predator and prey:

resource-based mechanisms and implications for stage-structured dynamics. Ecology 76:1758–1771.

Olson, M. H., S. R. Carpenter, P. Cunningham, S. Gafny, B. R. Herwig, N. P. Nibbelink et al. 1998. Managing macrophytes to improve fish growth: a multi-lake experiment. Fisheries 23(2):6–12.

Ondok, J. P., J. Pokorný, and J. Květ. 1984. Model of diurnal changes in oxygen, carbon dioxide and bicarbonate concentrations in a stand of *Elodea canadensis* Michx. Aquatic Botany 19:293–305.

Osenberg, C. W., E. E. Werner, G. G. Mittelbach, and D. J. Hall. 1988. Growth patterns in bluegill (*Lepomis macrochirus*) and pumpkinseed (*L. gibbosus*) sunfish: environmental variation and the importance of ontogenetic niche shifts. Canadian Journal of Fisheries and Aquatic Sciences 45:17–26.

Osenberg, C. W., G. G. Mittelbach, and P. C. Wainwright. 1992. Two-stage life histories in fish: the interaction between juvenile competition and adult performance. Ecology 73:255–267.

Ostrand, K. G., B. J. Braeutigam, and D. H. Wahl. 2004. Consequences of vegetation density and prey species on spotted gar foraging. Transactions of the American Fisheries Society 133:794–800.

Otis, K. J., R. R. Piette, J. E. Keppler, and P. W. Rasmussen. 1998. A largemouth bass closed fishery to control an overabundant bluegill population in a Wisconsin lake. Journal of Freshwater Ecology 13:391–403.

Pace, M. L., S. E. G. Findlay, and D. Fischer. 1998. Effects of an invasive bivalve on the zooplankton community of the Hudson River. Freshwater Biology 39:103–116.

Page, L. M., and B. M. Burr. 1991. A field guide to freshwater fishes of North America north of Mexico. Houghton Mifflin (Peterson Field Guide Series), Boston.

Pardue, G. B., and L. A. Nielsen. 1979. Invertebrate biomass and fish production in ponds with added attachment surface. Pages 34–37 *in* D. L. Johnson and R. A. Stein, editors. Response of fish to habitat structure in standing water. American Fisheries Society, North Central Division, Special Publication 6, Bethesda, Maryland.

Parker, G. A. 1970. Sperm competition and its evolutionary consequences in the insects. Biological Reviews 45:525–567.

Partridge, D. G., and D. R. DeVries. 1999. Regulation of growth and mortality in larval bluegills: implications for juvenile recruitment. Transactions of the American Fisheries Society 128:625–638.

Paszkowski, C. A. 1986. Foraging site and interspecific competition between bluegills and golden shiners. Environmental Biology of Fishes 17:227–233.

Paukert, C. P., and D. W. Willis. 2002. Seasonal and diel habitat selection by bluegills in a shallow natural lake. Transactions of the American Fisheries Society 131:1131–1139.

Paukert, C. P., D. W. Willis, and M. A. Bouchard. 2004. Movement, home range, and site fidelity of bluegills in a Great Plains lake. North American Journal of Fisheries Management 24:154–161.

Paukert, C. P., D. W. Willis, and J. A. Klammer. 2002a. Effects of predation and environment on quality of yellow perch and bluegill populations in Nebraska Sandhill lakes. North American Journal of Fisheries Management 22:86–95.

Paukert, C. P., D. W. Willis, and D. W. Gabelhouse, Jr. 2002b. Effect and acceptance of bluegill length limits in Nebraska natural lakes. North American Journal of Fisheries Management 22:1306–1313.

Paxon, K. O., and F. Stevenson. 1979. Influence of artificial structures on angler harvest from Killdeer Reservoir, Ohio. Pages 70–76 *in* D. L. Johnson and R. A. Stein, editors. Response of fish to habitat structure in standing water. American Fisheries Society, North Central Division, Special Publication 6, Bethesda, Maryland.

Pearse, A. S. 1921. The distribution and food of the fishes of three Wisconsin lakes in summer. University of Wisconsin Studies in Science (3):5–61.

Peterson, M. S., N. J. Musselman, J. Francis, G. Habron, and K. Dierolf. 1993. Lack of salinity selection by freshwater and brackish populations of juvenile bluegill, *Lepomis macrochirus* Rafinesque. Wetlands 13:194–199.

Petraitis, P. S. 1979. Likelihood measures of niche breadth and overlap. Ecology 60:703–710.

Petranka, J. W., and K. Fakhoury. 1991. Evidence of a chemically-mediated avoidance response of ovipositing insects to bluegills and green frog tadpoles. Copeia 1991:234–239.

Pflieger, W. L. 1975. The fishes of Missouri. Missouri Department of Conservation.

Philipp, D. P., and M. R. Gross. 1994. Genetic evidence for cuckoldry in bluegill *Lepomis macrochirus*. Molecular Ecology 3:563–569.

Phillips, G. L., W. D. Schmid, and J. C. Underhill. 1982. Fishes of the Minnesota region. University of

Minnesota Press, Minneapolis.

Pierce, C. L., K. A. Musgrove, J. Ritterpusch, and N. E. Carl. 1987. Littoral invertebrate abundance in bluegill spawning colonies and undisturbed areas of a small pond. Canadian Journal of Zoology 65:2066–2071.

Pierce, C. L., M. D. Sexton, M. E. Pelham, H. Liao, and J. G. Larscheid. 2001. Dynamics of the littoral fish assemblage in Spirit Lake, Iowa, and implications for prey availability for piscivores. North American Journal of Fisheries Management 21:884–896.

Pohlmann, K., F. W. Grasso, and T. Breithaupt. 2001. Tracking wakes: the nocturnal predatory strategy of piscivorous catfish. Proceedings of the National Academy of Sciences 98:7371–7374.

Pompilio, L., A. Kacelnik, and S. T. Behmer. 2006. State-dependent learned valuation drives choice in an invertebrate. Science 311:1613–1615.

Popper, A. N., and R. R. Fay. 1973. Sound detection and processing by teleost fishes: a critical review. Journal of the Acoustical Society of America 53:1515–1529.

Popper, A. N., and C. Platt. 1993. Inner ear and lateral line. Pages 99–136 in D. H. Evans, editor. The physiology of fishes. CRC Press, Boca Raton, Florida.

Popper, A. N., R. R. Fay, C. Platt, and O. Sand. 2003. Sound detection mechanisms and capabilities of teleost fishes. Pages 3–38 in S. P. Collins and J. N. Marshall, editors. Sensory processing in aquatic environments. Springer-Verlag, New York.

Porath, M. T., and K. L. Hurley. 2005. Effects of waterbody type and management actions on bluegill growth rates. North American Journal of Fisheries Management 25:1041–1050.

Pothoven, S. A., B. Vondracek, and D. L. Pereira. 1999. Effects of vegetation removal on bluegill and largemouth bass in two Minnesota lakes. North American Journal of Fisheries Management 19:748–757.

Putman, J. H., C. L. Pierce, and D. M. Day. 1995. Relationships between environmental variables and size-specific growth rates of Illinois stream fishes. Transactions of the American Fisheries Society 124:252–261.

Pyke, G. H. 1984. Optimal foraging theory: a critical review. Annual Review of Ecology and Systematics 15:523–575.

Rach, J. J., and F. P. Meyer. 1982. Winter harvest of bluegills in 1976–1977 from Lake Onalaska, Wisconsin. North American Journal of Fisheries Management 2:28–32.

Radomski, P., and T. J. Goeman. 2001. Consequences of human lakeshore development on emergent and floating-leaf vegetation abundance. North American Journal of Fisheries Management 21:46–61.

Raikow, D. F. 2004. Food web interactions between larval bluegill (Lepomis macrochirus) and exotic zebra mussels (Dreissena polymorpha). Canadian Journal of Fisheries and Aquatic Sciences 61:497–504.

Rasmussen, J. B., and J. Kalff. 1987. Empirical models for zoobenthic biomass in lakes. Canadian Journal of Fisheries and Aquatic Sciences 44:990–1001.

Regier, H. A. 1962. Validation of the scale method for estimating age and growth of bluegills. Transactions of the American Fisheries Society 91:362–374.

Renfro, W. C. 1960. Salinity relations of some fishes in the Aransas River, Texas. Tulane Studies in Zoology 8(3):83–91.

Resetarits, W. J., Jr. 2001. Colonization under threat of predation: avoidance of fish by an aquatic beetle, Tropisternus lateralis (Coleoptera: Hydrophilidae). Oecologia 129:155–160.

Rettig, J. E. 1998. Variation in species composition of the larval assemblage in four southwest Michigan lakes: using allozyme analysis to identify larval sunfish. Transactions of the American Fisheries Society 127:661–668.

Rettig, J. E., and G. I. Mittelbach. 2002. Interactions between adult and larval bluegill sunfish: positive and negative effects. Oecologia 130:222–230.

Richardson, R. E. 1910. A review of the sunfishes of the current genera Apomotis, Lepomis, and Eupomotis, with particular reference to the species found in Illinois. Bulletin of the Illinois State Laboratory of Natural History 7(Article 3):27–35.

Richardson, R. E. 1913. Observations on the breeding habits of fishes at Havana, Illinois, 1910 and 1911. Bulletin of the Illinois State Laboratory of Natural History 9(Article 2):405–416, plate.

Richardson, W. B., S. J. Zigler, and M. R. Dewey. 1998. Bioenergetic relations in submerged aquatic vegetation: an experimental test of prey use by juvenile bluegills. Ecology of Freshwater Fishes 7:1–12.

Ricker, W. E. 1942. The rate of growth of bluegill sunfish in lakes of northern Indiana. Investigations of Indiana Lakes and Streams 2(Article 11):161–214.

Ricker, W. E. 1945. Natural mortality among Indiana bluegill sunfish. Ecology 26:111–121.

Robison, H. W., and T. M. Buchanan. 1988? Fishes of Arkansas. University of Arkansas Press, Fayetteville.

Rodeheffer, I. A. 1939. The use of brush shelters by fish in Douglas Lake, Michigan. Papers of the Michigan Academy of Science, Arts, and Letters 25:357–366.

Roff, D. A. 1984. The evolution of life history parameters in teleosts. Canadian Journal of Fisheries and Aquatic Sciences 41:989–1000.

Rohde, F. C., R. G. Arndt, D. G. Lindquist, and J. F. Parnell. 1994. Freshwater fishes of the Carolinas, Virginia, Maryland, and Delaware. University of North Carolina Press, Chapel Hill.

Rold, R. E., T. S. McComish, and D. E. van Meter. 1996. A comparison of cedar trees and fabricated polypropylene modules as fish attractors in a strip mine impoundment. North American Journal of Fisheries Management 16:223–227.

Rosine, W. N. 1955. The distribution of invertebrates on submerged aquatic plant surfaces in Muskee Lake, Colorado. Ecology 36:308–314.

Ross, S. T. 2001. The inland fishes of Mississippi. University Press of Mississippi, Jackson.

Sadzikowski, M. R., and D. C. Wallace. 1976. A comparison of the food habits of size classes of three sunfishes (*Lepomis macrochirus* Rafinesque, *L. gibbosus* (Linnaeus) and *L. cyanellus* Rafinesque). American Midland Naturalist 95:220–225.

Santucci, V. J., Jr., and D. H. Wahl. 2003. The effects of growth, predation, and first-winter mortality on recruitment of bluegill cohorts. Transactions of the American Fisheries Society 132:346–360.

Sarker, A. L. 1977. Feeding ecology of the bluegill, *Lepomis macrochirus*, in two heated reservoirs of Texas. III. Time of day and patterns of feeding. Transactions of the American Fisheries Society 106:596–601.

Sarnelle, O. 1992. Nutrient enrichment and grazer effects on phytoplankton in lakes. Ecology 73:551–560.

Savino, J. F., and R. A. Stein. 1982. Predator-prey interaction between largemouth bass and bluegills as influenced by simulated, submersed vegetation. Transactions of the American Fisheries Society 111:255–266.

Savino, J. F., and R. A. Stein. 1989a. Behavioural interactions between fish predators and their prey: effects of plant density. Animal Behaviour 37:311–321.

Savino, J. F., and R. A. Stein. 1989b. Behavior of fish predators and their prey: habitat choice between open water and dense vegetation. Environmental Biology of Fishes 24:287–293.

Savitz, J., and J. Janssen. 1982. Utilization of green sunfish and bluegills by largemouth bass: influence of ingestion time. Transactions of the American Fisheries Society 111:462–464.

Schellart, N. A. M., and R. J. Wubbels. 1998. The auditory and mechanosensory lateral line system. Pages 283–312 *in* D. H. Evans, editor. The physiology of fishes, 2nd edition. CRC Press, Boca Raton, Florida.

Schneider, J. C. 1999. Dynamics of quality bluegill populations in two Michigan lakes with dense vegetation. North American Journal of Fisheries Management 19:97–109.

Schneider, J. C., and R. N. Lockwood. 2002. Use of walleye stocking, antimycin treatments, and catch-and-release angling regulations to increase growth and length of stunted bluegill populations in Michigan Lakes. North American Journal of Fisheries Management 22:1041–1052.

Schoener, T. W. 1970. Nonsynchronous spatial overlap of lizards in patchy habitats. Ecology 51:408–418.

Scholik, A. R., and H. Y. Yan. 2002. The effects of noise on the auditory sensitivity of the bluegill sunfish, *Lepomis macrochirus*. Comparative Biochemistry and Physiology 133A:43–52.

Schramm, H. L., Jr. 1989. Formation of annuli on otoliths of bluegills. Transactions of the American Fisheries Society 118:546–555.

Schramm, H. L., Jr., and K. J. Jirka. 1989. Epiphytic macroinvertebrates as a food resource for bluegills in Florida lakes. Transactions of the American Fisheries Society 118:416–426.

Schramm, H. L., Jr., K. J. Jirka, and M. V. Hoyer. 1987. Epiphytic macroinvertebrates on dominant macrophytes in two central Florida lakes. Journal of Freshwater Ecology 4:151–161.

Schrenkeisen, R. 1938. Field book of fresh-water fishes of North America. G. P. Putnam's Sons, New York.

Schulte-Hostedde, A. I., and G. Burness. 2005. Fertilization dynamics of sperm from different male mating tactics in bluegill (*Lepomis macrochirus*). Canadian Journal of Zoology 83:1638–1642.

Scott, W. B., and E. J. Crossman. 1998. Freshwater fishes of Canada. Galt House, Oakville, Ontario.

Seaburg, K. G., and J. B. Moyle. 1964. Feeding habits, digestive rates, and growth of some Minnesota warmwater fishes. Transactions of the American Fisheries Society 93:269–285.

Semlitsch, R. D. 1987. Interactions between fish and salamander larvae. Costs of predator avoidance or competition? Oecologia 72:481–486.

Sheldon, R. B., and C. W. Boylen. 1977. Maximum depth inhabited by aquatic vascular plants. American Midland Naturalist 97:248–254.

Shiozawa, D. K., and J. R. Barnes. 1977. The microdistribution and population trends of larval *Tanypus stellatus* Coquillett and *Chironomus frommeri* Atchley and Martin (Diptera: Chironomidae) in Utah Lake, Utah. Ecology 58:610–618.

Shoup, D. E., R. E. Carlson, and R. T. Heath. 2004. Diel activity levels of centrarchid fishes in a small Ohio lake. Transactions of the American Fisheries Society 133:1264–1269.

Siefert, R. E. 1972. First food of larval yellow perch, white sucker, bluegill, emerald shiner, and rainbow smelt. Transactions of the American Fisheries Society 101:219–225.

Simon, J. R. 1951. Wyoming fishes, Revised edition. Wyoming Game and Fish Department, Bulletin No. 4, Cheyenne.

Simpson, J. C., and R. L. Wallace. 1982. Fishes of Idaho. University Press of Idaho, Moscow.

Sivak, J. G. 1973. Interrelation of feeding behavior and accommodative lens movements in some species of North American freshwater fishes. Journal of the Fisheries Research Board of Canada 30:1141–1146.

Smith, G. R., J. E. Rettig, G. G. Mittelbach, J. L. Valiulis, and S. R. Schaack. 1999. The effects of fish on assemblages of amphibians in ponds: a field experiment. Freshwater Biology 41:829–837.

Smith-Vaniz, W. F. 1968. Freshwater fishes of Alabama. Auburn University Agricultural Experiment Station, Auburn.

Søndergaard, M. 1981. Kinetics of extracellular release of ^{14}C-labeled organic carbon by submerged macrophytes. Oikos 36:331–347.

Stacey, P., and D. Chiszar. 1975. Changes in the darkness of four body features of bluegill sunfish (*Lepomis macrochirus* Rafinesque) during aggressive encounters. Behavioral Biology 14:41–49.

Standen, E. M., and G. V. Lauder. 2005. Dorsal and anal fin function in bluegill sunfish *Lepomis macrochirus*: three-dimensional kinematics during propulsion and maneuvering. Journal of Experimental Biology 208:2753–2763.

Stein, R. A., D. R. DeVries, and J. M. Dettmers. 1995. Food-web regulation by a planktivore: exploring the generality of the trophic cascade hypothesis. Canadian Journal of Fisheries and Aquatic Sciences 52:2518–2526.

Stevenson, F., W. T. Momot, and F. J. Svoboda, III. 1969. Nesting success of the bluegill, *Lepomis macrochirus* Rafinesque, in a small Ohio farm pond Ohio Journal of Science 69:347–355.

Stoner, A. W. 1982. The influence of benthic macrophytes on the foraging behavior of pinfish, *Lagodon rhomboides*. Journal of Experimental Marine Biology and Ecology 58:271–284.

Storck, T. W., D. W. Dufford, and K. T. Clement. 1978. The distribution of limnetic fish larvae in a flood control reservoir in central Illinois. Transactions of the American Fisheries Society 107:419–424.

Swaffar, S. M., and W. J. O'Brien. 1996. Spines of *Daphnia lumholtzi* create feeding difficulties for juvenile bluegill sunfish (*Lepomis macrochirus*). Journal of Plankton Research 18:1055–1061.

Swift, C., R. W. Yerger, and P. R. Parrish. 1977. Distribution and natural history of the fresh and brackish water fishes of the Ochlockonee River, Florida and Georgia. Bulletin of the Tall Timbers Research Station, Tallahassee, 111 pp.

Swingle, H. S. 1946. Experiments with combinations of largemouth black bass, bluegills, and minnows in ponds. Transactions of the American Fisheries Society 76:46–62.

Swingle, H. S. 1959. Determination of balance in farm fish ponds. Transactions of the North American Wildlife Conference 21:298–322.

Swingle, H. S., and E. V. Smith. 1942. Management of farm fish ponds. Agricultural Experiment Station, Alabama Polytechnic Institute, Auburn.

Swisher, B. J., D. A. Soluk, and D. H. Wahl. 1998. Non-additive predation in littoral habitats: influences of habitat complexity. Oikos 81:30–37.

Taborsky, M. 1994. Sneakers, satellites, and helpers: parasitic and cooperative behavior in fish reproduction. Advances in the Study of Behavior 23:1–100.

Taborsky, M. 1997. Bourgeois and parasitic tactics: do we need collective, functional terms for alternative reproductive behaviours? Behavioral Ecology and Sociobiology 41:361–362.

Taborsky, M. 1998. Sperm competition in fish: "bourgeois" males and parasitic spawning. Trends in Ecology and Evolution 13:222–227.

Tamura, T., and W. J. Wisby. 1963. The visual sense of pelagic fishes especially the visual axis and accommodation. Bulletin of Marine Science of the Gulf and Caribbean 13:433–448.

Tátrai, I., E. H. Lammens, A. W. Breukelaar, and J. G. P. Klein Breteler. 1994. The impact of mature cyprinid fish on the composition and biomass of benthic macroinvertebrates. Archiv für Hydrobiologie 131:309–320.

Taubert, B. D., and D. W. Coble. 1977. Daily rings in otoliths of three species of Lepomis and Tilapia mossambica. Journal of the Fisheries Research Board of Canada 34:232–240.

Taylor, F., and A. C. Hendricks. 1987. The influence of fish on leaf breakdown in a Virginia pond. Freshwater Biology 18:45–51.

Thorp, J. H., E. M. McEwan, M. F. Flynn, and F. R. Hauer. 1985. Invertebrate colonization of submerged wood in a cypress-tupelo swamp and blackwater stream. American Midland Naturalist 113:56–68.

Thorpe, W. H. 1963. Learning and instinct in animals, 2nd edition. Harvard University Press, Cambridge, Massachusetts.

Titus, J. E., and M. S. Adams. 1979. Coexistence and the comparative light relations of the submersed macrophytes Myriophyllum spicatum L. and Vallisneria americana Michx. Oecologia 40:273–286.

Toetz, D. W. 1966. The change from endogenous to exogenous sources of energy in bluegill sunfish larvae. Investigations of Indiana Lakes and Streams 7(Article 4):115–146.

Tomasso, J. R., Jr., and M. Grosell. 2005. Physiological basis for large differences in resistance to nitrite among freshwater and freshwater-acclimated euryhaline fishes. Environmental Science and Technology 39:98–102.

Tomcko, C. M., and R. B. Pierce. 2005. Bluegill recruitment, growth, population size structure, and associated factors in Minnesota lakes. North American Journal of Fisheries Management 25:171–179.

Tomcko, C. M., R. A. Stein, and R. F. Carline. 1984. Predation by tiger muskellunge on bluegill: effects of predator experience, vegetation, and prey density. Transactions of the American Fisheries Society 113:588–594.

Tomcko, C. M., and R. B. Pierce. 2001. The relationship of bluegill growth, lake morphometry, and water quality in Minnesota. Transactions of the American Fisheries Society 130:317–321.

Tou, S. K. W. 1991. A statistical and experimental study on fish response subject to vortex ring motion. Journal of Environmental Science and Health 26A:755–775.

Trautman, M. B. 1981. The fishes of Ohio. Ohio State University Press, Columbus.

Trebitz, A. S., and N. Nibbelink. 1996. Effect of pattern of vegetation removal on growth of bluegill: a simple model. Canadian Journal of Fisheries and Aquatic Sciences 53:1844–1851.

Trebitz, A., S. Carpenter, P. Cunningham, B. Johnson, R. Lillie, D. Marshall, et al. 1997. A model of bluegill-largemouth bass interactions in relation to aquatic vegetation and its management. Ecological Modelling 94:139–156.

Tsuda, A., H. Saito, and T. Hirose. 1998. Effect of gut content on the vulnerability of copepods to visual predation. Limnology and Oceanography 43:1944–1947.

Tucker, R. P., and S. P. Woolpy. 1984. The effect of parthenogenic eggs in Daphnia magna on prey location by the bluegill sunfish (Lepomis macrochirus). Hydrobiologia 109:215–217.

Turner, A. M., and G. G. Mittelbach. 1990. Predator avoidance and community structure: interactions among piscivores, planktivores, and plankton. Ecology 71:2241–2254.

Valley, R. D., and M. T. Bremigan. 2002. Effects of macrophyte bed architecture on largemouth bass foraging: implications of exotic macrophyte invasions. Transactions of the American Fisheries Society 131:234–244.

VanderKooy, K. E., C. F. Rakocinski, and R. W. Heard. 2000. Trophic relationships of three sunfishes (Lepomis spp.) in an estuarine bayou. Estuaries 23:621–632.

Vanni, M. J. 1987. Effects of food availability and fish predation on a zooplankton community. Ecological Monographs 57:61–88.

Vince, S., I. Valiela, N. Backus, and J. M. Teal. 1976. Predation by the salt marsh killifish Fundulus heteroclitus (L.) in relation to prey size and habitat structure: consequences for prey distribution abundance.

Journal of Experimental Marine Biology and Ecology 23:255–266.

Vinyard, G. L. 1980. Differential prey vulnerability and predator selectivity: effects of evasive prey on bluegill (*Lepomis macrochirus*) and pumpkinseed (*L. gibbosus*) predation. Canadian Journal of Fisheries and Aquatic Sciences 37:2294–2299.

Vinyard, G. L., and W. J. O'Brien. 1976. Effects of light and turbidity on the reactive distance of bluegill (*Lepomis macrochirus*). Journal of the Fisheries Research Board of Canada 33:2845–2849.

Wahl, D. H., and R. A. Stein. 1988. Selective predation by three esocids: the role of prey behavior and morphology. Transactions of the American Fisheries Society 117:142–151.

Wainwright, P. C., C. W. Osenberg, and G. G. Mittelbach. 1991. Trophic polymorphism in the pumpkinseed sunfish (*Lepomis gibbosus* Linnaeus): effects of environment on ontogeny. Functional Ecology 5:40–55.

Walters, D. A., W. E. Lynch, Jr., and D. L. Johnson. 1991. How depth and interstice size of artificial structures influence fish attraction. North American Journal of Fisheries Management 11:319–329.

Walton, W. E., J. A. Emiley, and N. G. Hairston, Jr. 1997. Effect of prey size on the estimation of behavioral visual resolution of bluegill (*Lepomis macrochirus*). Canadian Journal of Fisheries and Aquatic Sciences 54:2502–2508.

Walton, W. E., N. G. Hairston, Jr., and J. K. Wetterer. 1992. Growth-related constraints on diet selection by sunfish. Ecology 73:429–437.

Walton, W. E., S. S. Easter, Jr., C. Malinoski, and N. G. Hairston, Jr. 1994. Size-related change in the visual resolution of sunfish (*Lepomis* spp.). Canadian Journal of Fisheries and Aquatic Sciences 51:2017–2026.

Weaver, M. J., J. J. Magnuson, and M. K. Clayton. 1997. Distribution of littoral fishes in structurally complex macrophytes. Canadian Journal of Fisheries and Aquatic Sciences 54:2277–2289.

Webb, P. W. 1984. Body and fin form and strike tactics of four teleost predators attacking fathead minnow (*Pimephales promelas*) prey. Canadian Journal of Fisheries and Aquatic Sciences 41:157–165.

Webb, P. W. 1986. Effect of body form and response threshold on the vulnerability of four species of teleost prey attacked by largemouth bass (*Micropterus salmoides*). Canadian Journal of Fisheries and Aquatic Sciences 43:763–771.

Webb, P. W., and D. Weihs. 1994. Hydrostatic stability of fish with swim bladders: not all fish are unstable. Canadian Journal of Zoology 72:1149–1154.

Wege, G. J., and R. O. Anderson. 1979. Influence of artificial structures on largemouth bass and bluegills in small ponds. Pages 59–69 *in* D. L. Johnson and R. A. Stein, editors. Response of fish to habitat structure in standing water. American Fisheries Society, North Central Division, Special Publication 6, Bethesda, Maryland.

Weithman, A. S., and R. O. Anderson. 1977. Survival, growth, and prey of Esocidae in experimental systems. Transactions of the American Fisheries Society 106:424–430.

Werner, E. E. 1974. The fish size, prey size, handling time relation in several sunfishes and some implications. Journal of the Fisheries Research Board of Canada 31:1531–1536.

Werner, E. E., and D. J. Hall. 1974. Optimal foraging and the size selection of prey by the bluegill sunfish (*Lepomis macrochirus*). Ecology 55:1042–1052.

Werner, E. E., and D. J. Hall. 1976. Niche shifts in sunfishes: experimental evidence and significance. Science 191:404–406.

Werner, E. E., and J. D. Hall. 1977. Competition and habitat shift in two sunfishes (Centrarchidae). Ecology 58:869–876.

Werner, E. E., and D. J. Hall. 1979. Foraging efficiency and habitat switching in competing sunfishes. Ecology 60:256–264.

Werner, E. E., and D. J. Hall. 1988. Ontogenetic habitat shifts in bluegill: the foraging rate-predation risk trade-off. Ecology 69:1352–1366.

Werner, E. E., and M. A. McPeek. 1994. Direct and indirect effects of predators on two anuran species along an environmental gradient. Ecology 75:1368–1382.

Werner, E. E., D. J. Hall, D. R. Laughlin, D. J. Wagner, L. A. Wilsmann, and F. C. Funk. 1977. Habitat partitioning in a freshwater fish community. Journal of the Fisheries Research Board of Canada 34:360–370.

Werner, E. E., D. J. Hall, and M. D. Werner. 1978. Littoral zone fish communities of two Florida lakes and a comparison with Michigan lakes. Environmental Biology of Fishes 3:163–172.

Werner, E. E., G. G. Mittelbach, and D. J. Hall. 1981. The role of foraging profitability and experience in habitat use by the bluegill sunfish. Ecology 62:116–125.

Werner, E. E., G. G. Mittelbach, D. J. Hall, and J. F. Gilliam. 1983a. Experimental tests of optimal habitat use in fish: the role of relative habitat profitability. Ecology 64:1525–1539.

Werner, E. E., J. F. Gilliam, D. J. Hall, and G. G. Mittelbach. 1983b. An experimental test of the effects of predation risk on habitat use in fish. Ecology 64:1540–1548.

Werner, R. G. 1969. Ecology of limnetic bluegill (Lepomis macrochirus) fry in Crane Lake, Indiana. American Midland Naturalist 81:164–181.

Werschkul, D. F., and M. T. Christensen. 1977. Differential predation by Lepomis macrochirus on the eggs and tadpoles of Rana. Herpetologica 33:237–241.

Wetterer, J. K. 1989. Mechanisms of prey choice by planktivorous fish: perceptual constraints and rules of thumb. Animal Behaviour 37:955–967.

Wetterer, J. K., and C. J. Bishop. 1985. Planktivore prey selection: the reactive field volume model vs. the apparent size model. Ecology 66:457–464.

Wiener, J. G., and W. R. Hanneman. 1982. Growth and condition of bluegills in Wisconsin lakes: effects of population density and lake pH. Transactions of the American Fisheries Society 111:761–767.

Wildhaber, M. L. 2001. The trade-off between food and temperature in the habitat choice of bluegill sunfish. Journal of Fish Biology 58:1476–1478.

Wildhaber, M. L., and L. Crowder. 1990. Testing a bioenergetics-based habitat choice model: bluegill (Lepomis macrochirus) responses to food availability and temperature. Canadian Journal of Fisheries and Aquatic Sciences 47:1664–1671.

Wildhaber, M. L., and L. . Crowder. 1991. Mechanisms of patch choice by bluegills (Lepomis macrochirus) foraging in a variable environment. Copeia 1991:445–460.

Wildhaber, M. L., and L. B. Crowder. 1995. Bluegill sunfish (Lepomis macrochirus) foraging behavior under temporally varying food conditions. Copeia 1995:891–899.

Wildhaber, M. L., R. F. Green, and L. B. Crowder. 1994. Bluegills continuously update patch giving-up times based on foraging experience. Animal Behaviour 47:501–513.

Williamson, M., and A. Keast. 1988. Retinal structure relative to feeding in the rock bass (Ambloplites rupestris) and bluegill (Lepomis macrochirus). Canadian Journal of Zoology 66:2840–2846.

Wilson, D. S., P. M. Muzzall, and T. J. Ehlinger. 1996. Parasites, morphology, and habitat use in a bluegill sunfish (Lepomis macrochirus) population. Copeia 1996:348–354.

Wilson, E. O. 1975. Sociobiology: the new synthesis. Belknap Press, Cambridge, Massachusetts.

Windell, J. T. 1966. Rate of digestion in the bluegill sunfish. Investigations of Indiana Lakes and Streams 7(Article 6):185–214.

Wohlschlag, D. E., and R. O. Juliano. 1959. Seasonal changes in bluegill metabolism. Limnology and Oceanography 4:195–209.

Wood, C. M. 1989. The physiological problems of fish in acid waters. Pages 125–152 in R. Morris, E. W. Taylor, D. J. A. Brown, and J. A. Brown, editors. Acid toxicity and aquatic animals. Cambridge University Press, Cambridge, U.K.

Wright, D. I., and W. J. O'Brien. 1982. Differential location of Chaoborus larvae and Daphnia by fish: the importance of motion and visible size. American Midland Naturalist 108:68–73.

Wright, D. I., and W. J. O'Brien. 1984. The development and field test of a tactical model of the planktivorous feeding of white crappie (Pomoxis annularis). Ecological Monographs 54:65–98.

Wydoski, R. S., and R. R. Whitney. 1979. Inland fishes of Washington. University of Washington Press, Seattle.

Yan, H. Y., M. L. Fine, N. S. Horn, and W. E. Colón. 2000. Variability in the role of the gasbladder in fish audition. Journal of Comparative Physiology 186A:435–445.

Yonekura, R., K. Nakai, and M. Yuma. 2002. Trophic polymorphism in introduced bluegill in Japan. Ecological Research 17:49–57.

Young, J. 2005. Numerical simulation of the unsteady aerodynamics of flapping airfoils. Doctoral dissertation, School of Aerospace, Civil and Mechanical Engineering, University of New South Wales, Australian Defence Force Academy, Canberra.

Zaret, T. M. 1972. Predators, invisible prey, and the nature of polymorphism in the Cladocera (class

Crustacea). Limnology and Oceanography 17:171–184.

Zaret, T. M. 1980. Predation and freshwater communities. Yale University Press, New Haven, Connecticut.

Zaret, T. M., and J. S. Suffern. 1976. Vertical migration in zooplankton as a predator avoidance mechanism. Limnology and Oceanography 21:804–813.

Zhu, Q., M. J. Wolfgang, D. K. P. Yue, and M. S. Triantafyllou. 2002. Three-dimensional flow structures and vorticity control in fish-like swimming. Journal of Fluid Mechanics 468:1–28.

Index

Page numbers followed by *f* indicate figures and those followed by *t* indicate tables.

A

M

N

O

P